A BOOK OF OBJECT-ORIENTED KNOWLEDGE

A BOOK OF OBJECT-ORIENTED KNOWLEDGE

Object-Oriented Analysis, Design and Implementation: A new approach to software engineering

B. Henderson-Sellers

PRENTICE HALL

New York London Toronto Sydney Tokyo Singapore

Acquisitions Editor: Andrew Binnie.
Production Editor: Fiona Marcar.
Cover design: Kim Webber.
This book was typeset in Australia by the author using T$_E$X.
T$_E$X is a trademark of the American Mathematical Society.

Printed in Australia by Macarthur Press Sales Pty Ltd,
  Parramatta, NSW

1 2 3 4 5 96 95 94 93 92

ISBN 0 13 059445 8.

**National Library of Australia
Cataloguing-in-Publication Data**

Henderson-Sellers, Brian.
  A book of object-oriented knowledge : object-oriented
  analysis design and implementation, a new approach to
  software engineering.

  Bibliography.
  Includes index.
  ISBN 0 13 059445 8.

  1. Software engineering. I. Title.

005.1

**Library of Congress
Cataloging-in-Publication Data**

Henderson-Sellers, Brian.
  A book of object-oriented knowledge : object-oriented
  analysis, design, and implementation : a new approach
  to software engineering / B. Henderson-Sellers.

  p.   cm.
  Includes bibliographical references and index.
  ISBN 0-13-059445-8

  1. Software engineering. 2. Object-oriented
  programming. I. Title.

QA76.758.H46   1991   91-25629
005.1--dc20   CIP

Prentice Hall, Inc., *Englewood Cliffs, New Jersey*
Prentice Hall Canada, Inc., *Toronto*
Prentice Hall Hispanoamericana, SA, *Mexico*
Prentice Hall of India Private Ltd, *New Delhi*
Prentice Hall International, Inc., *London*
Prentice Hall of Japan, Inc., *Tokyo*
Prentice Hall of Southeast Asia Pty Ltd, *Singapore*
Editora Prentice Hall do Brasil Ltda, *Rio de Janeiro*

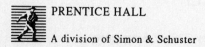 PRENTICE HALL

A division of Simon & Schuster

To Laura and Pat

Contents

Preface

What is this book about? I have tailored it to be a basic introduction to the object-oriented approach to software engineering, emphasizing analysis and design at the expense of the syntax of object-oriented programming languages (OOPLs). Why? Firstly, there are many (some may say too many) books on specific languages, especially C++ and Smalltalk. Secondly, it has become my conviction that learning about object-oriented software engineering techniques through a specific language is difficult, especially since the perfect object-oriented (OO) language has yet to be developed. So you may miss part of the overall paradigm by focusing too early on present-day language support. There is currently a dearth of books describing analysis and/or design, although they are coming rapidly. So far, however, most of them concentrate in great detail on, say, analysis and totally neglect design and implementation.

The format of the book is perhaps a little unusual and the reader deserves an explanation. The rapid growth of interest in all things object-oriented has led to an increase not only in training courses run in both universities and outside but also in-house training whereby an individual in an organization is mandated to "find out everything about object-orientation" and then present this material to his/her colleagues. In this latter case, I know of several presenters who make such a presentation based on only one or two research articles focusing on a small area of OO, articles not intended to provide the tutorial type of overview that is required. Consequently, the "training" that they would be capable of must be severely limited. This book aims at providing both teaching material to the second category and learning material to the first. To do this, I have ensured that all diagrammatic material occupies a full page that can easily be blown up on a copier at a constant magnification (about 1.6) and made into an overhead transparency. The "novice" OO lecturer then has a ready-made course supplemented by the textual material. Moreover, this course has been tried and tested (by myself) on many occasions in both commercial and university contexts. Of course, I cannot offer a cast-iron guarantee that people using this material will be 100% successful in getting across the OO message (if you'll pardon the pun). The diagrams are therefore annotated only with an exhibit number and do not have the normal figure legend. Please feel free to reproduce them (one copy only for copyright reasons) and use them in developing your courses, maintaining my own copyright legend, please. If you are buying this book as a student with little intention of teaching, then these figures, both diagrammatic and textual, will serve as a set of "key points" for your revision and more rapid learning. These figures abstract out the most salient features of the course (and we can regard it as a course whether we are using the book as supportive teaching material or as a learning text).

The book contains a description of the basic ideas of analysis, design, *and* implementation, together with lots of references for more detailed study. It is fashioned on my experience of teaching both university students and groups of professional MIS executives, managers, and programmers/coders. It is enhanced by my participation in recent OO conferences in Australia, North America, and Europe and is presented in a very personal style, adding in some unpublished views that I have gleaned in all these capacities over the last few years. I have found in teaching that the best way seems to be using a sort of "spiral" method — introducing many ideas early in a loose fashion and then tightening up definitions later. Consequently, certain critical ideas will be repeated, in varying degrees of detail, in several places in the book. Again, this sort of reinforcement I have found to be beneficial to the student of this fascinating subject. In the same vein you will find lots of cross-references. As the phases in an object-oriented life cycle are found to be highly merged with each other, blurring the boundaries between analysis, design, and programming, so must any discussion of object-oriented software engineering. Thus the five-chapter structure imposed on the material should be regarded as fluid. Indeed, in presenting my one-day seminar version of this material, I give the participants a choice of the order of these four basic chapters (Chapters 2–5) (called modules in a seminar setting) in pairs of 2/3 or 3/2 followed by 4/5 or 5/4 (the introductory, first chapter material is given as a prelude to the four main modules). In presenting this material in a one-day (6–7 hour) seminar time slot, I use about 50% of the material presented here, which in totality would occupy a two-day seminar with a few more practical examples thrown in. I have also utilized some of the material for a 60–90 minute introductory overview. The Exhibits I have found useful here are Exhibits 6, 10, 12, 16, 18–19, 21, 38, 59–64, 76–77, 88–93, 105, 107, 109–111, 113, 140, 142–143, 146–148. For a half-day introduction I suggest Exhibits 2, 8, 10, 12, 13, 16, 19, 24, 26, 38, 41, 45, 47, 59, 61–64, 68–69, 76–77, 84, 88–89, 91–92, 101, 103–105, 107, 109, 140, 145–147, 156, 163, 166.

This book is aimed at an introductory level and covers only basic object-oriented knowledge. I skim over such topics as genericity, exception handling, specific language implementations, detailed design considerations, and management issues in an attempt to give an overall picture of object-orientation as it is currently practiced. More detailed texts and papers are referenced at appropriate places. Neither will I consider object-oriented databases (except in passing), the use of formal methods, or the use of OO techniques in artificial intelligence (AI) or expert systems (ES). If the programming and the systems analysis communities are only just converging (as exemplified in this book), then the data modelers and the database community as well as the AI and formal methods communities still tend to be discrete, if convergent, entities. Although I choose not to encompass these communities in this book, I recognize their worth and include additional reading material in the Annotated Bibliography. However, if the object-oriented paradigm is to be adopted in these, as well as other areas such as management information systems (MIS), then it is still imperative that the basic knowledge, as presented here, is understood *first*.

It is hard to be definitive on what software skills the reader should possess in order to gain full advantage from both this text and the utilization of object-oriented software engineering. Certainly, I will presume the reader is reasonably familiar with computers, software, and the associated technical terminology. I will presume the reader has either several years' professional experience in software development (presumably in a structured development environment) and/or has participated in first-year, university-level courses in at least one programming language and/or information systems course.

In preparing and presenting this book, I wish to acknowledge the stimulation and ideas from all my seminar participants (now several hundred in number), from students at the University of New South Wales and from the coauthors of research papers, some of whose material is abstracted in some brief detail. In the last category I would like to express thanks to Larry Constantine for the collaboration related in Section 4.3.5 and to Julian Edwards for Sections 4.2, 4.3.2, 4.4, and 4.5. I am also grateful to, in alphabetical order, Grady Booch, Tan Dang, Julian Edwards, Brian Siu, and Rebecca Wirfs-Brock for commenting constructively on earlier drafts of this book and also to the Series Editor, Bertrand Meyer, for his advice. In addition, I wish to acknowledge the following copyright holders for permission to reprint copyright material: Addison-Wesley Publishing Company Inc. for part of Exhibit 2 and the code example on page 252; Larry Constantine for part of Exhibit 20; Larry Constantine and Computer Language Magazine, Miller Freeman Inc. for parts of Exhibits 91 and 98; ACM for Exhibit 29; Kent Beck and Ward Cunningham for Exhibit 40; Grady Booch and The Benjamin/Cummings Publishing Company Inc. for Exhibit 42 and part of Exhibit 90; International Business Machine Corporation for Exhibit 45(a);

Rob Thomsett and Associates for Exhibit 45(b); Ed Seidewitz and Michael Stark for Exhibit 80; Springer for part of Exhibit 62; IEEE for part of Exhibit 91; Addison-Wesley and AT&T Bell Laboratories for Exhibit 147; and Peter Wegner for the quote on page 247 and for Exhibit 154. Finally, thanks to Ann for being Ann; and to Kendal for dreaming up the BOOK's title — no doubt in retaliation for all the other OO acronyms that abound in my work.

The following trademarks are used in the text: Objective-C is a trademark of The Stepstone Corporation; Eiffel is the trademark of the Non-Profit International Consortium for Eiffel; C++ and Unix are trademarks of AT&T; Classic Ada is the trademark of Software Productivity Solutions, Inc.; MacApp and Macintosh are trademarks of Apple Computer, Incorporated; Actor is the trademark of The Whitewater Group; Simula67 is the trademark of Simula AS; VAX and VMS are trademarks of the Digital Equipment Corporation; ORACLE is the trademark of Oracle Corporation Inc.; Miranda is the trademark of Research Software Limited; Visual BASIC and Extended Visual BASIC are trademarks of Microsoft; Turbo Pascal is the trademark of Borland International Inc.; Smalltalk-80 and Smalltalk/V are the trademarks of ParcPlace Systems Inc. and Digitalk Inc., respectively.

Glossary of Terms

abstract data type (ADT): a description of a class (q.v.) but with no implementation details, thus providing the specification. Perhaps better thought of as a "user-defined" type.

class: a description of characteristics common to a set of objects. The class is the coded "template" and therefore includes full implementation details while remaining in conformity with the specification of the appropriate ADT. A "deferred" or "abstract" class is one in which some services are not implemented, this being deferred to a subclass. Such deferred classes cannot therefore be instantiated (q.v.) themselves.

classification: abstract notion of grouping like objects into classes.

generalization: creating superclasses within the inheritance structure (upward).

inheritance: equivalent to a taxonomic relationship between "parents" and "children," possibly over many "generations."

instantiation: creation of an individual instance (a run-time "object") from the class template.

message: the request by one object for the services/assistance of a second object — roughly equivalent to a subroutine CALL in a procedural language.

method: a procedure or function specified within the object class. Also known as a routine.

object: at run-time, a single instantiation of the class template.

object/class (O/C): a collection of like things. Used in analysis and design. Also can be referred to as "object" or "entity."

polymorphism: the ability to refer to an object whose compile time class is unknown i.e., not known until run-time. In many OOPLs, polymorphism is restricted to classes belonging to the same inheritance hierarchy (known as inclusion or limited polymorphism).

specialization: creating superclasses within the inheritance structure (down-
ward).

Glossary of Abbreviations

3GL: Third-generation language (a procedural language like COBOL, FOR-TRAN, BASIC)

4GL: Fourth-generation language (many fourth-generation languages are database query languages)

ADT: Abstract data type

AI: Artificial intelligence

ATM: Automated teller machine (in banking example)

CACM: *Communications of the Association for Computing Machinery*

CASE: Computer aided software engineering

CI: Class interface (diagram)

CRC: Class, responsibilities, and collaborations

DBMS: Database management system

DD: Design diagram

DFD: Data flow diagram

DP: Data processing

EDFD: Entity data flow diagram

EER: Extended entity relationship (data modeling)

ERD: Entity relationship diagram

ES: Expert systems

F-O-O: Functional analysis, object-oriented design, object-oriented programming

ID: Inheritance diagram

IFD: Information flow diagram

IS: Information systems

KBIS: Knowledge-based information systems

MI: Multiple inheritance

MIS: Management information systems

MISA: Mortgage investment savings account

O/C: Object/class

ODBMS: Object database management system

OMT: Object modeling technique

OO: Object-oriented (adjectival) or object-orientation (noun)

OOA: Object-oriented analysis

OOD: Object-oriented design

O-O-F: Object-oriented analysis, object-oriented design, functional programming

O-O-O: Object-oriented analysis, object-oriented design, object-oriented programming

OOP: Object-oriented programming

OOPL: Object-oriented programming language

OOPSLA: Object-Oriented Programming, Systems, Languages, and Applications. This is an annual conference organized by the Association of Computing Machinery (ACM)

OOSD: Object-oriented structured design

PDL: Program design language

PL: Programming language

SRS: Software requirements specification

STD: State-transition diagram

TOOLS: Technology of Object-Oriented Languages and Systems. A series of conferences held in Europe, Australia, and the U.S.A.

VDU: Visual display unit

Chapter 1

PREAMBLE

1.1 An Historical Perspective

I should, perhaps, begin this Preamble with a little history. You will be well aware of the hype of object-oriented approaches which has built up over the last few years. One of the questions that I often get asked is "Why all the hype in the last 2–3 years when the object-oriented languages have been around for over 20 years, since 1967 (the language Simula)?" I see this surge of interest as being brought about by a combination of factors. Since much of the object-oriented paradigm really originated in programming language environments (Simula, Smalltalk, C++, Objective-C, Eiffel, Interlisp), many recent ideas have came from the "language people," with a "computer science" bias, rather than an "information systems" (IS), applications-oriented, bias. Percolating from the back end of the software life cycle (coding), where the ideas were exploited largely in the domain of experimental computer science areas, the potential of OO[1] is only now being realized in an industrial/commercial applications area. It is from this perspective that I will speak: from an information systems (IS)/applications viewpoint and not as a theoretical/research computer scientist.

Object-oriented ideas first emerged in 1967 in the context of the language Simula67 (Exhibit 1), developed by Ole-Johan Dahl and Kristen Nygaard in Norway. While being a general-purpose language, its main use over the next decades was in simulation modeling. However, its design had a significant influence on later object-oriented programming languages (OOPLs), such as Smalltalk and Eiffel (as well as the object-based language Ada). In the early 1970s, a group at the University of Utah led by Alan Kay, who later formed the nucleus of the group including Adele Goldberg and Daniel Ingalls at Xerox in Palo Alto, formulated the basic rationale underlying the Smalltalk language and environment. This development remained as a research tool until the mid-1980s, when

---

[1] OO = object-oriented or object-orientation, dependent only on the grammatical context.

HISTORY OF OBJECT-ORIENTED LANGUAGES

1967	Simula	Dahl and Nygaard
early 1980s	Smalltalk	Kay, Goldberg, Ingalls
late 1980s	C++	Stroustrup
	Objective-C	Cox
	Eiffel	Meyer

EXHIBIT 1   Copyright © B. Henderson-Sellers, 1991

Xerox formed a subsidiary company, ParcPlace Systems, to turn Smalltalk into a commercial-quality product.

The coincident rise of interest in the C programming language led several people to design languages that utilized the systems programming capabilities of C and augment these with object-oriented features. Notable examples are C++, developed by Bjarne Stroustrup at AT&T, and Objective-C, developed by Brad Cox of Stepstone Corporation. The current version of C++, 2.0, was released in 1989 and is available on a wide variety of platforms. More recently, a new language, also strongly influenced by Simula, became available commercially. Developed by Bertrand Meyer, the language Eiffel provides an alternative environment in which OO ideas are well supported. Indeed, in Eiffel (or indeed in Smalltalk) it is virtually impossible to "slip back" to procedural programming, as it is in the hybrid C-extensions.

I therefore think that the two basic reasons for a rapid increase in interest in OO over the last few years for applications software development (as opposed to research) have been the wider availability of these languages plus supporting environments for the object-oriented paradigm, and the existence of higher powered hardware (cf. Trowbridge, 1990). However, the object-oriented paradigm is just that: it's a way of looking at the whole of the software life cycle. It's therefore *much* more than just a language. You can do object-oriented analysis and object-oriented design, and yet implement in a non-object-oriented programming language, such as FORTRAN or C — it's just that's it's relatively hard to do that: to translate from an object-oriented design into a non-object-oriented language (this will be discussed in Section 4.3.4). Object-oriented ideas are applicable throughout the life cycle of software development, not just coding.

With the advent of good, commercially available, object-oriented languages in the mid-1980s, there was sufficient language support, with a group of four or five OO languages, to permit the commencement of full commercial exploitation of the object-oriented paradigm. Future exploitation depends not only on language availability but also on the development of CASE tools, object-oriented databases, and OO development methodologies and notation.

The object-oriented philosophy will be increasingly adopted across all facets of an organization's software operations. Consequently, the requirement for an object database management system (ODBMS) will be paramount in a significant number of commercial, MIS groups. The arrival of commercially available ODBMSs in recent years, although they are generally acknowledged as being in their infancy, provides this opportunity. In an ODBMS, the characteristics of object-orientation[2] (as discussed here) need to be combined with database management requirements, i.e., persistency, secondary storage management, concurrency, recovery, and an *ad hoc* query facility (Loomis, 1990a), coupled with reasonable performance (at least as good as currently available relational database

---

[2] I don't really approve of the phrase "object-orientation." However, as the only noun available, it is probably better than having to use an adjectival "object-oriented" since the following noun can be too specific. At least as a noun, "object-orientation" must encompass *all* aspects of the object-oriented approach to software engineering.

management systems) and schema modification (e.g., Dobbie, 1991).

Two approaches are possible: (i) to extend an OOPL by adding persistency, data sharing control (concurrency), and a query facility, etc. (e.g., Lahire and Brissi, 1991); (ii) to rework existing relational DBMSs to support object-oriented structures. For instance, there is already a class *STORABLE* in Eiffel that can be used to save objects "as is" rather than to translate them into flat files, although fully persistent object support is not yet available commercially. To date, most existing ODBMSs have arisen along the latter path. Detailed examples of products can be found in, e.g., Heintz (1991) and Bancilhon and Delobel (1991), and general discussions in, e.g., Stein (1988), Dittrich (1988), Kim and Lochovsky (1989), Winblad *et al.* (1990), Loomis (1990b), and Khoshafian (1990).

An anticipated timetable for these innovations is given by Winblad *et al.* (1990) (Exhibit 2); and Collins (1990) reports forecasts that by the year 2000 over half of all systems built will be based on the object-oriented approach. Such changes are certainly supported by the computer industry, as reflected by the rapid growth in the industry's Object Management Group (Barber, 1991).

The second factor contributing to the rise of OO in the last two or three years is the availability of relatively inexpensive workstation hardware, which is powerful enough to absorb the extra overhead of many of the new OOPLs (Yamazaki *et al.*, 1990, claim empirical evidence for a 10% slower execution time with a source code 1.6 times larger than a comparative procedural programming language). Pure OOPLs rather than hybrid OOPLs especially need more computing resources (see Section 5.10 for more details on specific languages). Consequently, most of the language implementations have been targeted at the middle range of workstations (usually under Unix). There is very little OO support on mainframes at the moment, although a VAX/VMS port of Eiffel was announced in April 1991 and ports to mainframes running Unix certainly exist. There are also some versions of the languages available on small personal computers (e.g., several versions of C++, Smalltalk, Actor, and Eiffel). In some cases performance may be severely degraded on a machine the size of the PC running at only one or two Mips. The availability of Unix workstations at a reasonable price, I believe, coincided with the arrival of the languages, creating a synergistically receptive hardware/software environment for all these new OOPLs.

Finally, the last few years of the 1980s saw software developers, enthused in part by their use of OOPLs, asking questions regarding analysis and design methodologies. Many in-house, *ad hoc* methodologies were used owing to the dearth of widely acceptable and publicly endorsed approaches to analysis and design. The first published methods or partial methodologies appeared in 1990 (e.g., Booch, 1991; Wirfs-Brock *et al.*, 1990; Henderson-Sellers and Edwards, 1990a; Berard, 1990a, b; Coad and Yourdon, 1990) and are likely to mature rapidly in the near future. Still (at the time of writing) to be developed are OO metrics to assess productivity and assist in project management (some of these issues will be discussed in Section 3.11).

RAPID INCREASE OF INTEREST IN OBJECT-ORIENTED TECHNIQUES

1) LANGUAGE SUPPORT

2) HARDWARE SUPPORT

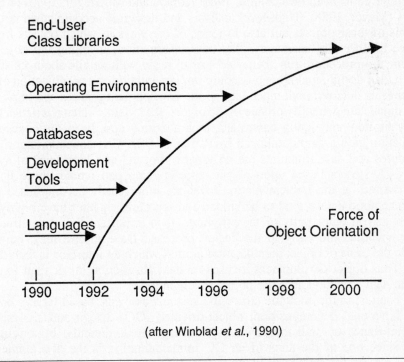

(after Winblad *et al.*, 1990)

EXHIBIT 2   Copyright © B. Henderson-Sellers, 1991

1.2 A First Look at the Object-Oriented Paradigm

Object-orientation is a way of thinking, not tied to any particular language, merely a mindset which is itself supported *better* by more recent languages. It is this new way of thinking that I will urge on you, the reader, rather than language syntax. One of the better ways to develop this new mode of thinking about software is firstly to avoid becoming embroiled in "language wars" or "notational wars" (for example, the so-called bubble wars) and secondly to try to assimilate the underlying concepts of the paradigm. Consequently, the emphasis in this book is on understanding through analysis and design rather than concentrating on language syntax (cf. Wybolt, 1991). Once these ideas become "natural," the learning of a language syntax becomes much easier (e.g., Waldo, 1990) — there are many excellent language specific texts on the market. These are discussed in the Annotated Bibliography to be found on pages 283 to 286.

The object-oriented paradigm (Exhibit 3), at its simplest, takes the standard components of any software system — data and procedures — but de-emphasizes the procedures, stressing instead the encapsulation, in an autonomous module, of data and procedural features *together*, exemplified by the clear and concise specification of the module interface. In a systems decomposition based on an object-oriented approach, the system is viewed as a collection of objects, sometimes referred to as entities (Bailin, 1989; Korson and McGregor, 1990) or object classes (Meyer, 1988). High-level analysis and design is accomplished not only in terms of these objects but also in terms of the ways in which objects interact with each other via "messages" that pass information, invoking the objects to implement a procedure (its "behavior") or to reply with details about its state.

Detailed design, including procedure implementation and specification of data structures, is deferred until much later in the development process and implementation details are generally private to the object, the "visible" characteristics being strictly limited and tightly controlled, thus adhering strictly to the concepts of information hiding as promulgated by Parnas (1972). Consequently, algorithmic procedures and data structures are no longer "frozen" at a high level of system design. A system based upon object representation can remain more flexible since changes at the implementation level are more easily accomplished since implementation details tend to be hidden and therefore changes have highly limited impact on other parts of the program. It is important that data structures not be specified too early in the design process. Data entities may, however, provide the basis of object identification around which an interface is then developed. Thus object development focuses on data abstraction rather than freezing specific data structures into the object specification.

In contrast to the common structured systems analysis, based largely on top-down functional decomposition, object-oriented (OO) design and analysis has many attributes of both top-down and, perhaps predominantly, bottom-up design. Since one of the aims of an OO implementation is the development of generic classes for storage in libraries (the software engineering "holy grail" of true *reusability*), an approach that considers both top-down analysis and bottom-up design simultaneously is likely to lead to the most robust software systems.

OBJECT-ORIENTED PARADIGM
— A FIRST LOOK

Not language-specific
but a new way of looking at software development

Focus on objects as encapsulations of state
plus behaviour with tight, yet clear, interfaces

Stresses

> Information hiding
> Reusability
> New analysis and design methodologies
> New style of programming

EXHIBIT 3   Copyright © B. Henderson-Sellers, 1991

Indeed, several authors (Malhotra *et al.*, 1980; Jackson, 1983; Turner, 1987; Constantine, 1989b) suggest that in reality, practitioners purporting to be following a strictly top-down approach actually utilize a mixed mode of operation between top-down, bottom-up, and middle-out.

Since a significant portion of object-oriented systems development is bottom-up, the differentiation between program design and coding is much less distinct than in a procedurally based systems life cycle (e.g., Meyer, 1989a). However, at this later stage, it would seem reasonable that *within individual code modules* the tools developed for high-level functional decomposition and top-down system design, such as DFDs, can still be found to be useful. Other graphical tools that are useful at different stages within the OO systems life cycle are object-relationship graphs, client–server diagrams, object design diagrams, class interface diagrams, inheritance charts, or collaboration graphs (Wirfs-Brock and Johnson, 1990; Wirfs-Brock *et al.*, 1990).

1.3 Overview of Text

Exhibit 4 is an overview of the following four chapters. Chapter 2 is really an introduction to the jargon. One of the characteristics of the object-oriented philosophy is the synergism between new ideas, many old ideas reworked, and a lot of new jargon. Although many of the ideas, *individually*, will not be unfamiliar to you, when they are combined together they allow us to view programming as well as software design and analysis in a very new way. The object-oriented approach is sometimes called a revolution. It is not a revolution but an evolution (Cox, 1986). As such, it's therefore building on what we know already but is looking at it from a very different perspective. What I am therefore going to be asking you to do is to think differently. That makes it both hard and easy: it is hard because I am going to ask you to take what you know and really take a full step sideways and look at software engineering differently; it is easy because a lot of the things I will introduce will seem familiar. In many ways there is a lot to be learned from what we know already. However, be careful not just to think, "Aha, this is structured programming with a new name and new jargon just to confuse everybody." Of course, people aren't just going to throw away the last 20 years of the structured revolution (Henderson-Sellers and Constantine, 1991). However, it is a fine line between using old (structured) tools *"as is"* in this new (object-oriented) environment, learning about new tools, and (perhaps hardest) using parts of old tools in a completely new way.

So in Chapter 2, I will start by going through the jargon of object-orientation. Remember that this is still an evolving paradigm (and I use the word "paradigm" in its strict sense as really being a shift in the world view). In a software engineering context I (and many others, e.g., Rumbaugh *et al.*, 1991) believe that this shift in mindset is vital. We believe that once you have shifted your world view, understanding object-orientation is easy. However, if you insist on trying to look at object-orientation by sticking firmly in a procedural-based paradigm, you are going to find it difficult.

Overview

4 Modules

Chapter 2   An Introduction to the
            Object-Oriented
            Philosophy
            and Terminology

Chapter 3   Object-Oriented
            Software Engineering

Chapter 4   Object-Oriented
            Systems Development

Chapter 5   Some Implementation
            Concepts

EXHIBIT 4   Copyright © B. Henderson-Sellers, 1991

This text is aimed solidly at an introductory level, either for students or professionals of some standing and experience with the structured paradigm. It is, therefore, *not* my intention to attempt to present a compendium of knowledge on OO. If I do not delve enough into a particular aspect for your particular interests, then I suggest you check in the Annotated Bibliography for a more specific and more detailed text.

We will start by looking at what the word "object" means (Exhibit 5) — and that is not as easy as it sounds. Although the terminology has not been perfectly defined yet, there is now a reasonable consensus. Terminology will be introduced with respect to objects at an analysis and design level and to objects in programming. To do this, I will simply split the life cycle very roughly into those three phases: analysis, design, and programming. In object-orientation, those three merge together much more. Although that merging provides a much stronger base for software engineering, it actually makes teaching/learning the OO paradigm a little harder since you inevitably try and make chunks out of teaching/learning material (for instance, this book is in five chapters, with several subsections, not one continuous, unsectioned diatribe).

Firstly, we need to discuss what objects are at an analysis and design level. As we move from design to programming, the terminology that is used is classes; and then at programming and program execution time, we get back into the jargon of "object". Until that basic terminology is accepted and understood, the rest of the book will be hard going, so I will stress this nomenclature at several points in the early discussion.

Initially in this text I am going to be purposely a little loose in my terminology (Chapters 2 and 3), just to try and get basic ideas over, and I'll tighten up the terminology in later chapters.

Chapter 3 describes software engineering concerns: concerns of reusability, extendibility, reliability, etc., and describes how object-orientation helps in those areas. There are important questions as to how we actually utilize the object-oriented way of thinking in a fruitful way, especially since there is little (but rapidly growing) experience in the commercial world of how to do this. A lot of companies that I know of are so keen on it that they see it as a competitive advantage and are therefore very secretive about it, which in in itself tells you something about those companies that have already adopted the OO philosophy, identifying it as highly important to the critical success of their company. However, that can make it somewhat difficult to find out what's really happening in commercial MIS/DP departments. Nevertheless, published reports of both successes and failures with OO in large commercial projects are now becoming available. These tend to reveal management, rather than technical, issues. Presentation of these "real world" experiences is to be found in Section 3.11.3.

In Chapters 4 and 5 (essentially the second half of the book), I will present a much more detailed view. I cannot in the space of a single book hope to cover anything like the full spectrum of object-oriented design and programming. So remember, this aims primarily to be a "first course" in object-oriented analysis (OOA) and object-oriented design (OOD), together with some insights into object-oriented programming (OOP), and to provide synergistic links between

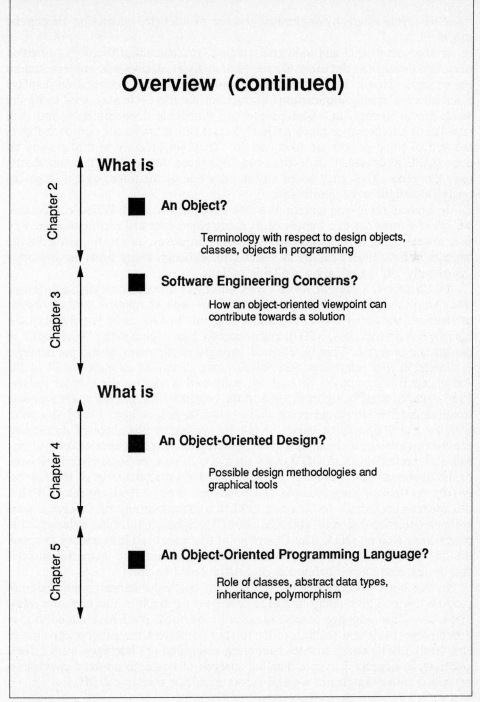

Overview (continued)

What is

Chapter 2

■ **An Object?**

Terminology with respect to design objects, classes, objects in programming

Chapter 3

■ **Software Engineering Concerns?**

How an object-oriented viewpoint can contribute towards a solution

What is

Chapter 4

■ **An Object-Oriented Design?**

Possible design methodologies and graphical tools

Chapter 5

■ **An Object-Oriented Programming Language?**

Role of classes, abstract data types, inheritance, polymorphism

EXHIBIT 5   Copyright © B. Henderson-Sellers, 1991

these life cycle stages by suggesting the use of a single, underlying conceptual model.

In the commercial and industrial context, you can adopt the object-oriented paradigm throughout the life cycle stages of analysis, design, and implementation (or coding). That is by far the neatest way because object-orientation displays a reasonably "seamless transition" throughout the life cycle stages by using the same model throughout. Can people use functional decomposition and then translate it into object-oriented design? Yes, taking a pragmatic approach that is the sort of thing people are likely to do. They are unlikely to throw away all their CASE tools and all their ideas and experience that have been accumulating over the years. They may adopt OO in only one of the three, rough, stages of analysis, design, or implementation.

In a recent survey we undertook in the state of New South Wales in Australia, we found 9 firms out of a sample of 51 using object-oriented methodologies, 8 of which were using it for production software. However, as yet, no methodology appears to have been adapted as a standard, although many firms are currently (as of early 1991) evaluating available options.

In Chapter 4, I present some views on object-oriented analysis and design. The "front end" of the life cycle is the least well developed part of object-orientation. As noted above, the initial impetus for OO came largely from the language end (e.g., Loy, 1990); only recently has it percolated "backward" to design and analysis. This is reflected strongly in the dates of the publications in Exhibit 6 (the references themselves being discussed in more detail in the Annotated Bibliography). Few of the published works on the subject predate 1986, most of them being from 1988 to the present. This follows much the same trend as did the structured revolution — the languages have forced the pace; analysis and design came later. At present we are in that stage of developing analysis and design techniques and methodologies. The first special issue of any technical journal on OOA/OOD that I am aware of was the September 1990 issue of the *Communications of the ACM* and a similarly oriented issue of the *Journal of Object-Oriented Programming* was published in early 1991. At the OOPSLA '90 meeting in Ottawa in October 1990, the great majority of delegates were computer-science-oriented. This was strongly emphasized, for me at least, in the panel discussion on OOA. The Chairman of that panel felt it necessary to spend the first ten minutes of the period explaining to the audience just what analysis and design really were, before the discussion could begin.[3]

In this book I do not intend "selling" any particular language and I do not propose even to give many language examples or much in the way of syntax. There are a few language-based examples in the book, but I have aimed to give pseudo-object-oriented code in order to try and present the general appearance and "feel" of OO code, without becoming embroiled in "language wars." Nevertheless, in Chapter 5 a more detailed analysis of language-oriented concepts is presented with examples in a small subset of all the available OOPLs.

---

[3]The Chairman, Dennis de Champeaux, did a good job and, flatteringly for me, used figures from one of our papers.

Object-Oriented Software Engineering

BACKGROUND READING

Books

Meyer, B., 1988, *Object-Oriented Software Construction,* Prentice Hall

Booch, G., 1991, *Object-Oriented Design with Applications,* Benjamin/Cummings

Rumbaugh, J., Blaha, M., Premerlani, W., Eddy, F., and Lorensen, W.,1991,

    Object-Oriented Modeling and Design, Prentice Hall

Wirfs-Brock, R.J., Wilkerson, B., and Wiener, L., 1990, *Designing Object-Oriented*

    Software, Prentice-Hall

Winblad, A.L., Edwards, S.D., and King, D.R., 1990, *Object-Oriented Software,*

    Addison-Wesley

Coad, P., and Yourdon, E., 1990,1991, *Object-Oriented Analysis,*

    Yourdon Press/Prentice Hall

Journals

Byte August 1986, March 1989 and October 1990

IEEE Software May 1988

CACM September 1990

Journal of Object-Oriented Programming commenced publication 1988

Hotline on Object-Oriented Technology commenced publication November 1989

Object Magazine commenced publication May 1991

EXHIBIT 6   Copyright © B. Henderson-Sellers, 1991

1.4 Adopting the OO Viewpoint

I feel it imperative that we learn the object-oriented *viewpoint*, not a specific language (a statement supported by Coppola, quoted in Stewart, 1991). I consider the OO mindset is best acquired through study and understanding of OOA and OOD (see also Goldstein, 1990) as well as pseudocode examples before studying the detailed syntax of any specific OOPL. It should be noted, on the other hand, that there is still a large emphasis on teaching object-oriented techniques as if they were applicable only to the program language/coding environment (e.g., Urlocker, 1989; Wegner, 1990); again probably reflecting the significant bias toward OOPL, rather than OOA/OOD, in both the literature and OO professionals/practitioners. I firmly believe teaching, and learning, about object-orientation is easiest if we avoid syntactic comparisons of OOPLs. Object-orientation is a paradigm — a set of coherent and cohesive ideas. Training in the paradigm should precede training in a new tool or new language (Hopkins, 1991; Stewart, 1991; Rumbaugh *et al.*, 1991); and it is this approach that is embodied in this book.

Object-oriented is a way of thinking, not just a language.

Chapter 2

AN INTRODUCTION TO THE OBJECT-ORIENTED PHILOSOPHY AND TERMINOLOGY

2.1 Paradigms and Programming

What do we really mean by the object-oriented (OO) philosophy or the object-oriented paradigm? Many people do not like the word "paradigm" used in this context. However, I believe that this is technically the best word, although I agree it is often misused and overused. The meaning of the word, as used in the discussion of paradigm shifts in science by Kuhn (1962), taken from *The Concise Dictionary of Earth Sciences* (Allaby and Allaby, 1990), is given as: "a large-scale and generalized model that provides a viewpoint from which the real world may be investigated." Similarly, the Macquarie Dictionary[4] gives: "a set of concepts, etc., shared by a community of scholars or scientists." In other words a paradigm is a commonly accepted model of some part of the world in which we are interested (another word may be *Weltanschauung* (Constantine, 1989a) or world view). As such, it explains observations. As more observations come to hand, it is possible that some of these observations seem to be contrary to the currently accepted theories, as embodied in the paradigm. Perhaps these are accommodated by a slight modification to the theory. However, as time progresses there are so many "exceptions" leading to modifications within the paradigm that the paradigm itself is no longer robust. A crisis point has been reached and is likely to lead to a revolution in the paradigm; in other words,

---

[4]The accepted Australian dictionary equivalent to Websters Dictionary in the United States

to replacement of the current paradigm by another, new paradigm (Kuhn, 1962; Cox, 1990a). Such paradigm shifts occurred in the Copernican revolution in astronomy, in Darwinian evolution, and in the adoption of the underlying ideas of plate tectonics in geology. The software crisis and the replacement of the structured paradigm by the object-oriented paradigm seem to be consistent with this discussion and with the use of the word "paradigm" in this context.

So much for paradigms, but this book is about one specific paradigm — object-orientation. This provides a new way of conceptualizing software development and, as such, stands in contrast to the alternative programming paradigms, which are predominantly procedural, logical, and functional. In a procedural paradigm, the language is essentially imperative, and control structures of sequence, iteration, and selection are available. Designs based on the procedural programming paradigm and the so-called functional decomposition methodologies form the basis of the structured approach to software development (e.g., Yourdon and Constantine, 1979). In the logical paradigm, programming languages, such as Prolog (e.g., Burnham and Hall, 1985), focus on rules and inferential relationships underlaid by the theories of propositional calculus. List manipulations and goal setting are major characteristics and recursion is usually very evident. Logic programming is also known as declarative programming. Finally, in a functional programming paradigm (e.g., Bird and Wadler, 1988) such as Miranda or Lisp, there are four components: (i) a set of primitive functions (predefined by the language), (ii) a set of functional forms, (iii) the application operation, and (iv) a set of data objects (Ghezzi and Jazayeri, 1987, p267). The programmer develops the functional forms using the predefined functions and the built-in mechanism of the application operation. Predefined (or primitive) functions may include selection operations (such as LAST, FIRST, TAIL), structuring operations (such as ROTATE RIGHT, LENGTH), arithmetic operations, predicate functions (i.e., those having a true/false value), logical operations (such as AND, OR, NOT), and identity functions. Assignments of procedural languages are replaced by function definitions. This all means that less emphasis is placed on the ideas of assignment of individual values to specific, named memory cells and instead the use of uniform data objects, such as sequences, lists, and arrays, permits the construction of more complicated data structures.

2.2 The Object-Oriented Triangle

Object-orientation is generally agreed as being the synergistic embodiment of essentially three concepts (Exhibit 7): some notion of encapsulation and/or information hiding; abstraction by classification, and polymorphism as implemented through inheritance. Although Exhibit 8 demonstrates that there is little tight agreement, and different authors emphasize different aspects of object-orientation, by grouping the concepts, as indicated, a consensus can be identified. The first group is that of information hiding, encapsulation, and objects — all related to the notion of a closely bound piece of code related to an identifiable "thing." I will tend to treat these first two terms as roughly synonymous, as does

3 BASES FOR OBJECT-ORIENTED

1) ENCAPSULATION AND

   INFORMATION HIDING

2) CLASSIFICATION AND

   ABSTRACT DATA TYPES

3) POLYMORPHISM

   THROUGH INHERITANCE

EXHIBIT 7   Copyright © B. Henderson-Sellers, 1991

MAIN CHARACTERISTICS OF OBJECT-ORIENTATION

	INFORMATION HIDING	ENCAPSULATION	OBJECTS	CLASSIFICATION	CLASSES	ABSTRACTION	INHERITANCE	POLYMORPHISM	DYNAMIC BINDING	PERSISTENCE	COMPOSITION
Pascoe, 1986	Y					Y	Y		Y		
Wegner, 1989			Y		Y		Y				
Collins, 1990		Y			Y		Y				Y
Winblad *et al.*, 1990		Y				Y		Y		Y	
Duff & Howard, 1990		Y					Y	Y			
Korson & McGregor, 1990			Y		Y		Y	Y	Y		
Potter, 1990			Y		Y		Y				
Borland, 1990		Y					Y	Y			
Loy, 1990		Y		Y			Y				
Meyer, 1988			Y		Y	Y	Y	Y	Y		
Stroustrup, 1988	Y	Y				Y	Y				
Blair *et al.*, 1990		Y				Y		Y			

EXHIBIT 8   Copyright © B. Henderson-Sellers, 1991

Thomas (1989b) who says that "encapsulation is the technical name for information hiding." Some people try to differentiate them conceptually as one being an idea and the other an implementation of the idea. Perhaps more strictly, code and data can be encapsulated together into an object (i.e., gathered together in a code module) yet remain visible to other objects (Exhibit 9) (e.g., Wirfs-Brock *et al.*, 1990, p18). In other words, encapsulation does not guarantee information hiding, although the reverse is essentially true, at least in OO. Exhibit 8 shows that all sources identify one of these three (information hiding, encapsulation, objects) as one of the three basic ideas of OO. Similarly, most authors include either classification or classes (obviously highly related and almost, but not quite, synonymous) or abstraction. Finally, almost all authors include inheritance. However, both Winblad *et al.* (1990) and Blair *et al.* (1990) identify inheritance as a basic *mechanism* (along with object, message and method, class and instance, in the former reference) rather than as a basic concept. Rather they identify as a basic concept that of polymorphism. Blair *et al.* (1990) suggest polymorphism is nearer the conceptual level and this is an approach adopted here. Other cited candidates for the object-oriented triangle are the implementation technique of dynamic binding and, interestingly, one source cites persistence (perhaps prescriptive rather than descriptive). Only one includes composition, which we will see from Chapter 4 is important in designing systems and subsystems. Perhaps this, again, should be thought of as a technique rather than an underlying basic principle.

It thus seems reasonable to summarize this broad consensus diagrammatically using the "Object-Oriented Triangle" (Exhibit 10) and describe the concepts associated with each vertex in the next three subsections.

2.2.1 Encapsulation and information hiding

Bjarne Stroustrup, from AT&T, the developer of the language C++, said in the May 1988 issue of *IEEE Software*, "decide which modules you want; partition the program so that data are hidden in modules" (Exhibit 11). This is the first difference from a procedural computing environment — it's gluing together data and functionality in some sort of encapsulating, modularized format (a notion that will be progressively refined and tightened up as we progress through this book).

Encapsulation, modularization, and information hiding are not new, but the ways they are used in object-orientation take these ideas to an extreme length that becomes highly beneficial. You can modularize in almost any language, but many programmers don't — it's not enforced *on* the programmer *by* the language. Encapsulation and modularization are ideas of tying things very closely together with an interior that can then also be hidden from view. Since these ideas are around in procedural languages, I will introduce appropriate procedural language analogies. For example, if FORTRAN subroutines were written with very tight interfaces, no global COMMON blocks, and a very small argument list, then this would be well on the way to being object-oriented (strictly, object-based — see Section 5.1). Although these OO ideas are mostly implementable in those 3GLs, the languages also make it easy to violate these rules/concepts (cf., for example,

ENCAPSULATION

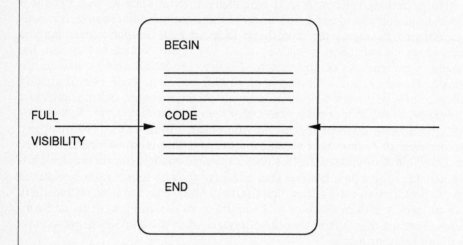

INFORMATION HIDING

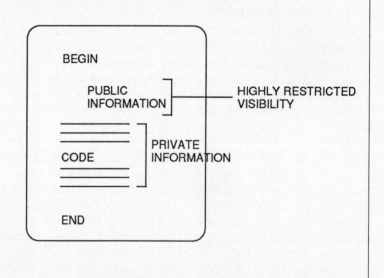

EXHIBIT 9   Copyright © B. Henderson-Sellers, 1991

OBJECT-ORIENTED TRIANGLE

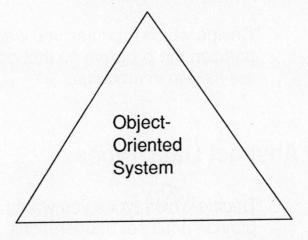

POLYMORPHISM

Object-
Oriented
System

ENCAPSULATION   ABSTRACTION

EXHIBIT 10   Copyright © B. Henderson-Sellers, 1991

Object-oriented philosophy builds on:

(i) Encapsulation (Data Hiding)

"Decide which modules you want; partition the program so that data are hidden in modules."

(ii) Abstract Data Types

"Decide which types you want; provide a full set of operations for each type."

Object-Oriented

"Decide which classes you want; . . . make commonality explicit by using **inheritance.**"

(Stroustrup, May 1988, IEEE Software)

EXHIBIT 11

Stroustrup (1988) and Korson and McGregor (1990)). Indeed, some commercial developers see the *enforcement* of encapsulation as one of the major features of an OO software engineering environment (Winston, 1990).

2.2.2 Abstraction and classification

Modularization uses the notion of an abstract data type (ADT): another, more transparent, phrase would be *user-defined type* (D. McIlroy, cited in Stroustrup, 1988). An ADT can best be considered from a programming language point of view: I will presume here that you're familiar with *INTEGER, CHARACTER, REAL*, etc., as basic language types. An ADT extends this idea and allows you, the user, to define your own type and to use it just as if it were a basic language type. This user-defined type can be anything, e.g., *TABLE, CHAIR,* or *CABBAGE*. That's the nub of an object-oriented program: thinking of your object classes as object types and using them just as you would any other type. (The notation and nomenclature of abstract types and objects will be tightened up later in this chapter and then even more tightly in Chapter 5.)

Bjarne Stroustrup (Exhibit 11) said "decide which types you want; provide a full set of operations for each type." So thinking in terms of types, an object is not just data and functionality bundled together in any old fashion, but is tightly related to the idea of an abstract data type: a user-defined type. We can identify objects with a real-world collection of things. It is therefore much more of a modeling approach. You look at the real world. You look around and see objects in the real world. You do not see functionality. I see people and chairs in a lecture room and *then* I think, what do these people and chairs do? That's the view I am asking you to take.

The second basic concept (Exhibit 10) is that of classification, building on this notion of abstraction. Classification is the idea of grouping software ideas into classes of things. So we deal with not just a piece of code that represents this table or what you can do with this particular table (as you would in the procedural approach) but a generic set or collection of all tables because they all look much the same, they support the weight that we are putting on them, they have a tablecloth on them, and so on. There is the same difference between any English word (or any word in any language), any noun that actually represents a collections of objects. When we say the word "dog," we may mean dogs in general, a collection of all dogs we've ever met. But we can also use the word "dog" in a very specific sense, meaning this one here at my heel. In OO we have the same sort of dual meaning. As we progress, we need to try to differentiate between when we are speaking about sets of objects and when we are speaking about individual objects. This may appear to be arcane initially, but once you get used to the paradigm (say by Chapter 3) it becomes fairly easy. Since we are using the same words (object) all the way through the life cycle, i.e., the same model of an object, the overall approach is often referred to as a "seamless paradigm" or a "seamless transition" from analysis, through design to programming. This is in contrast to a procedural decomposition, where you often use data flow diagrams and perhaps hierarchy charts in analysis and/or design and then have to translate these two very different models into a third model for detailed design and coding, taking into account the restrictions imposed by the procedural language of your choice as you start to code.

The use of a single model throughout the life cycle means that you can use essentially the same words because you are handling the same basic idea throughout. Conversely, if you are using the same words, i.e., using the word object for design objects, analysis objects, and run-time objects, there may be a problem of identifying readily the relevant stage of the life cycle. This is not so obtuse as it might at first seem, because any discussion often pertains primarily to one particular stage and the meaning of the word "object" becomes obvious. However, from a teaching and learning point of view we need, at least initially, to be very clear what we are talking about; so I will continue to reiterate the appropriate "object" terminology as a function of life cycle stage throughout Chapters 2 and 3.

2.2.3 Polymorphism and inheritance

The third vertex of the triangle of underlying OO ideas (Exhibit 10) is polymorphism and inheritance. Although we noted on page 19 that the basic concept is itself polymorphism, it is easier to understand polymorphism *after* you have understood software inheritance, which is a concept more likely to be related to your world experience. For this reason, I will defer the real discussion of polymorphism until later (Section 5.7) and concentrate on inheritance in this section. Suffice it to say here that polymorphism is the ability of abstractions to share properties. Sharing is then accomplished through the inheritance hierarchy.

Inheritance is a brand new idea available in OOPLs. In contrast, the ideas of abstract data types and classification are to some degree already in existence (for example, structures in C and even records in COBOL have some relevant characteristics); the idea of encapsulation is around (Modula2 and Ada are highly encapsulated languages); inheritance isn't. Inheritance in programming languages can be found only in object-oriented programming languages (OOPLs). Inheritance is simply a software analog of a taxonomic inheritance in a biological sense. However, in biological inheritance, traits are inherited from two parents, who themselves inherit from their parents, etc., back in time "up the ancestral tree." Most inheritance in the software world is from a single "parent" (single inheritance). However, increasingly OOPLs are beginning to support multiple inheritance, where features can be inherited from two or more "parents."

An inheritance structure is one of the ways of offering reusability, extendibility, and lower maintenance cost, and of achieving the software engineering goals we have been aiming at for 20–30 years (see Chapter 3). Stroustrup (1988) summarized these views in his statement that to be object-oriented you need encapsulation and abstract data types, and then you need to add in the third leg, inheritance (Exhibit 11): decide about your classes and make commonality explicit by inheritance.

Inheritance thus provides a method of relating classes in a way that is semantically sound. Such relationships, which parallel taxonomies most closely, are evident throughout the OO life cycle. Additionally, in programmer application, inheritance comes to be viewed as a method of sharing code.[5] It is a method of saying, "Here I have a piece of code representing people, and here I have a piece of code representing people attending a seminar/reading this book. This subgroup is a subset of all the people in the world. They're much like all people except they have one extra attribute: they're attending the seminar/reading this book, today. I don't need to rewrite all the code to describe what people can do — eat, breathe, sleep, and so on — in order to describe my seminar attendees/readers, since most of the characterization of 'seminar attendees' can be inherited from 'people' in general. They simply need an additional attribute value to reflect how they differ from people in general, i.e., some attribute to denote their specific temporal/spatial location."

For example, in terms of bank accounts (Exhibit 12), you define common information relevant to all bank accounts in the topmost class. (Here I am using "top" in the sense of top of the page in the appropriate cited figure, which is essentially the most general, basic class — a convention also used by Wirfs-Brock *et al.*, 1990.) Some bank accounts earn interest (and can be classified as savings accounts) and some don't (checking accounts). Thus both savings accounts and checking accounts inherit from a "parent" bank account. Consequently, checking account can be viewed as a "child" or "descendant" of bank account. The relationship is, in fact, often referred to as an "is-a" relationship.[6] Using inheritance we can say checking account inherits everything that is known about bank account, e.g., it has a balance, you can withdraw money from it (and similarly for savings account); but, in addition, there are some special rules for checking accounts and savings accounts: you cannot write a check on a savings account. These rules are, then, very specific to certain subcollections of bank accounts. Thus the higher level ("parents" and "ancestors") classes tend to be more abstract than the "children" and "descendant" classes, which are much more specific (Harmon, 1990). Savings accounts can also have "different flavors." For instance, a saving investment account will be just like a passbook account except it has a different minimum period of investment, a different interest structure, etc., and both are subsets of all savings accounts. In a savings investment account you probably have to keep your money in the bank for a certain period of time before you earn interest (at a higher rate), but otherwise all the other rules hold. The code for the bank account will have information about things that are common to all these subsets of different sorts of bank accounts (checking and the various types of savings accounts); the code for savings account will modify code with rules about interest; and the code for savings investment accounts is likely to include also rules on minimum deposit periods.

Furthermore, when you design a new account, let's call it a "super savings

---

[5] There are two basic types of inheritance: specification (more closely related to subtype hierarchies of highly related object classes) and implementation (more blatant code reuse, including ideas of "mixins," as discussed later.) The differentiation between these two types of inheritance is a little more advanced and will not be analyzed in detail in this text (see, e.g., LaLonde and Pugh, 1991).

[6] For a more advanced discussion of this, see LaLonde and Pugh (1991).

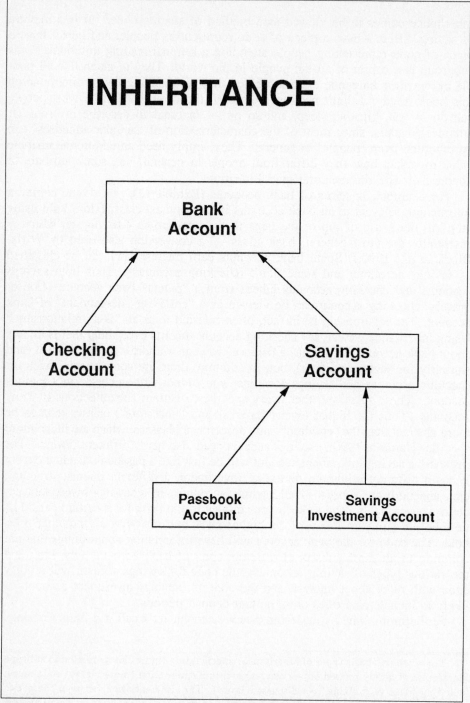

INHERITANCE

EXHIBIT 12   Copyright © B. Henderson-Sellers, 1991

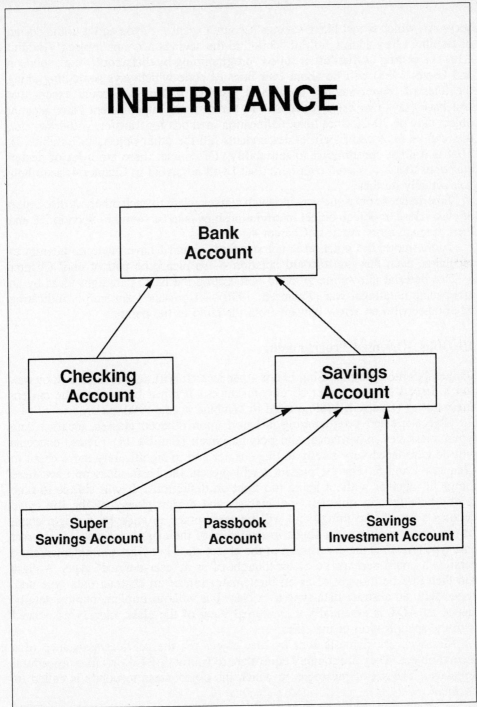

INHERITANCE

EXHIBIT 13

account", which is just like a savings account except . . . , you add it to the design of Exhibit 12 by adding a third "child" to the savings account "object" (Exhibit 13). The coding of that (often called "programming by difference," e.g., Johnson and Foote, 1988) will be about four lines of code which says something along the lines of "super savings account is just like a savings account except that you have (say) two extra features." In contrast, the super-parent bank account object may be 20–30 lines long, delineating methods for transfer, withdraw, etc., that can be *inherited* by all its descendants (all the other objects in Exhibit 13). That is a great contribution to reusability. Of course, there are a lot of design questions that I've skated over here (that I will not avoid in Chapter 4) as to how you actually do that.

Inheritance is only one way in which classes relate to each other. A discussion of class–class or object–object interrelationships is to be found in Section 2.6 and then in much more detail in Chapter 4.

Furthermore, the notation is not standard — and I have made no attempt to regularize even this nonstandard notation — so please be patient until Chapter 4. This deferral allows me to avoid obfuscating the basic paradigm ideas by an internecine notational war (Thomsett, 1990). At present I am simply indicating inheritance with an arrow upward from the child to the parent.

2.3 Object-Oriented Programming

"Object-oriented programming is not a panacea. It will not serve as a floor wax and a dessert topping under all circumstances. It's just better than the current alternatives" (Deutsch, 1989, quoted in Winblad *et al.*, 1990, p210).

Object-oriented programming is based upon objects, classes, abstract data types, messages, inheritance, and polymorphism (Exhibit 14). These concepts will be introduced very briefly in this chapter and in significantly more detail in Chapters 4 and 5. For the present I will present the basic ideas on how these things fit together without being too tight on definitions. It will suffice to note briefly here that an object in the analysis and design phases of the life cycle denotes a set of like things that will be represented in code by a single class. At run-time, an object is a single instantiation of the class template. An abstract data type (ADT) is the description of the object class but with no implementation details. It could perhaps be better thought of as a "user-defined" type. A class can therefore be thought of as an implementation of an abstract data type and, conversely, an abstract data type as a class but without implementation details. Hence an ADT is essentially the external view of the class, closely associated with the specification of the class.

Messages are requests sent by one object for the services/assistance of a second object. They are roughly equivalent to subroutine CALLs in a procedural language. The set of messages to which the object/class responds is called its *protocol*.

Inheritance is a key concept in object-orientation. As noted above, in an OOPL it is essentially a coding technique that permits reuse of code by creating new classes by extending existing classes using taxonomic relationships.

Object-oriented programming is based on:

Objects

Classes

Abstract Data Types

Messages

Inheritance

Polymorphism

EXHIBIT 14   Copyright © B. Henderson-Sellers, 1991

2.4 A Seamless Transition

In addition to the technical terms introduced above, we should also note that there is a strong overlapping nature to the object-oriented approach, because of the seamless transition, mentioned earlier, that uses the same model at the analysis, design, and programming stages (Exhibit 15). There is a basic idea of a common thread throughout the life cycle. Consequently, much of the jargon is applicable at most stages, sometimes making it a little hard to be categoric and say, "Now I am going to speak about analysis," "Now I am now going to speak about design" or "Now I am going to speak about programming" — these are gray shades. Indeed, one current topic of discussion is whether it is even necessary to include an explicit analysis and an explicit design stage or whether the two overlap and merge so much that there is no real differentiation other than a smooth transition from the beginning of analysis in problem space to the completion of a detailed diagram in solution space. Although we will, in this present discussion, stick with the terms "analysis" and "design" as independent notions, our discussions in Section 4.4 will tend to merge these two phases significantly and they will only essentially be differentiated during our discussion of appropriate notation (Section 4.5) and the relationship to problem or solution space.

A seamless transition means that objects identified during analysis will still be easily discerned throughout design as essentially the same entities, and during coding these will emerge identified with class code. This must assist auditability, both for the software engineer and for the user. The user will be able to see in the final design and implementation strong characteristics of his or her original problem. However, although the transition is significantly smoother than in a top-down procedural decomposition life cycle, the mapping between analysis objects and coded classes cannot be truly one-to-one. As we will see later (Chapter 4), during design many object classes *not* components of the original analysis will appear as abstract superclasses (although some authors prefer to differentiate by introducing an instance symbol different from the class symbol, e.g., Booch, 1991; Rumbaugh *et al.*, 1991). In other words, the final design will contain more object classes than were identified in analysis. Such abstractions aid reusability, efficiency, size, etc., but do not significantly erode the aforementioned promise of auditability.

Finally, I would like to remind you of the brief details of inheritance in Exhibit 12. The point I wish to make about this figure here in the context of a seamless transition is that in Exhibit 12 we are designing a set of bank accounts and yet when the system is run, these charts (especially Exhibit 12) could equally well describe a set of instances. This is another example of what is meant by a seamless transition: that the same graphical model is essentially equally applicable to sets of things, at analysis and design, and to individual things — individual object instantiations at run-time. That's great, because it saves all the hassles over how you get from DFDs to code and so on. Again the obverse of that is that an initial inspection of an object chart like this does not immediately tell you whether we are using it for analysis, design, or coding (but see Section 4.5).

A "SEAMLESS TRANSITION"

ESSENTIALLY SAME UNDERLYING MODEL USED THROUGHOUT LIFE CYCLE

ASSISTS AUDITABILITY

CAVEATS

- Some extra classes appear during design

- Relationships currently supported in OOPLs fewer than in analysis

EXHIBIT 15

2.5 Object/Class Nomenclature

In Exhibit 16 is outlined a meaning (if not yet a definition) of the key word "object." An object is essentially an encapsulation of data and functionality.

You should recall that much of the impetus in OO has come from programming, so people have looked primarily at programming objects. When you run a program using objects, you are describing individual examples: particular objects, particular people, particular bank accounts, particular cabbages. However, when you do analysis and design, you are generally not interested in single objects but in a more abstract notion of the set, or *class*, of all similar objects.

Finding the objects is loosely based upon identifying the nouns (Abbott, 1983; Booch, 1983) in the requirements specification, i.e., the user's description of the system. This usually contributes a "first pass" for the top-level objects in the system. These tend to be objects identifiable by substantive nouns. However, abstract nouns are just as likely to be candidates for becoming objects (e.g., Harmon, 1990). Indeed, as systems are analyzed and designed, it is often those more abstract concepts that emerge during system refinement. During system development those "first pass" objects (substantive and abstract) will be significantly augmented by objects created as artifacts of creating the conceptual model.

If you are designing a bank account system, for example (and an example to be used throughout this book on the assumption that you all know a little bit about that because we all have at least one bank account), you are not particularly interested in designing just for your collection of particular bank account(s); you are more interested in designing something that is generically applicable to everybody's bank account. Consequently, when you do the analysis and design you are interested in sets of things, in collections of bank accounts. At the analysis and design stages we are still talking about collections of like things. We often use the word "object" at the design and analysis stage to mean "collection" — it is an overloading itself of the word "object" just as "dog" is. You can say "dog," meaning a collection of all dogs, or you can mean just one specific dog. So in analysis and design you tend to draw your objects, with whatever icons you are using (see Section 4.5), to represent a set of all objects describing, for instance, bank accounts, bank teller, bank customer, automated teller machine (ATM), and so on. At run-time and execution we are interested in particular customers and particular bank subbranches and particular teller machines. We are interested in objects that are individual instantiations: in other words, instances. ("Instantiations" is the technical word that is used.)

At the analysis stage, other words are often used, including the words "entity" and "object class." My caveat with the word "entity" is really a teaching one and if I say "we are using entities" at the design stage, people may think "Ah, we are doing that already with data modeling; it is just data modeling but a different name." Data modeling has, indeed, a lot to offer, especially extended entity relationship (EER) modeling, but object-oriented analysis is not just data modeling with a different name. Furthermore, in explaining these ideas one has got to be very careful in drawing a fine line between using words and concepts the student ("student" used in a very general sense here of anyone pursuing new

What is an Object?

Object = Data + Functionality + Encapsulation

LIFE CYCLE STAGE	NOMENCLATURE	EXAMPLE

Analysis and Design	Objects or
	  Entities or
	    Object Classes (O/Cs)
		Bank Accounts

Design ⟶ Code	Classes A class is an implementation of an abstract data type (ADT)	Code describing *all* personal bank accounts ADT describes "Account" type: interface and features but not implementation
Run-time	Object A run-time object is an instantiation of a class	One specific bank account, belonging to one specific person

EXHIBIT 16   Copyright © B. Henderson-Sellers, 1991

knowledge) understands and changing that meaning or letting them feel that they already understand it so well that they do not see the new ideas. Notwithstanding, you will see "entities" used to mean "design object." So at the analysis and early design level you hear people talk about objects or entities (Exhibit 16) (see, e.g., Bailin, 1989; Korson and McGregor, 1990) or, to stress the idea of a consistent underlying model for design objects, which are classes, sets, or collections, and objects, which are run-time individuals, you often hear the term "object classes" (Meyer, 1988) or its abbreviation "O/C" (Henderson-Sellers and Edwards, 1990a) — object classes (O/Cs) being realized as a "set" concept in analysis, design, and coding; but as an "individual instance" concept when the program is executed (run).

As you move from analysis through design to coding, this notion of collection persists. What you actually write in an object-oriented program are classes. The coded class is a "template" from which we can instantiate individual examples of that class (this is emphasized by the use of the term "factory" in the language Objective-C). It's still that broad collection of things; it's a piece of code representing any bank account. We then, at run-time, take particular examples of "your bank account" and "my bank account," which are two individual run-time instantiations or run-time objects. So at run-time we use the word "object" to mean one specific instantiation, one particular example; here one specific bank account belonging to a specific person.

In fact, "object-oriented" is really a misnomer because what we really should be talking about is "class-oriented,"[7] since the essence of the object-oriented technique is actually the class. You can do objects in FORTRAN. What you cannot do in FORTRAN (easily) is create classes. In other words, I am differentiating here between an object in my hand, a single thing, and a class of all objects or a set of all objects. In FORTRAN you can quite easily write a tightly encapsulated piece of code about this *particular* thing, say a glass, but you can't then generalize and think about another one that is much the same but of a different color or filled with a different liquid (but you will be able to in FORTRAN-90, until recently called FORTRAN-8X; e.g., Wampler, 1990). So classes and abstract data types are actually central to the object-oriented approach, the abstract data type essentially being the formal specification of the object class.

On the other hand, the class is what you actually write as code. The class is thus the coded version of the set of objects that therefore includes code to describe the data associated with the object as well as its functionality (or behavior). In most OOPLs, the idea of a class and a user-defined type are closely linked — they are actually two different notions, but if you glue them together, you have the idea that a class is not just a piece of code that starts with a particular code word and ends with a different code word; it often represents a real-world object identified as an abstract data type (ADT), or may reflect a conceptual object

---

[7]Of course, if we changed the name to the "class-oriented paradigm," we would lose all those lovely double-O acronyms — but there are people who think that it would be ideal (e.g., Hecht, 1990).

identified in system development. This idea of abstraction is heavily embedded in object-oriented ideas.

2.6 Object Interactions

How do objects interact (Exhibit 17)? This is a difficult question and one we will return to later (see Section 4.5.2). There are three types of relationship generally recognized in data modeling (Loomis *et al.*, 1987) that are equally useful here: aggregation, association, and inheritance. Aggregation represents the **has_a** or **consists_of** relationship (e.g., a room consists of four walls, a floor, and a ceiling); association is the direct use of services of one object by another (e.g., a customer object uses the services of a bank object); and inheritance represents a taxonomic hierarchy or **is_a** relationship. These three relationships can be thought of as being, in some sense, mutually orthogonal, so that quasi-three-dimensional diagramming techniques are required (see Section 4.5). Although the current OO language model does not differentiate aggregation and association, such a differentiation has been found to be useful in analysis and broad (early) design. Currently, the OO programming model supports only a client–server relationship that serves to represent the "use" of one object by another, in a very general sense. In utilizing the aggregation/association discrimination possibilities in OOA, we can, for the present, consider the basic OO program language mechanism of client–server to be overloaded in OOA to permit representation of *both* aggregation and association relationships. The third relationship, inheritance, *is* supported by the current OO model.

At the language level, then, objects essentially interact in only two ways: inheritance and the client–server (Wirfs-Brock *et al.*, 1990) or client–supplier (Meyer, 1988) mechanism. This latter interaction forms the basis of viewing the overall design approach as being responsibility-driven — a term used in Rebecca Wirfs-Brock's work (Wirfs-Brock and Wilkerson, 1989b). Employing this type of thinking throughout the life cycle encourages the development of well-encapsulated classes, rather than considering encapsulation as an implementation concern only. This is essentially the approach used here, especially in relation to the analysis and design methodologies discussed in Chapter 4.

We can initially think of objects interacting as if they were a customer and a server, i.e., a client and a supplier. So the client goes along to the supplier (and these are objects, remember) and says, "I would like you to supply something to me." The supplier supplies that service back to the client. So, for instance, I could have a bank customer object that requested the services of the bank account object of, for instance, "tell me my balance" or it might request the service of "let me withdraw $500." The client in that case would be the bank customer and the supplier would be the bank account object. The request that the bank customer object sends to the bank account object is a message and that message can say "tell me my balance"; "withdraw $500"; "deposit $3000"; and so on.

The idea of object responsibilities is an important one. In life, if you go to a shop as a customer and you ask for a product, the supplier has a responsibility to give what you request and not some other thing. There is an analogy to

How do objects interact?

Modeling (analysis and design)

    Aggregation
    Association
    Inheritance

Language-level support

    Inheritance
    Client-server

EXHIBIT 17   Copyright © B. Henderson-Sellers, 1991

a regular, business contract (defined by Wirfs-Brock *et al.*, 1990, p117, as a coherent set of responsibilities). In this, there are obligations on both sides and benefits on both sides.[8] Here is an example (Exhibit 18) that I have made up in terms of a client who is a student and an instructor who is supplying some sort of service. The product here relates to examinations (an example devised at exam time, when exams were uppermost in my mind). Both parties to the contract have obligations and both receive benefits if the obligations are met. It's not always very easy to identify these and to pinpoint what they are, although they correspond roughly as shown. The obligation of the student is to attend an exam on a given day. If that student meets that obligation then the benefit to the supplier is that there is sufficient time in which to mark the exam. Hence the supplier can fulfil their obligation. If the student doesn't attend the exam, thus breaking their "contractual obligation", then there is no exam script to mark and the "supplier" need take no action. One of the benefits of that deal, of that contract, is a benefit to the students in that they receive their results by a given date. The results of breaking contracts, at the coding level, is discussed in Section 5.9.

In a more mathematical example, you might design a class that contains a method to calculate a square root. The client has an obligation to send a message to the supplier that has arguments that are positive; to say "tell me the square root of 10" or "tell me the square root of 3." If the client breaks that obligation by saying "tell me the square root of minus 3" then this regular square root method doesn't have any obligation. The client has broken its obligation, its part of the contract, to send a positive value and so there is no obligation on the supplier to make any response. Now in a procedural language, you could send a negative argument to a square root function and it would have to try to do something with it. Presumably, it will hit some run-time error as a result of the negative square root error, and collapse. Prevention is by individual hand coding of *IF x > 0 THEN ... ELSE ...* constructs, often prior to subprogam *CALL*. In a procedural language, then, such error-trapping code is indistinguishable from other code, whereas in an OOPL code to fulfill such contractual obligations is more clearly recognizable and more clearly models the specific situation.

You can code these responsibilities into a class (but not in all languages at present). The contract (set of responsibilities) therefore says, in essence, that the class functions are available only to you, as a client, if you fulfill certain obligations. There is therefore no obligation for the class to try and deal with situations for which it was not designed. A contract can be written using pre- and postconditions and invariants within the class (see Sections 3.1 and 5.9) that, of course, if you wish, you can neglect to write. Normally, what is recommended is that you write these in and use them at testing and development time and then once you are really convinced the class is working, you may wish to switch them off these checks if you, the programmer, think it appropriate and safe without them.

---

[8]In one of Meyer's papers (Meyer, 1989b) there is the example of a book publishing contract. If you are familiar with publishing, then it's a good example, otherwise it's not.

NOTION OF CONTRACTING AND RESPONSIBILITIES

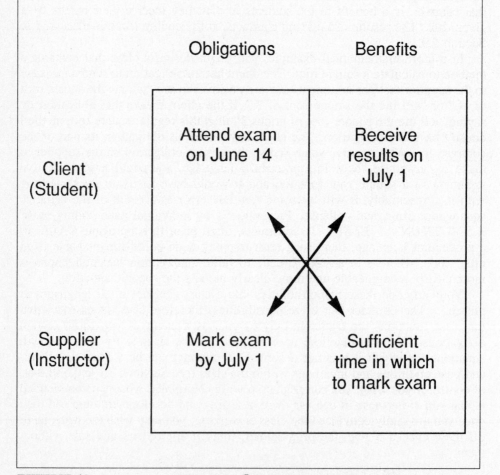

EXHIBIT 18 Copyright © B. Henderson-Sellers, 1991

The idea of contracting and subcontracting (Meyer, 1988) is an important one. Although not yet fully developed, it is one that will be stressed more in future methodologies and languages and is, in my opinion, crucial to reliable software engineering, contributing highly to software quality. Contracting with an object to provide a service places a responsibility on that object, as noted above. However, it is of no interest to the client whether the supplier fulfills its contract itself or by subcontracting to one or more other objects. Wirfs-Brock *et al.* (1990) view the case when the main supplier object uses the services of several other (subcontracted) objects in order to fulfill its own responsibility to the client as a "collaboration." In other words, a single responsibility may require several collaborations to be fulfilled. The idea of such a collaboration is, in many ways, analogous to the leveling diagrams discussed later in Section 4.5.4, where the construct used is that of aggregation. The differences between collaborations and aggregations are visible at the analysis stage but not the design stage. Conceptually, a collaboration involves several "uses" relationships, whereas an aggregation is compounded of several "consists-of" relationships. However, at a high level of abstraction, both can be viewed as a "subsystem" (Wirfs-Brock *et al.*, 1990, p30) such that only a very small number of icons for the topmost objects needs to be shown. Details of such collaborations, subcontracts, and aggregations can be fruitfully deferred until the detailed design stage.

2.7 Shift of Mindset

An abstract data type is strictly the interface of the features but not the implementation. It is the external view. Hence when you are designing, you are essentially designing the abstract data type. For example, I may describe a person object. A person is assumed to have characteristics of one head, two eyes, one mouth, two arms, two legs, and so on — and functionality such as eat, breathe, etc. At the abstract data type level, I am not interested in how you accomplish these functionalities. I do not know how your biology works. I do not know how you breathe and eat (and neither do I care — unless I am a doctor). Furthermore, I do not care if you suddenly decide to metabolize differently. You can change your metabolic implementation, so long as it doesn't affect the way you appear to me. In the real world (including the software engineer's world) we are really interested in the interface, i.e., what we can see. We are not interested in *how* things are accomplished, only that the functions of the interface *are* accomplished — and that is the switch of the paradigm (Exhibit 19). In contrast, in functional decomposition you always start with "How does this thing do it?", "What is the procedure?", "What is the function?", and then later you think of the data *with which* you can do it. In the object-oriented approach to software development you look at the thing and what it offers in terms of services (what it can supply to another object), and/or in terms of state (data) and behavior (functionality). I will define all these words more tightly later. For the moment, we can simply consider that the object is recognized by its external view, or specification, and all implementation is hidden away in a private part of the object class (e.g.,

Shift of Mindset

Procedural Mindset	Object-Oriented Mindset
What does system do?	Of what objects is the system comprised?
What is its purpose?	How can I model the system dynamically using objects, their behavior, and other objects they use?
How do I design and code to achieve this functional behavior?	
Focus on algorithms.	Algorithmic functions deferred.

Woodfield, 1990). A major advantage here is that you can change the implementation without affecting the interface. This has significant repercussions for software reliability, for reusability, for maintenance, and so on.

Procedural languages embody procedural design. The basic idea is to treat the data and the functionality differently and usually separately. You tend to do a functional decomposition and draw DFDs and so on, and then perhaps another team does the data modeling. Then in principle you bring these two together. In some firms I've seen, these two activities are undertaken in parallel and very seldom seem to meet. In OO that merging is done straightaway. First, shift your viewpoint. Instead of having a team doing a data flow diagram in a functional decomposition and a team doing data modeling, you bring the two together. That means that a lot of the people who have been doing data modeling bring significant experience and valuable information to OO. Indeed, there is a lot of work going on at present in examining data modeling ideas and seeing how they can be incorporated within the OO philosophy. However, beware of books and articles that purport to do this, while "serving up" fairly traditional data modeling but under the OO banner. For example, Winblad *et al.* (1990) note that the data-modeling-based tools of Shlaer and Mellor (1988) and Coad and Yourdon (1990), while containing many valuable ideas, essentially miss out on the basic OO philosophy of data-plus-functionality.

This is basically, then, what I am asking you, the reader/student, to do in terms of a shift of mindset. You have now begun to learn of some of the ideas regarding the contrast between a procedural and an OO mindset. We have all been used to designing and coding using procedural building blocks. This essentially starts off from a functional[9] idea and says, "What does a system do?", "What is its purpose?" You *then* ask, "How do I achieve this?", "How do I do my design and write my program to achieve this functional behavior?", deferring the implementation to a *very* late stage (e.g., Pokkunuri, 1989).

In a program constructed following any structured design methodology, data tend to end up being scattered around the program (Exhibit 20). We think of functionality first and what it operates on second. The focus is on writing a "neater" algorithm. Certainly, my experience in teaching functional decomposition in a procedural language over the last decade or so, has led me to realize that the students felt that was what they were really striving for in order to get "better grades": inventing a neater algorithm.

I am suggesting we move to an object-oriented mindset where we first of all ask, "Of what objects is the system comprised?" We look for the objects first: the real-world collections of things. Then we describe those collections of things: what they look like, how they behave (their behavior or functionality), and how they interact with other object classes. When we come to run-time, we implement a design based on classes and class–class interactions using the same model. Those algorithmic concerns are therefore deferred: the algorithms that

---

[9]Note that when I say "functional" I mean procedural and functional decomposition — I am not getting involved in functional programming languages at all. So "functional" and "procedural" as far as I am concerned are synonymous in *this* book.

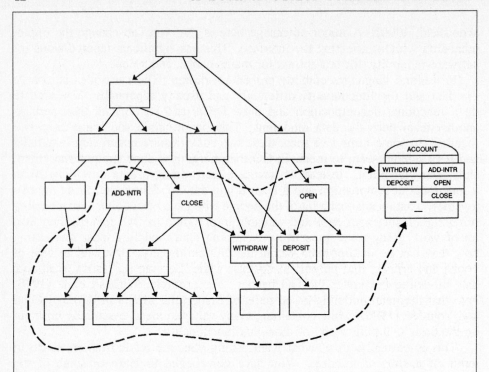

(after Constantine, 1990b)

Regrouping code parts from

functional hierarchy $\Longrightarrow$

Consider lots of different

subroutines

EXHIBIT 20   Copyright © B. Henderson-Sellers, 1991

implement the functionality are hidden deep inside the code of an object. There, you do see traditional, procedural code. Only at that stage do you use DFDs and other structured techniques. So OO is really a major reorganization of the *order* in which you do things, with a strong emphasis on deferring the decisions on functionality, algorithms, and data as long as possible. Indeed, the more deeply the implementation of the functionality is embedded and hidden away, the easier it must be to maintain the system. If you find a bug or you want to replace some part of the algorithm (which often a lot of us do when we invent a better, faster algorithm), we could just slip it in without affecting any interaction with the rest of the program.

A simple example might be in terms of a counter (Exhibit 21) (or maybe a flag, which I see used so many times in procedural languages). If you are coding in C or FORTRAN or COBOL, etc., inevitably you start to have flags that have zero/1, 1/2 values; maybe counters that have counter values 0–10 or 1–11. In a procedural language the way you do this is to define a variable counter to be of type *INTEGER*, initialize that counter, and then use the counter inside a loop. You count a number of times in the loop. The counter variable itself is likely to be embedded within the loop, in such a way that you modify the counter every time you go through the loop, incrementing it, usually by one, and somewhere you check that the counter value is still within the valid range. That check may be done implicitly as part of a DO loop, FOR loop, or whatever may be the technical word in any other language; or you may wish to do it yourself. You could have a construct that says counter equals zero, counter equals counter plus 1; if counter is less than 10 then carry on looping, else go off and do something else. In other words, it is the programmer's responsibility to implement an initialization, any modification, and repetitive checks on this counter variable.

One of the problems here is that we have defined our counter to be of type *INTEGER*. Let's assume our counter has valid values only in the range 1 to 7 to denote the days of the week. If I define my counter as an integer, then according to procedural language rules, if I have my counter with a value of 8 that's perfectly okay, since 8 is an acceptable value for an *INTEGER* variable. However, conceptually it is not satisfactory, because I am permitted only values 1 to 7 for days of the week. Thus a value of 8 does not make any sense in this real-world context. So we must continue to check for invalid values whenever, and wherever, this counter may be modified. This puts a large onus on the programmer to remember to implement all these checks. You will all, no doubt, be well aware of bugs that occur when you forget to do that check. Tracing back you find that the counter is out of range, but it is not picked up by the machine. Programmer responsibility, when using a procedural language, is very important.

In object-oriented languages, the responsibility is taken away from the programmer and put on the language. In an OOPL, in modeling this counter for the days of the week, you would define a class *WEEKLY_COUNTER* by setting a restricted range of integers of 1–7. This implies that, with this restricted range, if the counter variable goes beyond that range, an error is automatically flagged without the need to precede every use of the counter variable by a range validity check. Furthermore, I would probably also like to permit my counter to

Shift of Mindset
(Example of a Counter)

Procedural Language

> Define counter type integer
> Initialize counter
>
> Loop ⌐ Modify counter
>   └ Check counter is still within required range

(Error if modification to counter is illegal or illogical)

Object-Oriented

Model a counter as:

> a) Integer with restricted range
> b) Set of clearly defined operations

How these are implemented is irrelevant to users
of the services of this counter

EXHIBIT 21

have only clearly defined operations. For instance, if I have an integer counter in Pascal or FORTRAN or COBOL and if I multiplied my counter by another value, then that would be perfectly legal; the language syntax in a procedural language allows me to multiply and divide. However, it is reasonable to assume that my counter is just that, i.e., incrementing by plus 1 is OK, but multiplication is forbidden. Consequently, if I have a typographic error and type a star instead of plus, that will be accepted by the compiler (in a procedural language). On the other hand, in an object-oriented language, you clearly define the operations; you pick out from all the valid operations for *INTEGER* only those operations that are allowable. Here, the only valid operation would be plus.

Now you have defined a new type, an abstract data type, which is called *WEEKLY_COUNTER*. It is just like an *INTEGER* except (inheritance) it has got a valid range of only 1–7 (say) and has only got valid operations of increment and initialize. That is what is meant by tying together the functionality (the available operations) and the data in a new abstract data type: a new module or a new class. That new class is much safer to use, since it is now either a syntax or a run-time error when invalid ranges or operations are attempted. In a pseudocode fashion (Exhibit 22), you would define a new class *WEEKLY_COUNTER* as an integer, but with a restricted range of 1–7 together with legitimate operations of, here, increment (a simple count) and an initialization and that's all. That's the abstract data type notion that says to the user of this class that this weekly-counter can be used to count by incrementing the counter, it can be initialized, and its legitimate range is 1–7; it does not tell you anything about how that actually is coded. The ADT is the interface or the external view of this class. The class itself, which you write in your program, will have not only this statement about valid operations and valid ranges but also implementations of the two operations increment and initialize. So the class is the implementation of the abstract data type.

2.8 Summary

We have started on the road to understanding the basic concepts underlying the object-oriented philosophy, including ideas of run-time objects, coded classes, and design objects (Exhibit 23). The object-oriented triangle (Exhibit 10) reflects the synergism of information hiding, abstraction, and polymorphism. We have considered differences between nomenclature at analysis, design, and run-time, while noting the existence of a relatively seamless transition between these life cycle stages.

We have differentiated two run-time object–object interactions, noting especially inheritance, sometimes called an **is-a** relationship (for example, savings account is a bank account but slightly different), and the client–server relationship, intended as a **uses-the-services-of** relationship (in that I, a bank customer, have a bank account) and representing, at present, both association (**uses-a**) and aggregation (**consists-of**) analysis relationships. Further analysis of these various relationships is deferred until Chapter 4.

In pseudocode

CLASS WEEKLY_COUNTER

Integer range 1 . . 7

OPERATIONS

Increment

Initialize

END WEEKLY_COUNTER

Precludes accidentally using multiply or omitting initialization

EXHIBIT 22   Copyright © B. Henderson-Sellers, 1991

Chapter 2

Summary

Notion of run-time objects, classes, and design-level objects

Inheritance (is-a)

cf. Client– Server (uses-the-services-of)

cf. Association (uses-a)
cf. Aggregation (consists-of)

EXHIBIT 23   Copyright © B. Henderson-Sellers, 1991

concepts. The ramifications of adopting this new mindset will now be detailed in respect of software engineering concerns (Chapter 3), analysis and design (Chapter 4), and implementation and languages (Chapter 5).

Chapter 3

OBJECT-ORIENTED SOFTWARE ENGINEERING

3.1 Software Engineering Concerns

You've now heard some of the jargon and some of the concepts. Next we wish to step back and consider a systems point of view, i.e., a more abstract point of view. We ask, "What can the object-oriented paradigm offer in the software development process, in terms of software engineering goals?" First, let's state some standard software engineering goals (Exhibit 24) and then discuss how object-orientation can help to achieve these goals (see also Meyer, 1988). These, therefore, are not new goals but goals that an object-oriented viewpoint may help to achieve more readily than a traditional structured viewpoint.

1. We need software to be correct and verifiable — although the definition of these terms is not universally agreed upon. Software *quality* is a goal not always achieved, but potentially more attainable using an object-oriented approach (e.g., Henderson-Sellers, 1991c).

2. We want programs to be robust, in other words we want them to deal successfully with unusual cases so that, for example, if you have data outside the range, you expect that something sensible should happen.

3. We need systems generally to be extendible. Most of us when we develop a software system, although we achieve the goals stated in the original user's requirements specification, may anticipate that following delivery the user will return to us (the software developer) with new ideas about how the original success can be built on and the program developed to undertake new problem solving. This is likely to require the addition of extra program components. Using an object-oriented systems development methodology, this is easier and safer than in a more traditional functional

49

SOFTWARE ENGINEERING CONCERNS:

Systems should be

1) Correct/verifiable

2) Robust (with respect to abnormal cases)

3) Extendible (with respect to changes/modifications)

   (Important for large-scale programs)

4) Reusable

EXHIBIT 24   Copyright © B. Henderson-Sellers, 1991

decomposition methodology. So extendibility with respect to changes and modification is extremely important, especially when we consider *large* software developments.

4. Another major concern is that of reusability. Reusability is one of the major advantages that an OO approach can provide. Libraries of object classes and of object-oriented designs can be built up that can subsequently be reused. Remember that reusability includes not only reusability of code but also reusability of designs. Once again, this is not something we have never been able to do before — of course, we have been able to do this in structured design and programming. It's been very successfully implemented in FORTRAN NAG (Numerical Algorithms Group) libraries, in COBOL off-line modules, and in Ada modules. With OO, however, it becomes more feasible on a larger scale and outside of specialist software development teams, and it can be undertaken more safely and much more extensively. A lot of software development is oriented toward developing, on a large scale, systems that will allow reusability on that scale. We should not, of course, ignore the plethora of managerial problems with reusability. We have to consider whether we are talking about reusability within project groups, within a given organizational division, within a given organization; or whether we are talking about reusability between organizations. There are therefore lots of commercial questions regarding the reuse of code modules (see below).

Completing the list of software engineering goals (Exhibit 25), we note that:

5. Software systems should have integrity against unauthorized access of modification. Accidental modification of data values should not be possible.

6. A compatibility with other products is desirable. This can be in terms of OO code modules linking with non-OO code modules and, perhaps as an ultimate goal, different OO languages being able to work together.

7. Efficiency must always be a concern, although it depends very much on the environment; for instance, being more crucial in real-time control than in overnight "batch" processing. Language efficiency will diminish in significance as supporting hardware gets faster. However, the efficiency of supporting tools, including those for project management, library management, and debugging, will remain a critical concern in the adoption of OO technology.

8. Portability concerns are addressed both by the C-based hybrid OOPLs (C++, Objective-C, and their derivatives) and pure OOPLs such as Eiffel, which has an option to produce C code. These languages therefore link easily to other C modules.

9. Ease of use, or user friendliness, is certainly observed in pure OOPLs, although it does come at a price, as you might expect. Languages today come

5) Have integrity

6) Compatible (with similar products)

7) Efficient

8) Portable

9) Be easy to use

10) Maintenance is a **LARGE** % of
software engineering life cycle

EXHIBIT 25

with their own "environment" in which supporting tools can be accessed and many relate well to a window-based programming environment.

10. Finally, the literature stresses that around 70% of all costs are maintenance costs (e.g., Meyer, 1988). If you have a system that is more reliable, more easily extendible, then the maintenance costs should drop. The problem is that, although there are relatively large systems around (e.g., McCullough and Deshler, 1990) in all the currently available OOPLs, there are not yet anywhere near as many OO systems as there are systems implemented in COBOL, C, or Pascal. The small number of commercial systems in use means that there are no real hard numbers (metrics) yet to justify these claims of lower maintenance costs attainable with object-oriented systems. Indeed, the successful companies often regard their systems as confidential and as giving them a "competitive advantage," and thus their data are "commercial secrets."

How, then, are some of these software engineering concerns addressed by an object-oriented approach (Exhibit 26)? Groups of these goals are, in some cases, addressed by a single area in OO. Let's go through them in turn and see how OO fits in (Exhibit 27). Correctness can be addressed by the idea of assertions *within* the object that maintains quality, although it should be noted that the advent of assertions predates OOPLs being found in languages such as Alphard and Euclid (see Meyer, 1988, Chapter 7). Assertions include preconditions, postconditions, and invariants. A precondition is an entry test in a particular routine within the object and a postcondition is an exit test to ensure you have a correct answer. For example, you may have a condition that your bank balance must exceed some threshold value before you are allowed to withdraw. Class invariants can also be used that prevent specified constraints being violated at any time during the use of any part of the object class. They should be viewed as part of the class contract, i.e., essentially a part of the ADT specification and *independent* of implementation (see also Section 5.9 for a language-level view of assertions).

Robustness, extendibility, reusability, and integrity were items 2, 3, 4, and 5 in Exhibits 24 and 25. They're all essentially addressed by the concept of modularity and encapsulation, and by abstract data types. These are all slightly different ideas. Encapsulation and modularity have been considered important in procedural programs. However, identification of those modules in a procedural language need not be conceptually coherent. In those languages you can create a subprogram with a bit of a table, a bit of a dog, and a bit of a bank account. You cannot do this in an object-oriented approach. In OO, modularity is tightly tied to the idea of the abstract data type — a model of a real-world type. That, I think, is one of the key benefits.

In the following section, we explore each of these desirable characteristics (Exhibits 24 and 25) in turn.

How are these Software Engineering Concerns Addressed in an Object-Oriented Approach?

EXHIBIT 26   Copyright © B. Henderson-Sellers, 1991

1. Correctness

Assertions *inside* objects
maintain software quality

2. – 5. Robustness, extendibility, reusability, integrity

Addressed by
modularity/encapsulation
and abstract data types

3.2 Logical Modularity

Modularity (Exhibit 28) expresses the idea that each chunk of code should be autonomous and self-contained. Objects provide the basic modular building blocks containing both data and functionality relating to a particular concept. In some languages those modules are identical to classes; in others a class may be split between more than one module (e.g., interface and implementation separately modularized in C++); in others a module may contain more than one class. As can be seen, modules and classes are not identical concepts but in an OO framework they are often both the same. Consequently, in some OO language implementations you will find files located in a directory where each file is the code for a single class or implementation of an abstract data type (with the caveats listed above). Each object class contains coded and labeled routines, labeled attributes, and lots of hidden code that the clients don't need to know about. For example, a bank-account object in a library would be labeled as having, say, services of "withdrawal," "balance," "deposit," etc. That allows you then to actually start to consider building your system bottom-up as well as top-down. Everyone has been advised for the last twenty years or so that top-down is *the* way to build systems, although practitioners suggest that mostly a middle-out procedure is adopted (e.g., Jackson, 1983; Turner, 1987). In OO, both top-down and bottom-up construction have their roles (see Chapter 4). Once you have library classes, you can do much more bottom-up construction. That's what reuse is about — it's about taking the classes you've already built and refined that are sitting in the library and using them in different projects. Such library classes provide good bottom-up building blocks. The term "building blocks" is here very appropriate — indeed, the September 1990 issue of CACM, devoted to OOD and OOA, used Lego^{TM} building blocks as a motif throughout the issue and on the front cover (Exhibit 29).

Logical cohesion reintroduces the idea of a type rather than just any old "chunking" of the code. Types retain logical consistency, grouping data, and functionality together, where all these features are closely related to each other. I find it best to relate that simply to a user-defined type.

3.3 Information Hiding

Encapsulation and information hiding (Exhibit 30) have previously been possible in non-OOPLs. These relate to the idea of localizing things, protecting them from interactions with the environment. In OO you bind together data and procedures. You make that capsule as tight as possible so that the interface is as small as possible. You have an interface where the things that are allowed to be seen across the interface are very clearly defined. In a *pure* OOPL, there's no such thing as "global common" in the procedural language sense, although in a hybrid OOPL, such as C++, the capabilities of the C procedural rootstock still exist such that, if you wish to ignore the OO paradigm and just use C++ as a better C, you can continue to use global data. However, there are some classes that need to be accessed from a large number of places. Such classes in a pure OOPL are

Modularity

—— Autonomous
and Self-contained

—— Good Building Blocks

—— Logically Cohesive

EXHIBIT 28

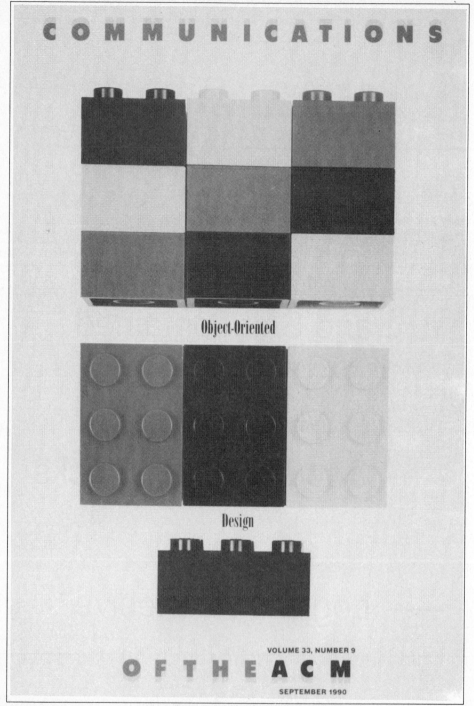

EXHIBIT 29

Encapsulation/ Information Hiding

—— Localizes data and procedures

—— Small but secure interface to outside (weak coupling)

—— Private part and public part (exported; interface)

—— Protected against changes in other parts of the program (cf. COBOL/FORTRAN Common/ C Globals)

—— Allows reusability; avoids redundancy

in some sense global, for instance, the common dictionary **Smalltalk** and the Eiffel class *ANY*, but are more akin to syntactic features of 3GLs, providing, for instance, some input/output, object comparison, copying features, and possibly some arithmetic features that would therefore never be interfered with or altered by the programmer. Everything that is shared is shared via a very tight interface. That way you know that if you alter a variable in one part of the program, the only effect it's going to have is on anything where information has been traded across that very small and well-defined interface. In C or FORTRAN that's what you're told to do, of course, but typically you don't. In an OOPL, such ideas are *enforced* by the language paradigm (and by the analysis and design methodologies, as we will see in Chapter 4) rather than being *permitted* in a procedural language like FORTRAN. This enforcement *requires* the clear specification of the encapsulated data and operations as well as their relationship to other similar groups of code. In addition, good examples of well-constructed classes are found in the extant OOPL libraries. No longer does the FORTRAN/C/COBOL programmer have to rediscover the art of good programming by personal experience but can "stand on the shoulders of giants" and thus progress much more rapidly to production of a high-quality software product.

In any class in any language there is what is usually known as a private part and a public part — the private part is where information is hidden (that's usually the implementation of the functionality and the attributes (the variables)); and the public part is the statement, the names, of the functions that this object will respond to messages about; in other words, that can be used by a client object. The visible portion of the class is also known as the exported part or the interface and is the code representing the class specification. Remember these functions and attributes are the exterior face to the world and the only ones that can be accessed by external objects (cf. friend and public member functions in C++). It is perhaps worth noting here that in Smalltalk, attribute values cannot be exported, whereas this is possible in Eiffel (read access only) and in C++ (read and write access). Nevertheless, it is good OO programming style to have no data members (attributes) publicly available directly (Wirfs-Brock and Wilkerson, 1989a).

If you do all that, as discussed above, then there's protection from the repercussions of changing functions in other parts of the program: the "domino effect" typified by COBOL in general, and by FORTRAN COMMON or C globals. In OO, you have a very tight interface to the object, which is itself the implementation of an abstract data type. Hence the class is of general applicability. The hard bit is creating generalized library classes that you're going to find useful later on in the project — or, indeed, in later projects. That's where the initial overhead lies, but that's where the longer term benefits definitely are. Note that in many language environments you are provided with a library of reusable object classes that are already highly tested. You may get several hundred object classes that do many of the things that we frequently want to do and can now therefore reuse very rapidly in your own applications program. Once you design your own systems, then you've got reusability on a large scale if you have previously made your library classes general enough, although the real benefits occur not on first reuse but on the second and subsequent reuse. Furthermore, you avoid redundancy because you don't have several objects with identical code in them.

3.4 ADTs and Classes

I've mentioned abstract data types and classes already (Exhibit 31). We will now start to tighten up the nomenclature. A module is a concept seen in many languages, e.g., a subroutine, Ada package, etc. However, in OO we now identify the module much more closely with an abstract data type. With information hiding and tight encapsulation, then that module can be identified, in many OOPLs, with the coded class; in others, like C++ or CLOS, the module is maintained as a separate language construct from class (see also Booch, 1991, p49). That's really the focus of OO programming, which is actually class-oriented programming: basing things around classes and then using them as a "template" to produce particular instantiations that conform to that class.

3.5 Reusability and Productivity

One of the most enticing "promises" of object-oriented systems is that of *real* reusability: reusability of code, reusability of program portions, reusability of designs. To date, reusability of code has been discussed in terms of the building of libraries of code modules (usually as object classes) (see also Section 3.11). Indeed, several language environments currently include a number (usually no more than a couple of hundred) of prewritten and (as users we trust) well-validated classes (Auer, 1989). The learning curve for any object-oriented language is therefore not just learning the syntax of the language, which in some cases is relatively easy, but learning to navigate through the existing libraries of prebuilt classes. The availability of these library classes, once learned, makes building new software systems through specialization and client–server implementations significantly easier than in the domain of procedural programming.

Reusability on a slightly larger spatial scale, that of program portions, occurs in the development of *frameworks*, such as MacApp, a framework for constructing Macintosh programs (Schmucker, 1986a, b). A framework is an application-specific class library (Winblad *et al.*, 1990); in other words, a grouping of classes tuned specifically to a single applications-oriented environment, but still general enough to be widely reusable. Another way of viewing this is as reuse of design (Johnson and Foote, 1988). (For further details see also Wirfs-Brock and Johnson, 1990.) It should also be noted that to use a framework, you must accept its model of the problem solution, but hopefully it will provide so much functionality that you are happy to accept its "structure" (Wirfs-Brock, pers. com., 1991). Reuse of detailed design is also seen at the program level when classes written in one language are translated into another OO language. On an even larger scale, off-the-shelf software (including software operating systems) can be viewed as reuse by procurement (Bollinger and Pfleeger, 1990).

Abstract Data Types and Classes

Module + information hiding
built around
Abstract Data Type (ADT)

Module now becomes a **Class**
in many OOPLs

Reusability now feasible from
previously developed library
classes

EXHIBIT 31   Copyright © B. Henderson-Sellers, 1991

Reusability, long promised (e.g., Wegner, 1990, pp15–16; Cox, 1990b), thus becomes feasible through the use of previous classes by instantiation and by new uses in aggregation and association configurations. Perhaps more significantly, reusability of code by taking a class and then specializing it via inheritance becomes a powerful, robust, and safe way of extending existing modular code without fear of "breaking" existing working modules. In this way, a new class that is just like its parent class, but with slight differences, is created. Reusability in the long term is in developing a library of classes from both commercially available classes and in-house developments (e.g., Goldberg and Rubin, 1990). In commencing a new project, commonalities with past projects are first identified and then the experience of those past projects is "reused" in terms of library object classes either directly or in terms of slight modifications, usually through inheritance.

In procedural libraries, code modules are well tested and then frozen in libraries for future use by others. Although this certainly provides some reuse, such modules are limited to highly specific applications areas insofar as the module has to be "perfect" as-is, or is essentially unreusable. However, in OO reuse, the "Open–Closed Principle" (Exhibit 32) can be applied: a principle that says that once a class is tested and accepted into a library, it should *not* need to be "opened up" (the "Closed Principle") while remaining "open" to further extendibility by inheritance. In other words, reuse is enhanced by the capability of building on and extending existing modules and "personalizing" them for the specific task in hand.

In terms of code and design elements there may now be two conceptual libraries to deal with: one for the project, storing revisions for the project under way, and one for components that are fully generalized. This product library would be where the components produced following generalization and acceptance testing (cf. the cluster model of Exhibit 62) would eventually reside ready to be accessed for other developmental projects (Meyer, 1989c, 1990a). In the object-oriented life cycle, more effort is required in the design phase and considerably less in program building and maintenance. Strategic planning is therefore required by an industry together with concomitant software metrics (see also Caldiera and Basili, 1991) in order for the actual productivity gain foreseen for large system developments using the object-oriented paradigm to be consistently evaluated.

The second caveat with respect to productivity and productivity metrics is to do with generalization: of building library classes. Building library classes is a production overhead; it's an overhead in the initial stages of the adoption of the OO philosophy, yet it's going to be a great advantage, giving a great benefit, later, when good, highly reusable classes are available in the library in significant numbers. Consequently, OO can be seen as much more of a strategic investment. There is more cost/effort initially in developing libraries of classes. The benefit is a long-term saving. This may often be regarded as a little difficult/strange for commercial IS managers — to consider a longer-term perspective rather than the next milestone/deadline/project completion and delivery (see Section 3.11). So a potential increase in productivity exists in that sense — in the

REUSE depends also on

"OPEN-CLOSED PRINCIPLE"

Once class is tested and accepted into library,

shouldn't need to be "opened up"

[CLOSED PRINCIPLE]

Yet can be extended by inheritance

[OPEN PRINCIPLE]

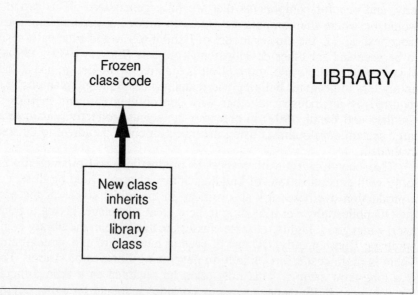

LIBRARY

Frozen class code

New class inherits from library class

EXHIBIT 32

longer term. Development of new OO metrics to aid in project assessment and project management is a topic of current concern (e.g., Goldberg and Rubin, 1990; Pfleeger, 1991; Henderson-Sellers, 1991a; discussions at OOPSLA '90 — see also Section 3.11).

Reusability, talked about for so long and always possible, if difficult, in 3GLs, becomes easier and well supported by the new language environments. In the longer term, increased productivity can be anticipated, largely as a result of the defunct need to "reinvent the software wheel" (Exhibit 33). When you employ this strategy, then reuse of library classes is a bottom-up reuse.

There are two productivity benefits. You can start to design while still analyzing. You can actually start to code very soon after you've started your detailed design, because now you can code in classes or clusters of associated classes. You don't actually have to have a full design. This allows you to test portions of the design with an implementation. The second benefit is that when you are well into design there is still the opportunity for user interaction. There's more chance that when users change their minds, they can still influence the design. You don't need to "freeze" the user requirement quite so early (see management issues in Section 3.11; also Section 4.3.2 and discussion of Exhibit 64). This is closely associated with a prototyping approach to building software. However, such rapidly constructed "prototypes" are really embryonic systems and can be demonstrated to management and end-users as a "working product"; that could lead to untimely expectations of system delivery. This results from an assumption, learned from procedural programming, that a working system is essentially a finished product. Such misconceptions have led to project slippage in organizations still in the adoption phase of the maturing technology (see, e.g., discussion in Chapter 3 of Jackson, 1986).

3.6 Data Dependency

Data dependency has long been an area of great concern in software engineering and, especially, in database management. To illustrate the problem, Exhibit 34 shows some pseudocode in a procedural language and in Exhibit 35 the equivalent in an OOPL to illustrate the extent of data dependency in the two paradigms. Here, consider a bank account that is a record and may have a type of *Checking* or *Savings* or *MISA* (Mortgage Investment Savings Account). It has a balance that is of type *Money*. I might identify procedures such as *deposit, withdraw, transfer*. In a procedural language, I would design a procedure (module) for *deposit*. With several types of bank account, it is likely that there may be slightly different rules for each type of bank account for each of these procedures. For instance, with the *MISA* type of account, often deposits and transfers have to be in multiples of say $500. Consequently, in a procedural sense you code it as procedure *deposit*. Unlike in an OOPL, in a procedural language we dive straight to the algorithm. So a `Case` statement is used dependent upon the type of bank account under consideration. Similarly, for procedure *withdraw*, the procedure has a `Case` structure, etc. In a procedural format, consider what happens when I invent a new bank account with new procedural implementations of *withdraw*,

Reusability and Productivity

Open-closed principle

Reuse of code, design,
   frameworks

Increased productivity
— less "re-inventing the wheel"

Building a system from
REUSABLE objects is
BOTTOM-UP

Data Dependency

```
Type
      BankAccount = Record
                Type:(CheckingAccount, SavingsAccount,
                                    MISAAccount);
            Balance: Money;
                . . . .
      End;

Procedure deposit(account:BankAccount,amount:Money)
Case BankAccount.Type of

      CheckingAccount:Checkdeposit(account,amount);
      SavingsAccount:Savingsdeposit(account,amount);
      MISAAccount:MISAdeposit(account,amount);
End;

Procedure withdraw(account:BankAccount,amount:Money)
Case BankAccount.Type of

      CheckingAccount:Checkwithdraw(account,amount);
      SavingsAccount:Savingswithdraw(account,amount);
      MISAAccount:MISAwithdraw(account,amount);
End;

Procedure transfer (. . . etc.)
```

New account (e.g., StudentSavingsAccount) must be added
separately to Case structure of **all** procedure definitions

EXHIBIT 34   Copyright © B. Henderson-Sellers, 1991

Problem avoided using OO

```
Type
    BankAccount = Record
Attribute
    balance
Routine
    withdraw
    - - algorithm to withdraw
    deposit
    - - algorithm to deposit
    transfer
    - - algorithm to transfer
End

Subtype
    Checking
Inherit
    BankAccount
End

Subtype
    Savings
Inherit
    BankAccount
Routine
    - - redefines withdraw
    withdraw
    - - new algorithm to withdraw
End
```

Adding new account, simply add

```
Subtype
    StudentSavings
Inherit
    Savings
Routine
    - - appropriate redefinitions or new features
End
```

deposit, etc. In that case, there has to be an entry into *every* `Case` structure — easy to miss one in a large program even with automated tools. In the original structure we had a three `Case` structure. Now we need four.

What would this look like in an OOPL (Exhibit 35)? There would be a *BankAccount* type with an attribute *balance* and routines *withdraw, deposit, transfer*, etc. Essentially, you can differentiate between attributes (data) and routines (functions or procedures) — see later discussions. The features have names and implementations. In OO, then, we have three subclasses: subclass *Checking*, subclass *Savings*, and subclass *MISA*. Each of those subclasses has a name. All of these inherit from *BankAccount* and they may or may not redefine the procedures. So class *Checking* inherits everything from *BankAccount*. It inherits the attribute *balance*; it inherits the routines *withdraw, transfer*, and *deposit*, and their implementations. In this case, there is no redefinition and, within the limits of the four declared features, there are no changes (presumably there are differences in other nonillustrated features or else there would be no real reason to have *Checking* as a different account from plain *BankAccount*). However, for the subclass *Savings*, Exhibit 35 shows that there is one redefinition of the procedure *withdraw*. This reflects the different rules the bank imposes on withdrawing from savings accounts, compared with those for withdrawing from other types of accounts.

Adding a new account class then becomes extremely easy. The bank decides to start a new *StudentSavings*. Rather than having to locate several `Case` statements scattered around a procedural program, in an OOPL a new account is added by declaring a new class *StudentSavings* that inherits from an existing class, *Savings*. Then the declaration simply says, in effect, this new account class is "just like a savings account" (the inherit clause), "but it has some slight redefinition of some or all the features."

3.7 A Better Model

It is proposed that an object-oriented model is a better model of the real world (e.g., Thomas, 1989b) (Exhibit 36). Object-orientation was, after all, originally developed in the simulation world, where modeling concerns are paramount. It is also a better software model insofar as it provides a "seamless transition" throughout the life cycle. In other words, the model we can now apply at the analysis and design phases of the life cycle is essentially the same as that applied for detailed design and coding, a model that can be exploited further in the life cycle methodologies and the notation discussed in Chapter 4. This is in contrast to functional decomposition and structured life cycle methodologies where different models are used at different life cycle stages: for instance, an entity-relationship diagram and data flow diagram in the analysis phase, a hierarchy chart in the design phase, and procedural syntax at the language level. These are all *very* different ways to view the world and hence to view the software model.

Viewing the world in terms of objects is claimed to be more natural. When I look around at the world I tend to see objects, things that have characteristics. The most immediate characteristic is how the object looks to me (its external

Better Model of Real World;

"Seamless Transition"

— seen as sets of interacting objects via their functionality

Compatibility

Links between OO environment and procedural environments

Ease of use

(depends on language and available tools)

interface). Then I notice how the thing behaves. In other words, I see state first and then behavior (see also apple example in Gibson, 1991). This is exactly the object-oriented approach, as discussed with respect to Exhibit 19. Objects are identified in the real world and translated *directly* (i.e., not through some intermediary akin to structure charts or DFDs) into software objects. These objects then interact with each other via their functionality, or behavior.

3.8 Compatibility and Ease of Use

While in a pure object-oriented language, it could be argued that there should be no linking with procedural code; in reality, there are strong links (Exhibit 36). In OOPLs that cannot be described as pure, but rather as hybrid languages, such as C++, both the OO and procedural paradigms can be used either singly or together. Furthermore, many of the language environments (Section 5.10) rely on routines written in a procedural language (often C) or assembler in order for them to work efficiently. This means that other coroutines written in, say, C can be included as part of the object-oriented system. Finally, it is a stated goal (and becoming increasingly feasible) to link in these languages not only with C (and also Ada) but also with FORTRAN and COBOL — the two languages with the most code currently still in use, written and accumulated over the last twenty or thirty years. Success in such interlinking could provide a likely path for migration in both the scientific environment (e.g., Rhoades, 1990) and the commercial MIS environment.

Other links between the object-oriented world and the procedural world are still being explored. At the OOPSLA '90 conference in Ottawa, one of the panel discussions was set up specifically to explore whether/where such commonalities exist (see also Henderson-Sellers and Constantine, 1991). Some of these cross-fertilizations are explored here in the section on convergent methodologies in the analysis and design chapter (Section 4.3.5).

Ease of use in an OO environment is something that comes with experience. The novice faces a stiff learning curve (see Section 3.10.2), although there is no evidence to suggest that this is significantly greater than one's first experience in learning a procedural language and structured analysis and design. Once past that initial barrier, informal information strongly supports the notion of easier coding, increased productivity, and lower maintenance costs (see also McCullough and Deshler, 1990). Finally, ease of use is not just about the language. Indeed, OO will become an arena not of language wars but of CASE (computer-aided software engineering) tools wars. The potential ease of use is so great that we are likely to see a programming style relying much more heavily on CASE tools, so that the *environment*, rather than the language, becomes the significant factor. At present, with few good CASE tools around, choosing a language should be strongly influenced by the available tools. These include browsers, dynamic debuggers (see, e.g., Purchase and Winder, 1991), and graphical tools to navigate amongst the classes — but beware of object-oriented CASE tools based on older functional decomposition CASE tools and evaluate them carefully!

3.9 Advantages of Object-Oriented Software Engineering

In her analysis of object-oriented project management, Goldberg (1991) asks the question "What do we value in software development project management?" She suggests (Exhibit 37) that satisfaction (to developer and/or end-user) derives from (1) delivering the product to the user on time; (2) ensuring that the products really do meet the user requirements; (3) responding in a timely fashion to user requests to modify the system and/or fix bugs in the current version of the software; (4) being able to offer increasingly sophisticated applications products to the marketplace; (5) keeping up with changes in standards and delivery technology; and (6) ensuring the project team feels both well motivated and successful.

Exhibit 38 summarizes the 12 basic advantages of using an OO approach to address the problem areas of software engineering outlined earlier. We can include:

1) More language support for correctness, for instance by using assertions (Meyer, 1989b), which ties in with the idea of a contract and the client–server diagram (Exhibit 18). If you can specify that a given object–object interaction is valid only for certain states of the object, and that there are obligations on the supplier and on the client, then it's easier to be sure that your object will react to bad data or an invalid state in an orderly fashion. In contrast, for example, in many BASIC interpreters, a division by zero will be flagged but essentially accepted and the program run does NOT terminate. To try to get away from this sort of error, it is necessary to have a strict and controlled way of dealing with errors that OO encourages and to flag errors very efficiently using a good trace-back mechanism and not just "pass the buck" as it is often claimed in Ada (Meyer, 1988), in which it may often be hard to locate the true source of any specific error.

2) Robustness, which relates to the program's behavior when exposed to abnormal conditions. A robust program will not only be resilient to abnormality but also, when it must fail, do so in a controlled and "graceful" way (e.g., Meyer, 1988, p4). Robustness is improved when you can safely modify a portion of your program that does not cause repercussions in distant parts of the program. Encapsulation helps achieve this goal.

3) Extendibility, for example, using inheritance to extend an existing bank-account object to a new object that is "just like a bank account but" has three extra lines of code. We can extend our systems in that way very quickly and very safely using those sorts of constructs.

4) Reusability, which is seen as so important by Brad Cox that he has made a trademark of the phrase "software IC" (IC = integrated circuit). His basic idea is that hardware works on the premise that you don't reinvent basic circuits every time; rather you take what already exists and you buy chips off the shelf and plug them together and build your "original" design of a "hardware box." Why can't we do the same with software? Let's move toward being able to do that so that we can go to a company and say, "I'd like to buy off your shelf a bank-account object." The idea is that of objects, being stored in libraries, which we can purchase from the vendors. So reusability is essentially concerned with

AIMS OF SOFTWARE DEVELOPERS

- Deliver product on time (and within budget)

- Ensure product meets user requirements

- Respond to user requests for changes

- Offer increasingly sophisticated applications

- Keep up with technological standards

- Ensure project team feel well-motivated and successful

(adapted from Goldberg, 1991)

Advantage of an Object-Oriented Approach (Summary)

1. Correctness (through assertions)

2. Robustness

3. Extendibility

4. Reusability (+ development of libraries of classes)
      (Software-IC™)

5. Have integrity (safe with respect to unauthorized
    access/modification)

Also

6. (Potential) increased productivity

7. Avoids data dependency problem

8. Better model of real world

9. One-to-one map between requirements and design
      and between design and coding ("seamless transition")

10. Compatibility (+ links with other language modules)

11. Ease of use (but cf. learning curve)

12. Competitive edge — "The Computing of the 90s"

EXHIBIT 38   Copyright © B. Henderson-Sellers, 1991

developing objects for and distributing objects from libraries. Meyer (1989c) epitomizes this as a shift from a *project* culture (non-OO) to a *product* culture (OO).

5) Integrity, in terms of unauthorized access. In other words, we return to the characteristics exemplified by encapsulation. If we now have a very small interface, then that gives the module a higher integrity so that it is now not easy to modify it accidentally, something that a language that supports globally scoped variables can very easily permit: for instance, FORTRAN COMMON blocks, C globals, and COBOL programs where variables are, for the most part, global. In such programs it is very easy to accidentally overload a variable name, with sometimes disastrous consequences.

Those are the *main* advantages presented by object-oriented software engineering. I also see other potential advantages that are perhaps less clear-cut. These include:

6) Productivity. It is foreseen (Thomsett, 1990) that there is, necessarily, an increased overhead in the design stage of OO with a concomitant decrease in coding/implementation and in maintenance. This contrasts with traditional methods where the maximum effort in design is less but the following phases (implementation, testing, and maintenance) continue to require large amounts of effort (traditional "Rayleigh" curve: Norden, 1958). This is discussed in more detail in Section 3.5 (productivity) and 3.11 (project management).

7) Data dependency problem. Discussed in Section 3.6, it brings back to mind the idea of encapsulation, whereby changing functions within an object have no repercussions elsewhere.

8) OO as a better model of the real world. Some people argue against that, but I would suggest that as you look around you, you first see objects, i.e., things, and only later do you look at their functionality explicitly. That means you can discriminate between analysis objects in the real world, transform them into design objects in the solution space — and you're using the same model. So you can use a software bank-account object to model the real-world, tangible bank-account object.

9) The same model for the different stages. There is a more or less one-to-one mapping between requirements and design and then between design and coding: a "seamless transition."

10) Compatibility. I think there are a lot of still unexplored advantages in terms of linkages with other languages. For instance, in Eiffel you can link in subprograms in C or assembler. This suggests a more open design in software development. This means that coding, which may be very difficult in the high-level OOPL, can be undertaken in a lower-level language and then successfully linked in to the OOPL. It also creates an heterogeneous debugging environment that requires either multiskilled programmers or specialized teams. Hence this compatibility comes at a price. Other packaging approaches can be explored in which procedural modules can be given interfaces compatible with objects in a system. This may provide a migration path from procedures to objects, as such encapsulated procedures gradually require replacement.

11) Ease of use. Again there is debate, because there must be a learning curve

for new ideas, which is after all why you bought this book![10] Initially, therefore, an OO environment must be harder to use simply because of its unfamiliarity. But once you get used to using it — and that may take a little while, depending upon how many hours per week you devote to learning it, perhaps a few months or up to a year to become really proficient — *then* you will find it a lot easier and more productive.

12) Competitive edge. I originally added a question mark in parentheses here. However, over the last year, from talking with representatives of industries in Australia, North America, and Europe, several of whom are very cautious about releasing details, it is clear that leading edge companies have no hesitation in regarding OO as giving them a competitive edge. Many are willing to talk once their product is released and their competitive advantage has been well and truly established (e.g., McCullough, and Deshler, 1990).

3.10 Areas of Debate

Although many tout OO as "the computing of the nineties and the next century" many will ask, "Why should we succumb to this new technology and adopt the object-oriented philosophy with all its investment in learning a new mindset?" "We only adopted a relational database two years ago; why should we now switch to an object-oriented database? Perhaps there'll be something even better in another couple of years." And how can we really tell? We don't know for sure, but it's the perception of many of us that the object-oriented approach to software engineering has a reasonably lengthy lifetime ahead of it. The recent emergence of the Object Management Group (Barber, 1991) within the computer industry, as well as a high degree of interest and involvement from all major hardware and software vendors, substantiate this forecast.

Some areas of interest and concern are shown in Exhibit 39. Some of these are now fading, some are rising, and consequently this table will be the first thing in the book to date. Those that are now becoming less important topics of "fiery debate" are listed at the top of the figure.

The top-down versus bottom-up debate stemmed partly from the ideas over the last few decades that we should all be doing top-down decomposition. I've already illustrated how it's necessary also to consider bottom-up design in order to optimize on design and code reuse. Hence this is not really an either/or, it's really an "and." The life cycle methodologies discussed in Section 4.3.2 start off being top-down and then migrate to being bottom-up. The merging of these two approaches is useful.

Meyer (1988, p332) asks the question "Would you rather buy or inherit?" This relates to the ongoing discussions about the apparent trade-offs between using client–server and using inheritance. In general, as noted elsewhere in this book, most cases are relatively clear-cut. They are either **uses-a** or **is-composed-of**, both of which use client–server; or they are **is-a**, which is inheritance. Some indecision and confusion can arise in special circumstances, but such cases are

---

[10]I hope you did buy it and not purloin it!

Recent and Current Areas of Interest and Concern in Object-Oriented Software Engineering

Recent

Top-down versus bottom-up

Object–object relationships ——
client or inheritance, which is preferable?

Current

Object-object relationships: what are they at analysis and design and what is appropriate notation?

Life cycle methodologies

Learning curve

How to find objects

Commercial programming in the large and project management

OO metrics

How do you make classes really reusable (including interface with other languages)?

Managing object libraries

EXHIBIT 39   Copyright © B. Henderson-Sellers, 1991

really outside the scope of this book. Meyer (1988) certainly notes that inheritance is a "more committing decision than 'buying' " — a further variable in the equation. Further discussion on this topic is also to be found in Rumbaugh *et al.* (1991, Chapter 10).

In a somewhat similar vein are discussions on the significance of the availability of multiple inheritance. While most languages have aimed to add multiple inheritance as an extra, much-needed language feature, there are still debates regarding appropriate cases of multiple inheritance (MI), especially since the overuse of MI leads to complex networks of classes that are likely to thwart class reusability. Meyer (1988) gives many examples of the use of MI in the Eiffel library classes. On the other hand, it has been argued that an apparent need for MI can equally well be coded using single inheritance (see also Snyder, 1986). There is, however, a growing consensus that MI is a valuable and powerful tool, yet should perhaps be used sparingly, only when really necessary.

3.10.1 Notation and methodologies

The relationships between objects (or classes) is still very much a research question, especially with respect to the notational aspects. At a special workshop session at OOPSLA '90, with the wonderful acronym of GOOSE (Graphics for Object-Oriented Software Engineering), several notations were proposed. Some of those are included in the discussion in Section 4.5. The question of whether we need different or similar notation for analysis, design, and implementation life cycle stages is still (at the time of writing) being hotly debated.

Another area of current concern is that of devising and testing design and analysis methodologies. As noted in Chapter 1, since the object-oriented "(r)evolution" has been led by the computer scientists, the areas of analysis and design methodologies have been somewhat neglected. Special issues of *Communications of the ACM* (September 1990) and of the *Journal of Object-Oriented Programming* (January 1991) are beginning to address the dearth of information in these important information systems areas. Some of these methodologies and guidelines are discussed in Section 4.3.

3.10.2 Learning languages

Learning the language syntax differs between languages and prior experience. It is said that learning an OOPL that is an obvious extension of a language you already know is tantamount to admitting defeat, since you will tend to continue to code in the paradigm with which you are already familiar (e.g., Antebi, 1990), rather than adopting the powerful new concepts embodied in the OOPL itself. Burton Leathers (pers. com., 1990) wisely suggests that if you want to learn C++, learn Smalltalk or Eiffel first, a sentiment echoed by Thomas (1989b), LaLonde and Pugh (1990), and Gibson (1991). C programmers might automatically drift toward C++, and indeed managers find it easier to support such a transition. However, experience is building (e.g., Waldo, 1990) to suggest that this can be a painful transition for the reasons outlined above. The need for *good* training was noted by Leathers (1990b), Wybolt (1990), Stewart (1991), and by many others at the OOPSLA '90 formal presentations and informal gatherings.

3.10.3 Finding objects

There is then the question of how to find object classes. No one yet has a definitive answer, although many have tentatively suggested answers. The first edition of Grady Booch's *Software Engineering with Ada* suggested looking at the requirements document and underlining all the nouns. This was omitted from the second edition, however, although it is a frequent topic of exchanges via the international electronic bulletin boards. This may only be a very coarse first step, since often in a requirements document there will be more nouns than those that will become objects, and conversely many objects in the final implementation will be more abstract notions not immediately identifiable at the requirements analysis stage of the life cycle. Abstract nouns will also become classes. Others say to find the objects, simply look around and there they are. Again, this can be at best a crude first approximation. Methodologies for finding the object are still required, although Rumbaugh *et al.* (1991, Chapter 8) give useful guidelines on how to eliminate unnecessary and incorrect classes from the object model.

Finding the objects and their interrelationships is not yet a secure art. Here is a second guideline tool. A method known as CRC cards, standing for "Class, Responsibility, and Collaborations", has been used in both teaching applications (Beck and Cunningham, 1989) and commercial environments (Wirfs-Brock *et al.*, 1990). This is a "low-tech" tool in a high-tech arena. A CRC card (Exhibit 40) is simply a personal filing card or index card, approximately 10 cm × 15 cm (4″ × 6″) on which class names, class responsibilities, and interacting or collaborating classes are named. Advantages claimed for this technique are the easily flexible rearrangements (usually by spreading the cards on a desk or the floor) and the possibilities of assigning the card completion across a larger team than would be possible to seat around a single VDU on which the project would be focused. Although hypermedia versions have been tested, the designers claim that users prefer the card variety. The use of CRC cards is seen as an early exploration tool in which key objects, key collaborations, and key subsystems can be identified in a highly interactive atmosphere, perhaps somewhat akin to "brainstorming." Disadvantages are that in the highly interactive nature of OOD, corrections and revisions to cards, possibly involving total rewrites as corrections to corrections to corrections become indecipherable, are finally harder than in a more flexible electronic-medium format. Final, agreed documentation would also be a problem if this technique were applied to later design work. Even as an exploratory tool, returning a stack of cards to the user for verification may not be very successful (Booch, pers. com., 1991).

3.11 Project Management

Commercial programming in the large (e.g., Wegner, 1990) and project management (Exhibit 41) are the upcoming topics in the object-oriented world. While initially the focus has been on the languages, now attention is moving first to analysis and design and then on to the scalability of successful OO pilot projects to large-scale, commercial applications. Although one of the promises of OO

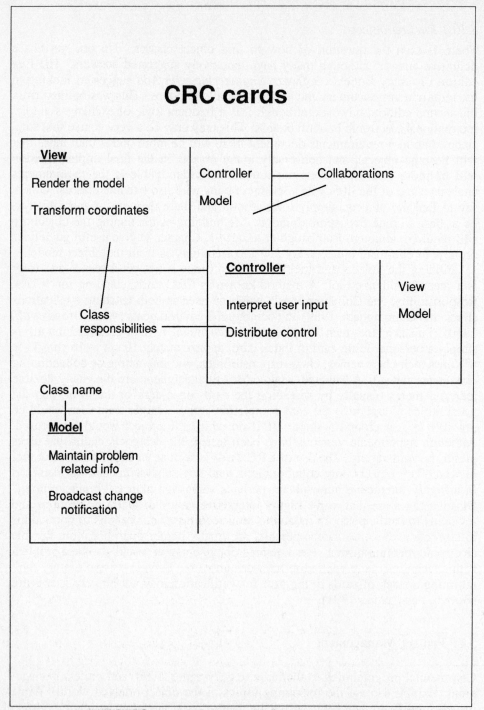

CRC cards

View

Render the model

Transform coordinates

Controller

Model

Collaborations

Class
responsibilities

Controller

Interpret user input

Distribute control

View

Model

Class name

Model

Maintain problem
    related info

Broadcast change
    notification

PROJECT MANAGEMENT

More effort in design

Less in testing/implementation

Much less in maintenance and
    reuse

EXHIBIT 41   Copyright © B. Henderson-Sellers, 1991

is greater safety, quality, and reliability in large and very large projects, there is, as yet, little empirical data to support that. It has become clear that initially small projects should be initiated using OO techniques (e.g., Goldberg and Rubin, 1990; Coleman and Hayes, 1991). When the first OO project attempted is a large-scale project, problems have been encountered with project management in the new environment, sometimes worsened by technical hitches (e.g., Leathers, 1990a), poor training, inaccurate estimates of effort, etc. (see also Stewart, 1991). However, there are a growing number of reports of highly successful use of OO techniques. In the cash management arena, McCullough and Deshler (1990) report that "prospective users were amazed" by the WyCASH+ system; and on-the-fly modifications/extendibility was proven in a short time in response to an initial customer query. Here, as elsewhere, a prototyping development environment was chosen for the OO implementation. Other successful projects are reported by Hopkins (1990a) in telecommunications, by Winston (1990) in a wide range of applications areas, by Wybolt (1990) in the development of CASE tools, and by Berman and Gur (1988) and Nurick (1990).

As noted in Sections 3.5 and 3.11, new perspectives are required in project management for setting goals and "deliverables." Booch (1991, p208 et seq.) notes the need to reconcile the incremental and iterative nature of object-oriented development with traditional "milestones" used by many organizations. He recommends more informal design reviews during development together with new metrics, focusing not on lines of code but, for instance, on the percentage of classes from the full number in the design implemented. In other words, emphasis in terms of project management and productivity is shifted from the coding phase to the design phase, which is the phase where more effort is concentrated. Typically (Exhibit 42), design effort may be 60–70% more than in a traditional structured development; coding may be 40% less; testing 25% less; and system integration 70% less (Booch, 1991, p207). As a second measure of progress, Booch recommends evaluation of the stability of the class interfaces. In addition, as the system is incrementally integrated and tested, a series of working "prototypes" may be viewable by the management and customer alike.

There are other management questions partly related to generalization, as an overhead to developing useful classes, especially with regard to appropriate metrics (see Sections 3.5 and 3.11.1). For example, there is a management question regarding the interface between two project teams (cf. Constantine, 1990c). If you are the project manager for one of those teams, you presumably want your team to succeed, even perhaps at the expense of your colleague's team. If that sort of corporate culture is in existence, then how do you allow one team to build generalized classes useful not for its own future projects, but for an alternative team's next projects? Since generalization decreases your own productivity (with the currently available metrics) yet reuse increases productivity, the "other team" will benefit from the first team's generalization efforts. Management will need to reassess how productivity, effort, and success are measured in an object-oriented software development environment (e.g., Hopkins and Warboys, 1990; Bollinger and Pfleeger, 1990). Thomsett (1990) evaluates the potential conflicts between two program development teams within the same organization. He recommends

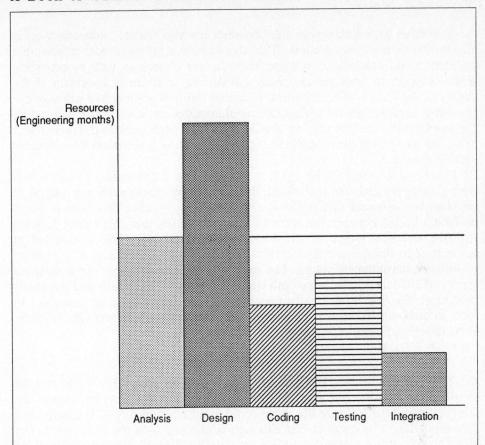

60 – 70% more design effort
40% less coding effort
25% less testing
70% less effort in system integration

EXHIBIT 42   Copyright © G. Booch, 1991

the institution of a linking-pin role between the two teams: someone who is responsible to both team leaders. This shared human resource will enhance the production and generalization of reusable library classes as well as providing central support to both teams. Such a reporting structure is necessary if the quality of software is to be enhanced by use of this new approach to software engineering: an approach for which traditional management structures are ill suited. Thomsett (1990) stresses that we should regard the object-oriented development paradigm as an *organizational* paradigm first, and as a technical development paradigm second.

Finally, since the OO life cycle is underlaid by a conceptual model which more closely parallels the real world, the need for including a domain analyst in the team is paramount (Wirfs-Brock *et al.*, 1990, pp14–15). This person would become a bridge between the software analyst and the user, becoming familiar with the technical jargon of the domain being modeled. This could lead to software specialists in certain domains perhaps working freelance to a number of software development shops. The existence of such a person in the software team will undoubtedly enhance both communication with the user and the user's confidence that the team "really understands" the user's specific problem. In such an ambience of mutual understanding and trust, qualify software is likely to be developed more effectively.

3.11.1 Metrics

Exhibit 43 is a schematic diagram of the components of the life cycle and the distribution of effort with time, i.e., productivity. This emphasizes that the different stages of the software life cycle could occur concurrently — the individual curves overlap. The result is that although at any one time the same amount of effort could be going into the project as with the "linear" life cycle, this effort is likely to be distributed more evenly across the project stages. The result is a reduction in the lapsed time taken to complete the project. Indeed, it is likely that the class design, together with class generalization in the latter part of the project, could take considerably longer, since genericity and code reuse is one of the aims of the object-oriented life cycle in order that maintenance costs (often, unwisely, excluded from project development costs) can be dramatically reduced. In addition, it is likely that system testing time will be considerably reduced (e.g., Booch and Vilot, 1990a). Consequently, the traditional software metrics, either in terms of source lines of code or function points, will inevitably indicate a further decrease of productivity (in addition to that mentioned above), since they do not address the subsequent phase of program maintenance. Thus again it may be that traditional metrics are of little direct applicability to OOD.

To date, then, no comprehensive methodology for size estimation of an object-oriented system has been successfully developed. Metrics for software designed and built using a functional decomposition approach are largely inappropriate for object-oriented software development (e.g., Moreau and Dominick, 1989).

As an example, consider working out a regular productivity metric in terms of lines of code delivered per unit effort (Exhibit 44). First, you do a regular

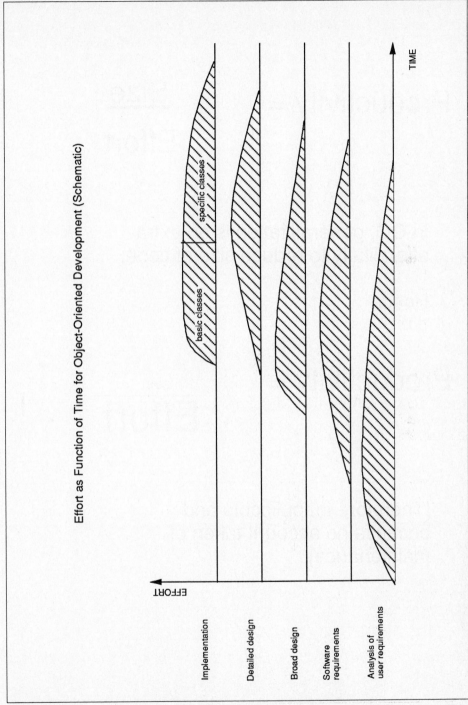

Effort as Function of Time for Object-Oriented Development (Schematic)

EXHIBIT 43   Copyright © B. Henderson-Sellers and J.M. Edwards, 1990

$$\text{Productivity} = \frac{\text{Size}}{\text{Effort}}$$

In OO, generalization is an extra effort likely to reduce size of code.

Hence

$$\text{Productivity} = \frac{\text{Size}}{\text{Effort}} \searrow \ !$$

[Therefore inapplicable and because no account taken of maintenance]

EXHIBIT 44

design and calculate productivity. If you then go further and spend effort in generalizing, this process will often reduce the number of lines of code. Thus in the ratio of lines of code to effort, the numerator has decreased and the denominator increased, suggesting a significant decrease in productivity (Meyer, 1989c).

New concerns need to be considered. These include allowing for code reuse, for effort spent in creating generalized classes for future use (to be stored in class libraries), as well as for the cost of storing and managing library modules. As in traditional metrics, the new metrics needed for object-oriented (OO) software development should be aimed at (1) size, complexity, and productivity — for overall project estimates; and (2) dynamic allocation of personnel at various stages in the life cycle. Exhibit 45 illustrates the need for a different model in the latter case and indicates schematically some of the areas to be considered. In addition to a different distribution of effort with time, the major differences lie in the *reuse of code* to achieve the same functionality and the additional effort required on project number i (on generalization) in order to reap the benefit of code reuse in projects $i + 1$ *et seq.* This suggests that an additional "metric" of $R = \frac{Reuse\ Savings}{Generalization\ Costs}$ should be calculated in some way in order to assess the viability of using the OO paradigm in any specific project, although it should be noted that if the long-term generalization costs exceed the long-term reuse benefits (that is, if the cost–benefit ratio is greater than unity), no productivity enhancement will be obtained (Balda and Gustafson, 1990; Bollinger and Pfleeger, 1990; Henderson-Sellers, 1991a).

Generalization costs are, at present, very difficult to assess empirically. Nevertheless, conceptually we can consider costing the development of reused classes *either* against the projects in which they are used *or* against the project in which they first arose. Although the former is more appealing, it is more difficult since (i) cost accounting could be difficult if the model remained unused for some time; and (ii) the cost should presumably be amortized over the number of projects that use this class, a number that in general is unknown. To do this then, some fixed and agreed depreciation rate and amortization period would need to be introduced. In the second (cost to the originating project), the current project would bear the cost of refining (generalizing) object classes for acceptance into the corporate library. In an organization where the software is to be developed for internal use, this presents little problem, but for third-party software developers and vendors such overheads are unlikely to find favor with the current clients.

All the metrics discussed by Henderson-Sellers (1991a), both traditional and object-oriented, essentially terminate when the product is delivered. Maintenance costs are not considered, although this has been an area of active research for some years (e.g., Card *et al.*, 1987). Since, as noted above, this can be significant cost to the software developer over time, and since this is an area where dramatic improvements are likely to follow upon the adoption of object-oriented techniques, it is also important for future development of object-oriented metrics that this maintenance cost be included in overall project costs (together with a concomitant introduction into structured systems development metrics in any comparative analyses between design and implementation environments).

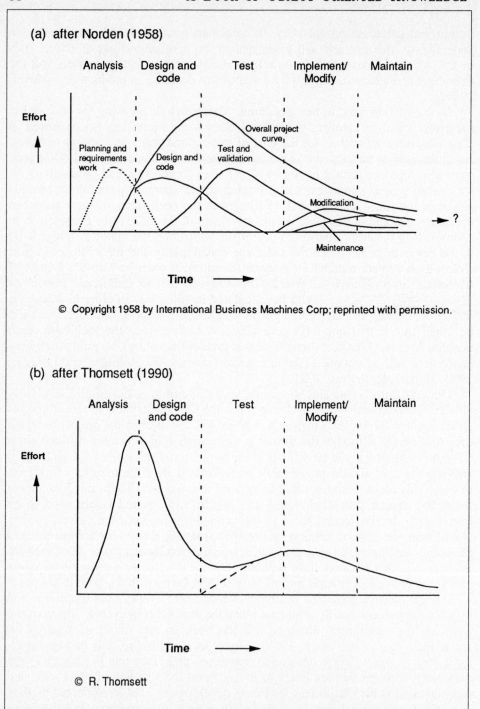

(a) after Norden (1958)

© Copyright 1958 by International Business Machines Corp; reprinted with permission.

(b) after Thomsett (1990)

© R. Thomsett

EXHIBIT 45   Copyright © B. Henderson-Sellers, 1991

3.11.2 Managing reusability

How do you make classes really reusable and how do you manage those class libraries (Exhibit 46)? Firstly, classes should conform strictly to the notion of being an implementation of an abstract data type. In other words, class builders should avoid the temptation, too easy in procedural languages, to lump together specific pieces of data and functionality in a single module "for convenience," i.e., an *ad hoc* design usually undertaken in the absence of any design procedure/methodology. Even perfectly designed and constructed classes will, however, need to be made readily available and "managed" (Meyer, 1990a; Gibbs *et al.*, 1990).

Reusable object classes are indeed seen as a major benefit of adopting the object-oriented paradigm in the commercial data processing and applications programming worlds. However, without some efficient and effective method of locating previously written classes, this benefit could too easily be lost since the ease of reprogramming a class will discourage spending time in locating existing code (cf. Prieto-Diaz and Freeman, 1987; Page-Jones, 1991a). Some type of classification structure seems vital for navigating around the class libraries prior to selecting the class you want. But does this relate to your own individual workstation, a divisional library, an organizational library, or a wholesaler's library (e.g., a global center for the resale of library classes in a given language environment)?

Library management requires a new structure within an organization. If an *organizational* library is to be constructed and maintained, then decisions have to be made regarding what classes go into the library. This requires planning and coordination between team members and also quality checking and validation of the library components themselves. Organizational (if not international) standards on documentation and naming conventions are required, as are management commitment and support for a policy of reuse, one that allows for creators of reusable classes to be suitably rewarded (e.g., Goldberg, 1991; Stewart, 1991).

Gibbs *et al.* (1990) describe class management not only in terms of database techniques, but also taking into account new concerns implicit in an object-oriented system. These relate to class evolution, class selection, and class packaging. In addition, there may be purely commercial concerns of pricing and licensing policies.

Technical issues relating to generalization of classes are raised by, e.g., Meyer (1990a). In terms of the fountain model of Henderson-Sellers and Edwards (1990a) applied to classes or clusters of classes (see especially their Figure 8), generalization follows class development and testing prior to inclusion in a project (or other) library. Meyer (1990a) details the necessary steps and some of the pitfalls. He stresses that although "it is always preferable, of course, to get the inheritance right initially," in practice this is rarely achieved and should not be regarded as an indicator of a software engineer's ability. (This is supported directly by Meyer's own library development work.) The final product is seen as more important than the process, although of course an efficient process is also to be encouraged. This again reflects a shift from a process-oriented software culture to a product-oriented one (Cox, 1990b).

Managing Reusability

Classification of object classes

Organizational libraries

Vendor libraries

Browsing and retrieval tools

A given system is probably going to consist of fewer objects than it would have had procedural subroutines (Constantine, 1990a). While learning to navigate around a class library of around 200 classes is not trivial, even with the use of available browsing tools, the anticipated advent of corporation libraries of several thousand or million classes, and the possibility of third-party class vendors providing off-the-shelf classes for purchase, both require some technique for locating the required class. Object cataloging and retrieval systems are currently being developed to address this challenge of large-scale reusability (e.g., Meyer, 1990a; Price and Girardi, 1990; Henderson-Sellers and Freeman, 1991). Finally, the problem of software quality in vendor libraries has yet to be addressed fully (Korson and McGregor, 1991).

3.11.3 Commercial Adoption

There is a growing experience in the commercial adoption of object-oriented software development techniques. While early experiences were either shared by word of mouth or retained commercial confidentiality, more developers are now willing to share their experiences, often learned the hard way, with other commercial companies. Many of these experiences are reported at conferences such as OOPSLA or TOOLS, or in journals such as *Hotline on Object-Oriented Technology*.

The general and growing consensus is that OO technology should be adopted NOW (e.g., Page-Jones, 1991a) even while it is not yet mature and still in the growth phase, probably in a small, important, yet not absolutely critical, project (Exhibit 47). In such a situation, the learning phase is encapsulated within a small group, thus avoiding the management and interpersonal problems of large groups, the members of which then become a resource for spreading the technology throughout the rest of the organization. Any problems that might arise, as they might with the adoption of *any* new technology, especially if the staff are not adequately trained and/or briefed, are again contained and can be dealt with promptly. The project should be of value to the organization, with the encouragement and backing of senior management and *should not* be a "mickey-mouse" project, simply invented as a test-bed. The counterargument to using a noncritical project is that a successful project therefore does not really provide the value to the company that it would have if it had been in a more critical area, thus delaying real adoption within the organization.

Project management, milestones, and metrics have been discussed above. Adoption of object technology must be viewed in the light of a strategic plan. Since it is almost impossible to gain advantage with the first project on account of both the learning curve and the unavailability of reuse from previous projects, the real savings must be in the longer term and indeed have been realized by many organizations that have already been investing in this new technology over the last few years.

New job specifications are needed in an object-oriented development environment. Page-Jones (1991a) lists some of these. Since the development of in-house library classes to supplement and complement those provided with the selected language or bought from third-party vendors is a major advantage realizable with

ADOPTING AN OBJECT-ORIENTED APPROACH

1) SMALL, NONCRITICAL (YET VALUABLE) PROJECT

2) PLAN FOR LONG-TERM COST SAVINGS FROM WIDESPREAD REUSE — OF CODE, DESIGNS, FRAMEWORKS

3) INSTIGATE

- Class librarian

- Class developers

- Class reusers

- etc.

4) ADOPT NOW — AND GROW AS THE TECHNOLOGY GROWS AND MATURES

object technology, it is important that one person be given responsibilities for the management of the organization's class libraries. Other responsibilities, in addition to operational management of libraries, include strategic planning of library development, the initiation and maintenance of standards (i.e., the vetting of classes submitted for inclusion in the library), and two groups of "programmers": one that will be skilled in class development, especially generalization, and one that will be skilled in class reuse. Providing such new challenges and revisions of job specifications will offer new challenges and new opportunities, although it must be stressed that rewards for reuse must be awarded by management in the same way that programmers are currently rewarded for their (often very individual) work. Finally, it must be stressed that skills already acquired under the structured development model will not be totally wasted. Although some retraining is vital, once the new mindset has been acquired, the types of skills currently available in the industry can be mustered, reworked, and reapplied to a whole range of new and exciting problems that previously could not have been even considered.

3.12 Summary

In summary (Exhibit 48), the software engineering concerns of correctness, extendibility, and maintainability tie up very closely with that of reusability, which is seen by many to be a major advantage of the OO approach to software engineering. To accomplish reusability, modules must be tightly encapsulated, using the Open–Closed Principle, and then stored in a library. The management of class libraries is becoming of increasing concern and requires a solution if we are to see a large-scale and successful adoption by commerce and industry of object-oriented software engineering. New management structures will need to be put into place, and new metrics and project management strategies employed. Overall, several writers urge the immediate adoption of object technology, even though it is in its infancy in terms of existing commercial experience, thus allowing the maturation of the firm's experience with OO along with the development of the technology itself. Indeed, one of the areas that will assist this is the current effort being expended in developing analysis and design methodologies, associated notation, and, ultimately, CASE tool support for a fully object-oriented software development environment. These topics are the focus of Chapter 4.

Chapter 3

Summary

Concerns of Correctness, Reuse, Extendibility, Maintainability

Encapsulation

Class Libraries

Chapter 4

OBJECT-ORIENTED SYSTEMS DEVELOPMENT

In this chapter (Exhibit 49), I will look at how we actually undertake an object-oriented systems design using, as a major ongoing example, the design of part of a banking system, augmented by smaller examples on the way. As noted earlier, analysis, design, and coding tend to merge. In this chapter we consider that merging in more detail and how it affects the object-oriented life cycle.

Before developing the object-oriented systems development life cycle, it is educative to consider how an object-oriented mindset contrasts with the current approaches to software engineering. In this context, we first look at an example based on a design from Jackson (1983), but viewed from an object-oriented standpoint. Secondly, we will begin our consideration of a banking example, an example which will be developed further later in this chapter (Section 4.6).

4.1 Brief Introductory Design Examples

These brief introductory design examples are highly simplistic and chosen to illustrate specific points rather than provide an overall rigorous description. This first example is from Jackson (1983) (Exhibit 50). If you are familiar with Jackson System Development (JSD) you will know that this approach has some small amount of object-orientation about it; it certainly takes a modeling approach, as does OO. However, it gets to the functionality very much faster than an OO design would and it has a strict chronology.

In this example, we are asked to consider the management of a pleasure lake with boats on it. People come to hire the boats for an hour or so. Our job is to develop and manage the software reporting to management, who have hired us to write it. In the requirements analysis given to us, we find that customers arrive at the booth and ask if there is a boat available. If so, information is keyed in about the customer to describe the time of hire and to allocate a session ID. On return

95

Chapter 4 Overview

■ **Examples of Object-Oriented, cf. Functional Designs**

■ **Proposed Systems Development Methodologies**

■ **Compatibility with Current (Functional) Methodologies**

■ **Available Notation**

Some Brief Design Examples

Example 1 (based on an idea from Jackson, 1983)

Boat hire on pleasure lake

Customer asks if boat available
        If so, information keyed in about time session
        starts and session ID

        On return of boat, total time is calculated
        and customer pays

Management now requests reports on:

1) Number of hiring sessions

2) Average session time

EXHIBIT 50

of the boat, this time is keyed in, the total time is calculated, and the hire charge (pro rata) is calculated. For example, a customer hires a boat at 12.12 p.m., is the third customer of the day, and returns the boat at 1.30 p.m. Management asks us to prepare some software to provide some reports giving the number of hire sessions per day and the average session time — a very simple problem for us to design. Hardware and software are available to identify times and customer IDs. The number of hire sessions is dead easy — a simple count (Exhibit 51) using the current facilities of the system.

The second part is to calculate the average session time over a day. The average time is thus simply the total hire duration divided by the number of sessions. We have a value for the denominator directly from the hire count. For the numerator we have that for each hire session, the hire duration is the return-time less the hire-time. Hence the total hire duration is $\sum$ return-times $- \sum$ hire-times. In a functional world, this "neat algorithm" may well be found. (This is of course not the only way.) Although we are considering analysis and design in this chapter, it might assist the reader to relate this design, briefly, to code. In this vein, the pseudoprocedural code is shown in Exhibit 52. The main body of the code is a loop until the end-of-day, which increments a counter for each customer, adds in an end time, and subtracts a start time for each customer to give the total time. So long as there has been at least one customer, then the average session duration is easily calculated. If there are no customers, a message to that effect is printed. Also note that before this loop there is a necessary initialization of the counter and the total time variable. Success!

Management is flushed with success. If that was so easy (they say to us), then let's have more reporting information. What is the longest session and what are the average session times in the morning and in the afternoon (Exhibit 53)? How do we extend the existing code to calculate this? It's difficult without totally rewriting the code since the code bears little resemblance to the real world; there is no variable which represents the "session time." This is because we went immediately for a neat functional algorithm.

What would be the OO design? Well, we would model the session directly, depicting session as an object (Exhibit 54). Consequently, when an extension to the design (and hence the code) was requested, a model of the session would already be available. It would therefore be much simpler to extend the OO design to include additional reports by incorporating those "subsessions" via inheritance: adding in subclasses of morning session and afternoon session as "children" of session. We could, of course, have done this in procedural code if we'd been determined, but it would have been much harder. This extension using inheritance in OO is significantly easier and neater.

The second example relates to the banking system (Exhibit 55) — at least the basics common to (almost) all cultures. Although I haven't included a full requirements analysis, let's consider the modeling of the essentials of a banking system as viewed from the perspective of a person with personal accounts. What are our objects (actually O/Cs, of course)? Customers, tellers, bank accounts, checks, money, and ATMs could all provide candidate O/Cs. Let's consider just a few of these to make our design problem tractable in a limited time and

Algorithms Sought For:

1) Simple Count
2) Average Time = Total Time/Session Count

Now Total Time = (End Session 1 — Start Session 1)
                 + (End Session 2 — Start Session 2)
                 + ...

Neat Algorithm

$= \Sigma$ End Session Times
$- \Sigma$ Start Session Times

Pseudoprocedural code

```
NUMBER: = 0;
TOTALTIME: = 0;
DO WHILE not-end-of-day
      NUMBER = NUMBER + 1;
      TOTAL TIME = TOTAL TIME + END TIME
      – START TIME;
ENDDO
PRINT "number of sessions = ",  NUMBER;
IF NUMBER ≠ 0
      THEN PRINT "Average session time = ",
      TOTALTIME/NUMBER;
      ELSE PRINT "No hirings today";
ENDIF
```

Success

EXHIBIT 52   Copyright © B. Henderson-Sellers, 1991

New Report

- —— Longest Session
- —— Average Session Times in
  morning, cf. afternoon

NOT Possible

Why? Because code bears little
relationship to real world

No variable corresponds to a
model of a "session"

EXHIBIT 53   Copyright © B. Henderson-Sellers, 1991

Simple Object-Oriented Solution

```
                    ┌─────────────────────┐
                    │                     │
                    │      Session        │
                    │                     │
                    └─────────────────────┘
                      ▲                 ▲
                     /                   \
          ┌──────────────────┐  ┌──────────────────┐
          │     Morning      │  │    Afternoon     │
          │  Hire Session    │  │  Hire Session    │
          └──────────────────┘  └──────────────────┘
```

EXHIBIT 54   Copyright © B. Henderson-Sellers, 1991

Example 2

Banking System

— Customers

— Tellers

— Bank Accounts

— Checks

— Cash

a) Identify real-world entities/objects

b) Model by software objects

c) Code objects

space. Having identified these real world objects, we then proceed to model those real objects with software objects, firstly in the design sense and then finally by implementing those objects in code.

These objects, then, constitute a very simple system, i.e., this is not a complete system design. Indeed, at this introductory stage, we are not even going to differentiate between analysis and design (this is deferred until later in this chapter). To do that, we must first introduce some appropriate notation (Section 4.5). Consequently, the notation in Exhibit 56 is NOT in any sense "recommended."

In our analysis/design, we first identify objects that interact with one another. We might draw lines to show such interactions (Exhibit 56). A teller might interact with cash as might a customer. "Customer" also interacts with ATM and directly with the teller (a two-way interaction). Both customer and teller might interact with savings account, the teller directly and the customer indirectly via an ATM or indeed via the teller. Drawing a selection of the objects as nodes and interactions as connecting lines provides a first, simple graphical representation of our system. In this figure we note that there is no indication of functionality, how a customer operates, or how an account operates, only the design level interactions. The procedural implementation remains hidden. Furthermore, it is obviously easy to add an additional type of account, say a checking account (Exhibit 57). Further detail about the type of relationship could be added by labeling the arcs. Such considerations of a development methodology and associated notation will be deferred until later in this chapter once we have defined the methodology and notation. It might also be noted that checking and savings accounts are likely to be related taxonomically, although such a realization is not crucial at an analysis stage. If not identified now, such a relationship would be sought directly in the design phase (see later discussions).

4.2 Software Life Cycle

We now want to look at some of the proposed systems methodologies (Exhibit 58). We start off by looking at the overall life cycle and the conceptual framework into which that fits and then look in a little more detail at some design issues and at some notation, remembering that in many of these areas, methodologies/notation are not yet finalized. As throughout this book, only introductory-level ideas are introduced — further details can be sought in the technical literature (see Annotated Bibliography).

We start with a familiar diagram, that of the waterfall model of the life cycle and ask, "How does the OO life cycle fit into this?" Exhibit 59 shows a simplistic view of the "waterfall." Shown here is a broad division of the life cycle into very roughly three stages: an analysis, a design, and an implementation phase (left-hand side). Obviously, there is a lot of iteration in this diagram, not just a single step through, and many of the "consecutive steps" actually overlap such that moving from one life cycle stage to the next is nowhere near as clear-cut as in a procedural life cycle (or as we have been led to believe in the procedural life cycle). Despite this overlap, several industries still have milestones: stages that must be reached successfully before the "next" phase can be commenced.

Simple Model

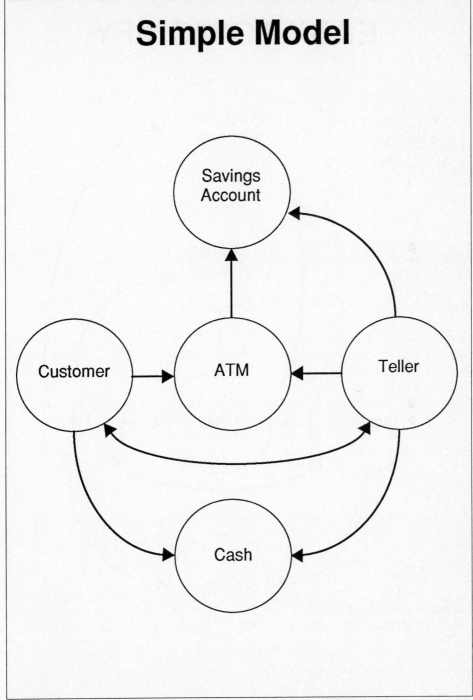

EXHIBIT 56

EASY TO MODIFY

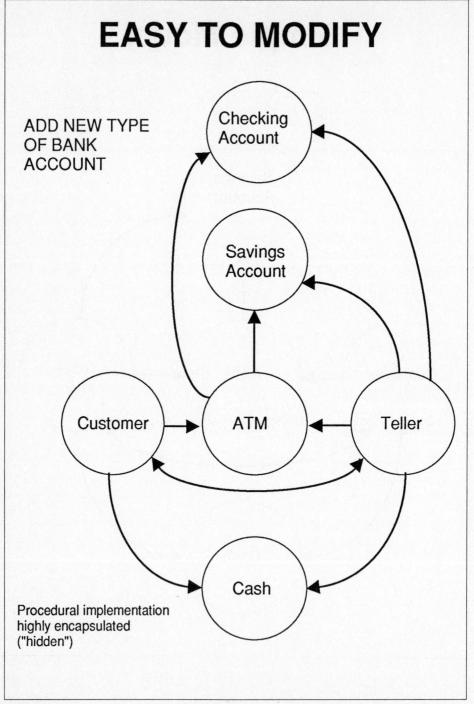

ADD NEW TYPE
OF BANK
ACCOUNT

Procedural implementation
highly encapsulated
("hidden")

EXHIBIT 57   Copyright © B. Henderson-Sellers, 1991

Proposed Systems

Development

Methodologies

EXHIBIT 58   Copyright © B. Henderson-Sellers, 1991

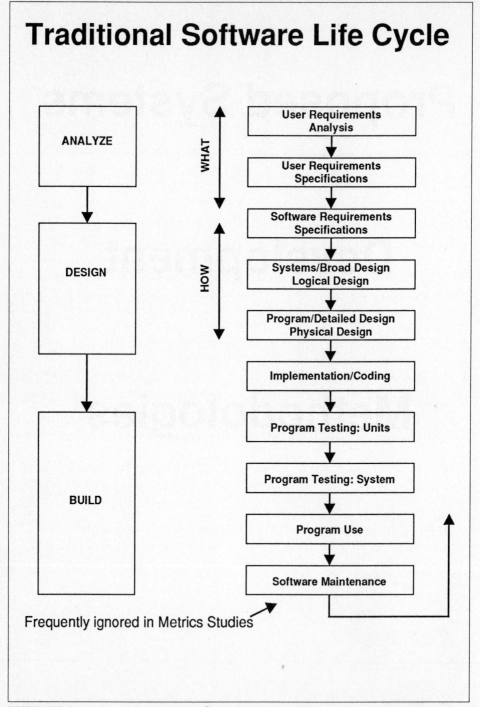

Traditional Software Life Cycle

EXHIBIT 59   Copyright © B. Henderson-Sellers and J.M. Edwards, 1990

In OO, as we have seen, overlaps become even more evident than in traditional methodologies — and traditional milestones substantially harder to identify.

In the more detailed description of the life cycle a number of subdivisions are identified (right-hand side of Exhibit 59). The number of these varies between authors. In general, the problem is first defined and an analysis of the requirements of current and future users undertaken, usually by direct and indirect questioning and iterative discussion. Included in this stage should be a feasibility study. Following this, a user requirements definition and a software requirements specification, SRS (Davis, 1988), are written.

In the analysis phase (e.g., Berard, 1990c), the problem is examined in terms of user requirements and therefore in the language of the user. This phase extends from the initiation of the project through to users' needs analysis and the feasibility study (cf. Davis, 1988), and is set firmly in the problem space (Exhibit 60).

Moving to the solution space gives a software solution, but now written in the language of the software developer rather than the software users. This transition roughly defines the progression from analysis to design. The design phase covers the various concepts of system design, broad design, logical design, detailed design, program design, and physical design. The design stage is perhaps the most loosely defined since it is a phase of progressive decomposition toward more and more detail (e.g., Sommerville, 1989) and is essentially a creative, not a mechanistic, process (Turner, 1987).

Following on from the design stage(s), the computer program is written, the program tested, in terms of verification, validation, and sensitivity testing, and when found acceptable, put into use and then maintained well into the future. Although you may wish to divide the life cycle into more phases in this way, most of the discussion in this book considers only the three broad stages on the left-hand side of Exhibit 59.

In an OO life cycle like this, there is significant merging between various stages of the life cycle and thus a high degree of iteration. So rather than the waterfall model, we use the fountain model (Henderson-Sellers and Edwards, 1990a) (Exhibit 61) as a graphic descriptor of the process. This is rooted in the real world at its base, emerges, builds through user requirements analysis, specification, etc., — the same sort of stages as before except now highly merged. For example, systems design to module design to coding occurs over a very short space. Modules are coded individually (actually often in clusters — see below) and then put together as a prelude to system testing. Following system acceptance, it is anticipated that maintenance costs will be less and extendibility significantly more feasible.

As indicated here, there is more emphasis on *classes* rather than systems. Consequently, it is more appropriate not just to consider the whole system at each stage of the life cycle, but rather to identify that individual classes or individual clusters of classes (Exhibit 62) go through their own *cluster life cycles*. Meyer (1988) identifies a life cycle for each cluster as (1) specification, (2) design and implementation, and (3) validation and generalization. The life cycles of different clusters are likely to be out of phase with each other such that, for example,

PROBLEM SPACE

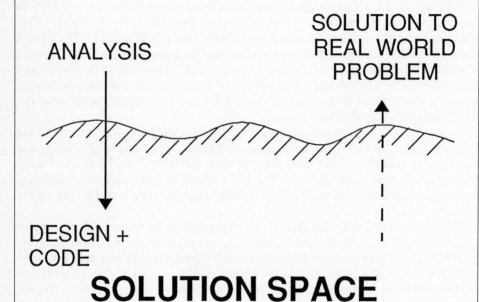

ANALYSIS

SOLUTION TO
REAL WORLD
PROBLEM

DESIGN +
CODE

SOLUTION SPACE

The Fountain Model for Object-Oriented Life Cycles

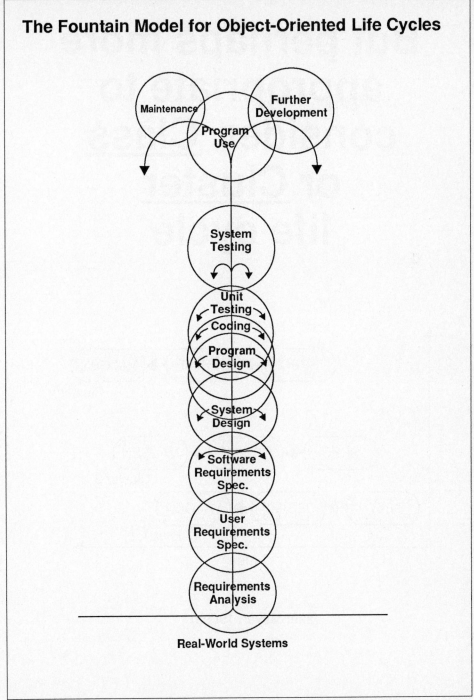

EXHIBIT 61   Copyright © B. Henderson-Sellers and J.M. Edwards, 1990

But perhaps more appropriate to consider <u>Class</u> or <u>Cluster</u> life cycle

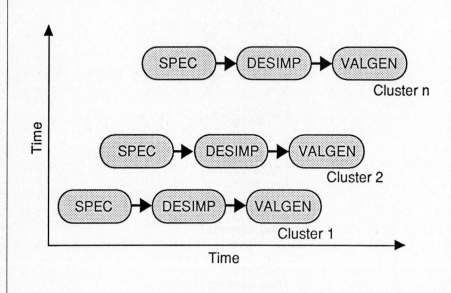

(after Meyer, 1989a)

EXHIBIT 62

while Cluster n is beginning specification, Cluster 3 has already completed this phase. If you consider any design problem with which you are familiar, you are likely to be able to identify groups of common blocks of code. In a banking environment, you might have a class for account, for teller, for ATM — all much of the same contextually — whereas payroll classes and international banking classes are conceptually far removed. Such commonality having been identified, these classes are thus developed as a cluster and stored, usually, in a single O/S directory. Then one project team would develop the home banking classes, another the international classes and a third the personnel system classes. From a project management point of view, this probably supplies a reasonable degree of independence and autonomy to the individual project teams (and the clusters of classes they are developing). This has repercussions for project management of object-oriented systems development in the commercial environment (see Section 3.11).

Exhibit 63 shows how the fountain model can be adapted either for a single class or more likely to a single cluster of classes (the word "module" is used in this diagram to mean either). This reflects ideas similar to those in the systems fountain model of Exhibit 61, but here we now include the cases of generalization and aggregation as a model for the fine-tuning of those classes for future use. Again that part is difficult. Meyer (1990b) describes his experiences in generalizing classes for the Eiffel library, which give real insight into the degree of difficulty in obtaining really generic and useful library classes. Finally, superimposed on these steps is the concept of iteration: a return from a "higher" to a "lower" phase, sometimes contiguous, sometimes further removed.

Putting all this together gives a relatively complicated, yet useful, diagram (Exhibit 64). Time is shown on the ordinate depicting evolution, with time, of both requirements and global design. Typically, requirements are frozen initially but tend to evolve. As you design, you may often give feedback that could offer the opportunity for the requirements analyst to identify some potential improvement. In an OO environment you can do that. Why? Because the worst that can happen is that some classes may have to be thrown away — although the extent of this will vary depending on the nature of the revision. It is most unlikely that the whole system design will be scrapped. In any case, the classes already implemented may be of use in future projects. There are more capabilities (i) not to have to freeze the requirements too soon; (ii) to have interactions between the design and the requirements much more than in a traditional life cycle; and (iii) to start the coding at an early design stage. It should also be noted that the object-oriented life cycle retains the advantages of the prototyping approach such that the user can develop a better understanding of the system before signing off the specification documents.

4.3 Systems Methodologies

4.3.1 Functional decomposition methodology

In a traditional approach, the analyst uses functional decomposition that starts with the WHAT and moves very rapidly to the HOW — How do I implement

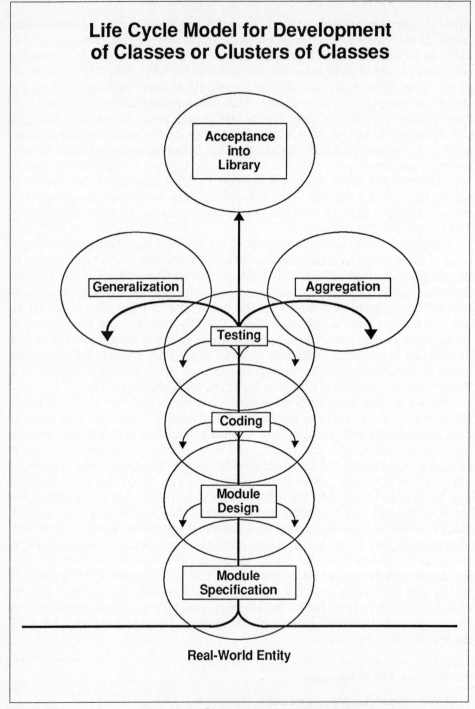

Life Cycle Model for Development of Classes or Clusters of Classes

Acceptance into Library

Generalization

Aggregation

Testing

Coding

Module Design

Module Specification

Real-World Entity

EXHIBIT 63 Copyright © B. Henderson-Sellers and J.M. Edwards, 1990

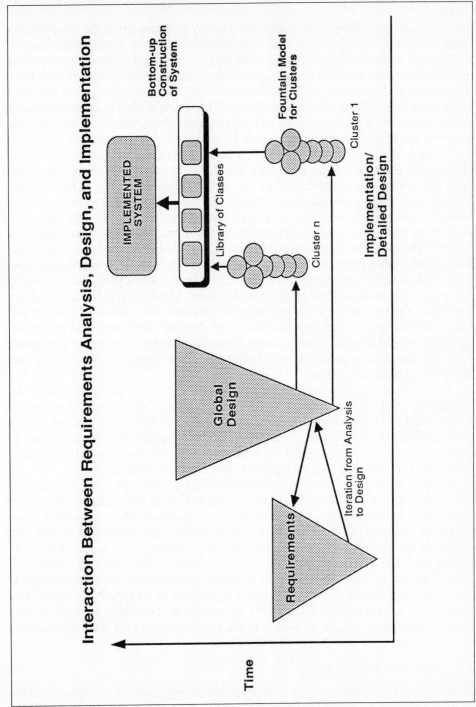

Interaction Between Requirements Analysis, Design, and Implementation this functionality? How do I design the system to accomplish the functionality I am concerned with? Functional decomposition is also a top-down analysis and design methodology. Although the two are not synonymous, most of the published systems analysis and design methods exhibit both characteristics (e.g., Yourdon and Constantine, 1979; DeMarco, 1978) and some also add a real-time component (e.g., Ward and Mellor, 1985). Top-down design does impose some discipline on the systems analyst and program designer; yet it can be criticized as being too restrictive to support contemporary software engineering designs.

What is wrong with that type of top-down functional methodology? Meyer (1988), identifies four basic flaws in a top-down functional decomposition (Exhibit 65). First, it tends to freeze in the requirements very early. There is very little account taken of evolutionary change and we all know that systems evolve. In traditional methodologies that is very difficult to accomplish. Second, it is difficult to identify a single functionality of a system. When a system has been designed, usually *the* functionality becomes modified to several functionalities. Third, based on a functional mindset, top-down functional decomposition identifies functionality and algorithms very early in the life cycle, indeed basing the whole design methodology on that construct. Meyer suggests that top-down functional decomposition often neglects the data structure, although it is perhaps more realistic to say that data structures are deferred until *very* late in the decomposition and design. Finally, there is no encouragement to develop reusable code; not that it's not possible, but there is no encouragement to do this and thus avoid "reinventing the wheel."

In functional decomposition, procedures and algorithms are uppermost in the designer's mind, as noted earlier (Chapter 2). Initially, the system is viewed at a high level in terms of what it is intended to *do* and then, at a detailed design stage, *how* it will accomplish these process-oriented goals. Design tools used to support this methodology, which is strongly based on *data flows*, include data flow diagrams (DFDs), data dictionaries, and structure charts.

Functional decomposition is well supported by the older procedural languages and is therefore a natural mode of design expression in that context. The incorporation of subroutines into these languages led to the ability to undertake some degree of autonomy and information hiding, while at the same time shared data tended to be placed in globally accessible data storage areas (e.g., COMMON blocks in FORTRAN, externals in C). This leads to the "stack of dominoes" effect familiar to anyone working in program maintenance whereby changes to one part of a software system often cause a problem in an apparently dissociated program area. Furthermore, a system envisaged as providing a single service (single function) is unable to evolve to take into account new data structures or new functions with any degree of robustness.

4.3.2 The O-O-O methodology

At present (Exhibit 66), we may thus conceive of object-oriented analysis (OOA) as relatively language-independent. Current work is aiming at consolidating language-independent analysis and if possible language-independent object-oriented design (OOD). That contrasts with a lot of the early work in OOD that came

Meyer (1988) identifies four flaws in top-down functional design

1) Takes no account of evolutionary change

2) System characterized by a single function —— a questionable concept

3) Based on functional mindset; data structure aspect often neglected

4) Does not encourage reusability

EXHIBIT 65 Copyright © B. Henderson-Sellers, 1991

At Present:

Object-oriented analysis language-independent

Object-oriented design tends to be language-dependent

—— Detailed design more so

e.g., Booch's Ada package notation

EXHIBIT 66   Copyright © B. Henderson-Sellers, 1991

from people first doing implementations in specific languages (much of it in Ada — a non-object-oriented language; but see Section 5.10) and growing "backward" to design, thus introducing an implicit language bias into the OOD. This language bias is evident in almost all texts that included chapters on OOD published prior to (but not including) 1990. More recent texts focus on design issues in a language-independent framework (e.g., Wirfs-Brock *et al.*, 1990). Certainly, at implementation, there must be a direct language dependency. Nevertheless, we can look at some of Grady Booch's Ada-based design work and generalize it (Exhibit 67). His 1987 OO methodology goes as follows:

1. Identify objects and attributes. In the first edition of *Software Engineering with Ada*, he suggests this can be done by underlining the nouns, an idea first proposed by Abbott (1983). This is now seen as oversimplistic, being unlikely to scale well beyond the trivial, while still providing a useful "first cut." There are also problems implicit in the modern (bad) habit of turning nouns into verbs and verbs into nouns indiscriminately (cf. Booch, 1991, p143 et seq.). There are still no clear methodologies on object identification but many guidelines (see also Section 3.10.3).

2. Identification of operations/functionality *after* the data/objects.

3. Establish the visibility/interfaces.

4. Establish that interface more closely.

5. Implement.

To my mind this isn't a really full life cycle. We're really talking there about detailed design. Steps 3–5 are really down to code module design. This, therefore, would at first sight appear to be a technique for more detailed design and not for systems development. Indeed, in his latest book Booch (1991) clearly states (e.g., p190) that the steps given above, now slightly modified, pertain solely to design. In his modified design methodology (Exhibit 68), he suggests the use of a "round-trip gestalt design" (akin to Berard's "analyze a little, design a little, implement a little, and test a little"; see below). Booch's four recommended steps are:

- Identify the classes and objects at a given level of abstraction.

- Identify the semantics of these classes and objects.

- Identify the relationships among these classes and objects.

- Implement these classes and objects.

In a "thoroughbred" object-oriented life cycle systems development (see also right-hand side of Exhibit 77, p135), the object-oriented paradigm is utilized during analysis, design, and coding, thus providing a single model valid *throughout*

Object-Oriented Development Methodologies:

1. Booch (1987)

1) Identify objects and attributes

2) Identify operations affecting objects

3) Establish visibility

4) Establish interface

5) Implement each object

Notes:

3 – 5 really detailed design, better suited to object design than to system analysis and design

EXHIBIT 67

Object-Oriented Development Methodologies:

2. Booch (1991) — round-trip gestalt **design**

    1) Identify classes and objects at given level of abstraction

    2) Identify semantics of classes and objects

    3) Identify relationship

    4) Implement/code

3. Berard (1990b) — recursive/parallel **life cycle**

> "Analyze a little,
> design a little,
> implement a little,
> test a little"

EXHIBIT 68

Object-Oriented Development Methodologies:

4. Henderson-Sellers and Edwards (1990a)

1) Systems requirements specification

2) Identify entities (O/Cs)

3) Establish relationships between entities (O/Cs)

4) Analysis merges to design

$\Rightarrow$ lower-level design diagram (DD)

5) Bottom-up design, use of library classes

6) Introduce inheritance relationships

7) Clustering/generalization

Iterative until new class acceptable for library inclusion

EXHIBIT 69

the life cycle stages. The use of this "seamless transition" permits a continuity across phase "boundaries" and also allows highly similar terminologies and graphical notation to be used at each successive stage.

In their analysis of the "thoroughbred" object-oriented (i.e., Object-oriented analysis, Object-oriented design, Object-oriented implementation, or O-O-O) systems development, Henderson-Sellers and Edwards (1990a) proposed a seven-step methodological framework (Exhibit 69) of the object-oriented life cycle, providing a very general, broad model for systems development. It recognizes the need to encompass both top-down decomposition and bottom-up synergistic system building simultaneously and is based to some extent on suggestions of Booch (1987, p48) and Bailin (1989) (graphical notation for these diagrammatic ideas will be developed in Section 4.5):

1. *Undertake system requirements specification* (Exhibit 70). This stage is a high-level analysis of the system in terms of objects and their services, as opposed to the system functions, based on a source document originating from the (future) users. However, if a great deal of OOA is undertaken, then the result may be an object-oriented requirements specification including timing details, hardware usage, cost estimates, and other documentation. Coad and Yourdon (1990) and Shlaer and Mellor (1988) both present OOA methods that may be of some use at this stage, although both sets of authors present methods more firmly grounded in data analysis ideas rather than an object-oriented "worldview."

2. *Identify the candidate objects.* At both the analysis and the high-level design stage, it is necessary to identify the objects (O/Cs) and the attributes and operations (the services) they provide. This is where the functional features will be defined, although no indication of implementation is required, this being one of the basic tenets of the object-oriented paradigm. Objects can often be identified in terms of the real-world objects, although as Meyer (1988) notes, abstract nouns often also provide excellent objects. As noted in Section 3.10.3, both abstract and substantive nouns can be found in the requirements specification, although these will not be the final total of objects in the implemented system. Attributes will be reflected to some degree by adjectives in the specification. In addition to real-world objects, Coad and Yourdon (1990) offer guidelines to identify further objects during object decomposition and identification. They recommend that events, roles played, locations, and organizations are also good candidates for objects. However, at this high level of abstraction it seems unnecessary to decompose the object and look for more primitive object representations, since these are more reasonably part of the detailed design stage. Here an object dictionary should be used as the object-oriented analog of the data dictionary.

Identification of appropriate objects must therefore not be undertaken solely on the objects identified in the requirements specification and at the analysis and design stage, since it is anticipated that well-designed object classes

Step 1

Systems requirements specification (SRS)

■ in language of users

■ source document to find objects

Step 2

Find candidate objects
(real-world objects)

■ First pass — nouns in SRS

+ verb   methods

+ adjective   attributes

■ Concrete *and* abstract

■ (Coad & Yourdon, 1990; Nerson, 1990)
e.g., Structure and classification
Events
Roles played
Location
Organization

will be used again and again. Such identification of generalizability (see also Steps 6 and 7), although encouraged in standard procedural language courses, has seldom taken seriously to date. Identification of objects and ultimately of classes will *de facto* define the operations affecting the objects, and the services they offer, hence defining the visible interface.

3. *Establish interactions between objects* (Exhibit 71) in terms of services required and services rendered, and depict these initially in a top-level object diagram (see Section 4.5.4). Although these may bear some slight resemblance, at first glance, to a version of a data flow diagram (DFD), perhaps interpreted following Bailin's (1989) EDFD (or entity data flow diagram), it is important to note that data are contained *within* an object and *do not* flow in the same sense as that described by a DFD in functional decomposition techniques. The interactions in the analysis phase (Exhibit 71) are those of classification, association, and aggregation. These static relationships are discussed in detail in Section 4.4, and the dynamics of object systems described briefly in Section 4.4.1. At the same time, various inheritance relationships may become very apparent. Although a systematic search for these, especially with respect to base library classes, can be deferred until later (Step 5), groups of object classes clearly related through inheritance should be identified as such as early as possible. In this sense, isolation of inheritance structure is used to clarify and simplify the analysis and design, in contrast to (i) the refinement of the inheritance hierarchies envisaged in Step 5 in which library classes are much used; (ii) the use of specialization and generalization (generalization is essentially going up the inheritance tree, specialization is going down — see further details in Sections 4.5.5 and 5.6) to create new often abstract (deferred) superclasses in Step 6; and (iii) the generalization, specialization, and testing of Step 7.

4. As the analysis stage merges into the design stage, high-level design diagrams (DDs) and increasingly *lower level DDs can be drawn* to illustrate more details of the objects. The transition from analysis to design is marked by the replacement of the three analysis relationships utilized in Step 3 by the two design relationships of inheritance and client–server (Exhibit 71). From this stage onward, bottom-up concerns should be taken into consideration. The identification of reusable design components, or classes, from previous designs is an important part of the OO strategy. In some languages (e.g., Ada and, to a limited extent, Eiffel) classes can be embedded inside other classes (e.g., Jalote, 1989). In a pure object-oriented life cycle (right-hand side of Exhibit 77), especially one that is using the same language for systems analysis, design, and implementation, the decision on whether to represent embedded classes or not will therefore reflect the language being used. Diagrammatically then, design-level objects would remain as individuals. However, at the top level an object of higher level abstraction would be represented by a single piece of notation (see, e.g., Henderson-Sellers and Edwards, 1990a, b, and Section 4.5).

Step 3:

Establish Interactions

Analysis relationships: Classification,

Association, Aggregation

Step 4:

Analysis merges to Design

Design relationships: Client-server
(with current OOPLs)

EXHIBIT 71

Step 5

Explore Existing Library Classes

Refine Design — now highly detailed

Step 6

Examine Class Network for more Inheritance Structures

This may introduce new classes and new interactions

Class Coded and Tested

5. At the same time, bottom-up concerns should be being realized insofar as objects are themselves often constructed bottom-up from libraries of more primitive objects (Exhibit 72) (not top-down as described by Winblad *et al.*, 1990, p33) using concepts of inheritance, as well as of client–server and contracting (Meyer, 1989b; Wirfs-Brock and Wilkerson, 1989b), the libraries themselves containing object classes created as one of the successful outcomes of a previous application of this (or other) proposed development methodology. Internal details of objects are specified using structured techniques, including entity relationship diagrams, DFDs, and hierarchy charts. Initial implementation (coding plus testing) of low-level classes may begin at this or the next stage, following the cluster model of Meyer (1989a) or the module version of the fountain model of Henderson-Sellers and Edwards (1990a).

6. As more objects are identified within the detailed design, reevaluation of the total set of classes will require an iterative analysis of whether new superclasses (parents) or new subclasses (children) will be useful (Exhibit 72) such that inheritance diagrams will be further developed and refined (see also Section 4.5.5). This process tries to develop a logical hierarchy (Exhibit 73) of objects such that there are no "missing" objects. This step is needed in order to provide a well-defined hierarchy so that future projects can reuse the structure without having to redesign the inheritance chart for themselves. This process will probably take place during the generalization phase of the cluster model of class development.

7. Aggregation and/or generalization of classes (Exhibit 74) relates to refinement work needed to ensure classes are reusable and augments the project-specific refinements of the inheritance hierarchy of Step 6. Such refinements may, of course, lead to iteration back and a reconsideration of the DDs describing the system. Clusters of classes will be identified and/or consolidated and documentation prepared. It may be that prototyping will already have commenced by this stage, providing constructive feedback to the potential users such that the requirements documents may require modification and clarification (e.g., Turner, 1987) leading to further development of the class specified. Although this is contrary to expectations of the traditional life cycle model, such feedback, essentially from one end of the traditional life cycle to the other, is made possible by the object-oriented techniques and is seen as providing a more reliable, robust, and useful software system.

In Step 7, the system classes that have been identified and developed should continue to be worked on until they are general, generic, and robust enough to be placed in a library of components. This may be simply a "honing" of existing objects or may require the introduction of additional classes (possibly of a deferred or abstract nature, i.e., ones that cannot be instantiated) (Exhibit 75) at intermediate levels in the class inheritance hierarchy. Sometimes objects may be overly complex and may require splitting into a

OFF-LINE INHERITANCE HIERARCHY

EXHIBIT 73   Copyright © B. Henderson-Sellers, 1991

Step 7

Further Refinement
beyond demands of
current project
in order to
facilitate later reuse

Cluster Identification

Documentation

EXHIBIT 74   Copyright © B. Henderson-Sellers, 1991

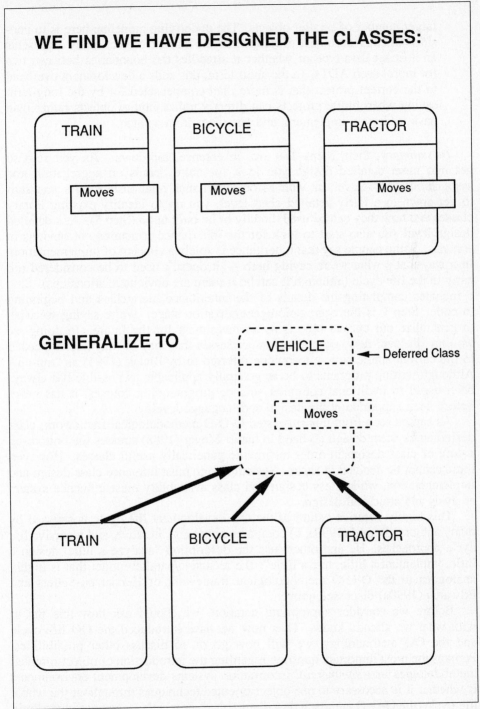

EXHIBIT 75

larger number of smaller objects. The underlying guideline here is to consider whether an object developed in the current project really represents an abstract data type or whether it straddles the boundaries between two (or more) such ADTs. In the short term, this adds a development overhead to the current project that is more than compensated for by the long-term saving when future projects can directly utilize library objects rather than have to design, implement, and test them from scratch.

In summary, then, Steps 1–4 are, in essence, top-down. As you start to get into more detailed design you look for more details on aggregation and association/client–server, as well as on inheritance relationships. As you start to get down to a fairly detailed class level, you try to identify existing library classes and how they can be used directly or be built upon (Step 5). At a detailed design level you also start to look for the inheritance structures not obvious in analysis. Some people say that inheritance is solely a concern of implementation. In a way that's what we're saying here — it doesn't need to be considered too early in the life cycle (although it can be if there are obvious relationships). Step 6 includes completing the details of the inheritance hierarchies and beginning to code. Step 7 is the aggregation/generalization stage. We're saying we wish to generalize our current objects as an investment for the future. In doing so, we may discover new, generalized superclasses that may or may not be needed in the current application, a technique referred to by Bielak (1991) as "top-up." Although writing programs to be as generally applicable as possible has always been urged in traditional computer science programming courses, it has never before been supported at the design and language levels.

As can be seen from this suggested O-O-O methodological framework, class design and system design go hand in hand. Meyer (1988) stresses the bottom-up nature of class design in order to provide generically useful classes. However, these cannot be decided *in vacuo*. System design must influence class design and implementation, while class design and class availability must influence system analysis and structural design.

This highly iterative nature of the OO development life cycle is stressed by many authors. Berard (1990a, b) compares sequential, iterative, and recursive life cycle approaches. He and others use the description "analyze a little, design a little, implement a little, test a little": the recursive/parallel model that is highly analogous to the O-O-O methodological framework of Henderson-Sellers and Edwards (1990a) discussed above.

Before we consider appropriate notation, we should ask how this fits in with what we already know. Thus now we have introduced the OO life cycle and the OO methodology, we will now go on to discuss other possibilities. Perhaps the most important question regarding the introduction of object-oriented methodologies into *commercial* information systems development environments is whether it is necessary to use object-oriented techniques throughout the whole life cycle (the O-O-O approach described above) or whether it is possible to "mix and match" with functional decomposition techniques to create a hybrid object-oriented/functional decomposition software systems development methodology

(Exhibit 76). Although it would appear that the former would be more self-consistent, the arguments for proposing the latter approach consider the reality of the large current investment in top-down functional decomposition, in terms of both expertise and front-end CASE tools, which many industries currently possess (e.g., Ward, 1989). Secondly, even if the OO design methods are viewed as "more natural," the investment in code in say COBOL leads to the question, can an object-oriented design (viewed as a better design) be implemented in a non-OO language?

In terms of possible OO/functional hybrid approaches, two major likely linkages can be identified in Exhibit 77: (i) from a functional description at the analysis stage that is then transferred to an object view at the design stage (Booch, 1987; Alabiso, 1988) (and presumably then an OO implementation) (referred to hereafter as the Functional analysis, Object-oriented design, Object-oriented implementation (or F-O-O) methodology); (ii) the implementation in a standard procedural language of an object-oriented design (O-O-F) (Exhibit 78). Either of these paths is indeed feasible. Convergent methodologies, using parts of object-oriented and parts of structured techniques, within the same life cycle stage may be useful, with care, in some circumstances (Henderson-Sellers and Constantine, 1991).

4.3.3 The F-O-O methodology

The rationale behind the F-O-O methodology is that since much of the enthusiasm in object-oriented techniques was generated in the latter stages of the life cycle with the advent of new object-oriented programming languages (OOPLs), software developers may have adopted the new paradigm at implementation and probably design stages. As these ideas start to percolate "upward" to the earlier life cycle phases, the question remains whether functional decomposition techniques will be retained or whether a fully object-oriented (O-O-O) methodology, using OOA methods, such as that of Bailin (1989) or Coad and Yourdon (1990), will be developed. In the transition phase, therefore, it is likely that structured techniques will continue to be used at the requirements specification and analysis stage and that techniques for "translating" these analyses into object-oriented designs will be sought.

Nevertheless, proceeding from a structured analysis to an object-oriented design can be awkward (Bailin, 1989; Coad and Yourdon, 1990) since different aggregation principles are involved in a functional-oriented, as opposed to an object-oriented, analysis. This is illustrated in Exhibit 77 by the wavy arrow from functional analysis to object-oriented design. In this diagram one-to-one ("seamless") mappings are indicated by straight arrows and disjoint mappings by wavy arrows. Each transition indicated by a wavy arrow in Exhibit 77 thus requires the development of a technique to "translate" between the functional and object-oriented worldviews.

Data flow diagrams (DFDs) are well known in functional/structured analysis (e.g., Yourdon and Constantine, 1979). Nodes (either round "bubbles" or rectangles) represent *processes* and connecting arrows data flows. These may be augmented to illustrate control flow, following, e.g., Ward and Mellor (1985).

Compatibility with Current (Functional) Methodologies

Role of Hybrid Methodologies to optimize current investments

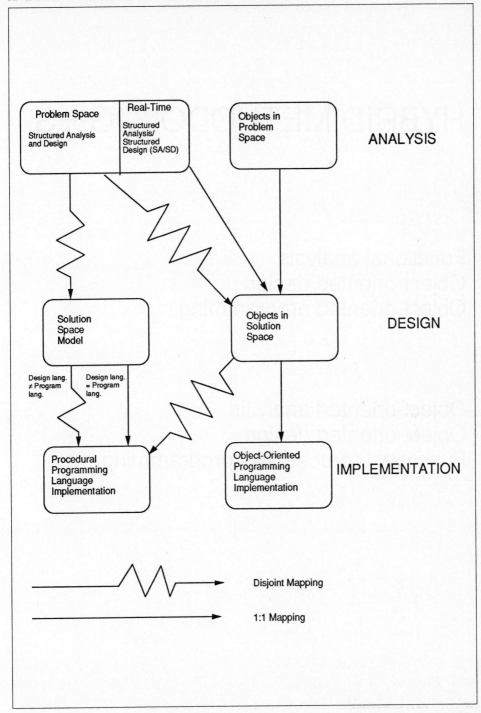

HYBRID METHODOLOGIES

Functional analysis
Object-oriented design
Object-oriented programming

Object-oriented analysis
Object-oriented design
Functional (procedural) programming

DFDs also have the advantage of being able to be "stacked" to represent analysis/design information at a set of *levels* of resolution (e.g., Bailin, 1989; Seidewitz, 1989; Laranjeira, 1990) (Exhibit 79). Methodologies to transform from a structured analysis to a structured design abound (e.g., Page-Jones, 1980); here the parallel transformation from a structured analysis to an object-oriented design is considered (see also Wasserman *et al.*, 1989; Seidewitz and Stark, 1987).

Ladden (1989) suggests that objects may be derived from DFDs in one of three ways:

1. From a single-level DFD, find one or more objects.

2. Objects may overlap more than one DFD.

3. One DFD process bubble may be allocated to more than one object.

At the same time, process bubbles map to object methods and their data stores to instance variables (Hopkins, 1990b). Exhibit 80 shows one such example of a DFD with five nodes and three files. Each of these files (data stores) thus forms the nucleus for an object. Three objects are therefore "carved" from this DFD. The original DFD node bubbles become methods associated with one particular object, and the data flows in the original DFD that now form inter-object connections must be clarified, possibly as client–server relationships.

Such regrouping may of course permit the use of the DFD style of notation to be adapted for object-representation in which the nodes become objects and the arrows messages (processes) (e.g., Ladden, 1989; Bailin, 1989). However, this does not easily permit the emphasis on "services offered," since the multiple labeling of a service used by several objects (since the arrow now represents the service) would soon detract from the needed comprehensibility of such diagrams (Exhibit 81) — a size problem also noted by Ladden (1989) with respect to Booch diagrams used in the Ada industry.

This method is complemented by the use of entity-relationship diagrams (ERDs) that provide the data component directly together with some client–server information and possibly some inheritance representation (e.g., Ward, 1989). (Further details of appropriate notation are given by Henderson-Sellers and Edwards, 1990b, and in Section 4.5 here.)

On the basis of the above analysis, the following 7-step F-O-O methodological framework (Exhibit 82) is therefore proposed (Henderson-Sellers, 1991b):

1. *Undertake system requirements specification and analysis* in terms of a functional mindset. At this stage this is a top-down functional decomposition and structured techniques are therefore used. This will involve identifying functional relationships, data stores, data flows, and probably a (semantic) data model. The analysis is undertaken in terms of real-world relationships prior to constructing analysis diagrams to represent these real-world relationships.

2. *DFDs are drawn* as part of the detailed analysis. These describe functional relationships, identifying processes graphically as nodes (some version of

DFD
LEVELING DIAGRAM

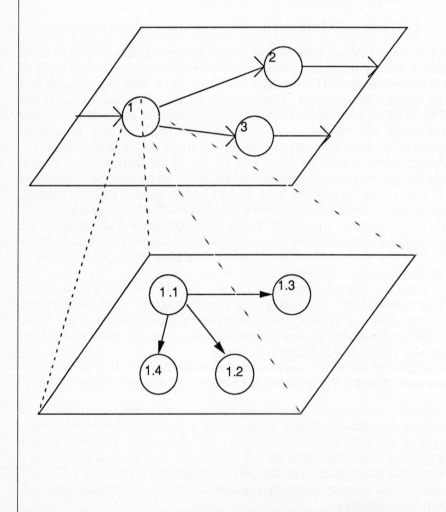

EXHIBIT 79   Copyright © B. Henderson-Sellers, 1991

Carving OO Requirements from DFDs

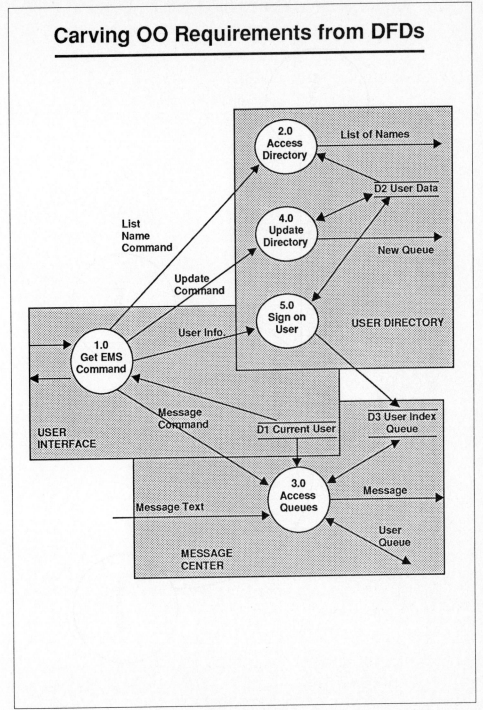

EXHIBIT 80 Copyright © E. Seidewitz and M. Stark, 1987

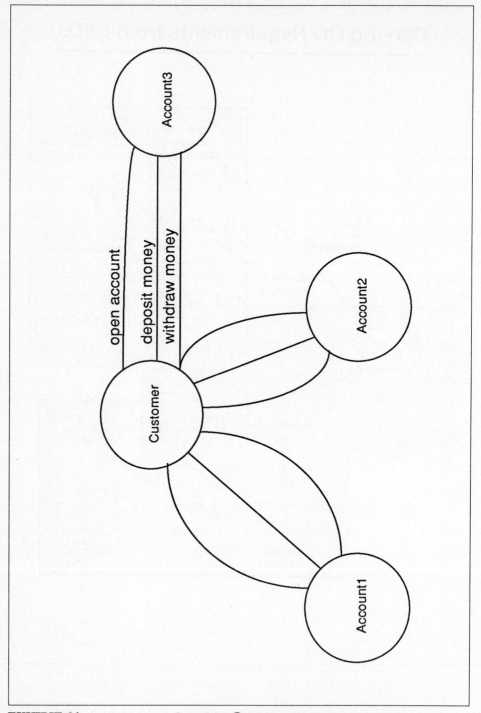

EXHIBIT 81   Copyright © B. Henderson-Sellers, 1991

7 steps in F-O-O methodology

1) Functional decomposition in analysis

2) DFDs for analysis

3) Semantic data modeling

4) Transform DFDs and ERDs into objects and DDs

5) Consideration of library classes

6) Object interactions and inheritance hierarchies

7) Generalization for reusability

"bubble" notation). The data themselves are stored in files that are identified by a terminator representation and data are pictured as "flowing" from node to node (process to process) — indicated by arrowed lines joining nodes.

3. At much the same time, *semantic data modeling* is undertaken. As a necessary adjunct, data relationships are evaluated and data modeling commenced. This uses a standard entity-relationship diagrammatic notation. If linkage to a standard relational database is envisaged, then the ideas of normalization will be included in the data modeling exercise.

4. *Transform DFDs and ERDs* into objects and O/C relationships (DDs). Once the DFDs and ERDs have been produced from a standard functional decomposition methodology, the difficult task of transforming into an object-oriented framework is commenced. As illustrated above, DFDs can be "carved" into objects. However, there is no guarantee that objects will be uniquely, or easily, related to the DFD nodes as in the simple example discussed above. In a large system, pieces of objects may be distributed widely throughout the design (Exhibit 20). Since objects are related to abstract data types, which contain both data and functionality logically bound together, this step is implicitly difficult since while ERDs, if undertaken carefully, can bear a strong similarity to objects, DFDs are not easily related in a modular fashion to the functionality of any particular object. The matching of functionality to appropriate object class is potentially an extremely difficult task in this F-O-O methodology and is therefore the crucial area of interest in authors in trying to propose workable F-O-O methodologies (e.g., Alabiso, 1988; Bailin, 1989; Ladden, 1989).

5. Once the difficult transition from a functional analysis to an object-oriented logical design has been made, then the Steps (5–7) of the O-O-O methodology can be used with ease (Section 4.3.2): i.e., consideration of the availability of library classes; O/C interactions and the use of DDs and inheritance diagrams; reusability concerns.

4.3.4 The O-O-F methodology

Conversely, you might say I have lots of active systems implemented in COBOL; therefore there is an opportunity to adopt OOA and OOD but not OOPLs. The rationale behind the O-O-F methodology (Exhibit 83) is that the novel ideas behind the object-oriented philosophy that permit the use of the same "model" throughout the systems development life cycle will be implemented to provide an object-oriented analysis (OOA), merging into an object-oriented design (OOD). As has been stressed by many authors (e.g., Mullin, 1989), the term "object-oriented" relates to this modeling philosophy; and it is essentially coincidental that, today, new languages structured on the same paradigm are available to complete the software development life cycle *entirely* within the OO paradigm. Nonetheless, with current large investments in procedural code and coding tools,

7 steps in O-O-F methodology

1) Object-oriented decomposition in analysis

2) Analysis/identification of objects

3) Identify object interactions

4) Analysis merges to design. More detail

5) Consideration of library classes

6) Reevaluate set of objects with respect to constraints of procedural language

7) Code objects into procedural language

especially the investment in COBOL in the commercial environment and Ada in the Defense environment, organizations may well be reticent to replace their language environment by one of the new OOPLs. A further concern is the nonstandard and evolving nature of these new programming environments.

In addition to the basic structure shown here, explicit addition of attributes and services permits the adoption of an entity-relationship (ER) notation (Coad and Yourdon, 1990) to illustrate n-ary relationship constraints and mandatory/ optional links. Exploring in full detail such synergism between object-oriented notation and data modeling notation is of current concern (e.g., Bailin, 1989; Ward, 1989; Henderson-Sellers and Edwards, 1990b).

In an O-O-F methodology (Exhibit 83), only one model is used in both OOA and OOD. The analysis-to-design transition is therefore straightforward and essentially a stage of progressively adding more objects required at the base level of object aggregates — significantly simpler than the disjoint transformation from DFDs to structure charts or from DFDs to objects (Coad and Yourdon, 1990, p163). Notationally, this requires the use of object leveling diagrams (Henderson-Sellers and Edwards, 1990b) — see Section 4.5.4. At the same time more services may need to be specified. The one-to-one mapping also ensures traceability — not possible in traditional functional-oriented analysis and design.

The O-O-F methodology maps analysis and design objects to the procedural implementation language that may support OO concepts to a varying degree. Stroustrup (1988) classifies such languages as supporting, for example, data hiding, data abstraction, modularity, and OO. While this path is feasible, it does not take full advantage of reuse and extendibility, which are at the heart of OO concepts.

Pragmatically, however, it should be recognized that the organization policy may be to implement in a 3GL, such as COBOL, or in a 4GL, such as Oracle, Coral, or Adabas. Millikin (1989) recommends that even in these cultural environments, object-oriented analysis and design techniques still provide a valuable precursor to implementation in a traditional language environment by providing a "better" design with a higher degree of encapsulation and information hiding (see also Rumbaugh *et al.*, 1991). The ease or difficulty of doing this implementation will, of course, be determined not only by the success of the OOA and OOD steps in producing a good detailed design but also the extent to which such design features are supported by the chosen language. Procedural languages traditionally support only procedural abstraction directly, so that data abstraction and encapsulation, while feasible, are the full responsibility of the programmer (an approach that has often been realized successfully within a non-object-oriented development environment). The O-O-F methodology is certainly one that has been adopted by some organizations (Coad and Yourdon, 1990, p173).

In summary (Exhibit 83), the following 7-step O-O-F methodological framework is therefore proposed (Henderson-Sellers, 1991b). The first five steps follow the corresponding steps in the O-O-O methodological framework. The final two steps are:

6. For implementation in a procedural language the created object-oriented

design must now be converted to a design suitable for coding in a procedural language. This is likely to require a reevaluation of the total set of objects identified in the design phase, perhaps regrouping and adding more procedural detail in order that OO concepts can be simulated within the target procedural language. The detailed approach of this step will be strongly language-dependent. In addition to the use of external, library classes, object messages could be replaced by additional arguments to subprogram "calls" which are then used to evaluate `Case`/`Switch` statements to access the appropriate method code unless multiple-entry subroutines (as in FORTRAN, for instance) are available. Similarly restricted ranges of values from basic language types (e.g., *INTEGER, REAL, ARRAY*) may require the extensive (and repetitive) use of conditional constructs. In some cases, objects can be to some degree mimicked by the use of arrays (Wampler, 1990), one for each feature.

7. Finally, the transformed *object-oriented design is coded into procedural modules*. The modular structure of the OO design should cause no problems with coding as subroutines in procedural languages and will enforce that modularity into the procedural language, a procedure that has always been possible within procedural languages but seldom previously encouraged. The resultant procedural program, based on an OO design, should be of a higher quality than if a structured design had been undertaken, even though it will not be possible to take full advantage of all the features of the OO paradigm, such as inheritance and polymorphism.

These three methodologies are contrasted in Exhibit 84. In the first four steps, the O-O-F and O-O-O approaches run in parallel, diverging thereafter. In contrast, the F-O-O steps merge with the O-O-O steps from Step 5 onward.

4.3.5 Convergent methodologies

In many object-oriented programming languages, the only available component is an object module or object class (Meyer, 1988). However, since object-structured organization can be mapped into or realized in almost any modern high-level programming language, in many implementation environments it is possible, in actuality, to mix purely functional or procedural components (Exhibit 85), such as a stand-alone or self-contained function, and object-oriented components. Indeed, the designer of Eiffel, Bertrand Meyer, foresaw the likelihood that users of Eiffel might wish to integrate Eiffel modules (classes) and procedural modules, written in, say, C. In addition, in one sense both the C-extension languages, like C++ and Objective-C, as well as one of the purer object-oriented languages, Eiffel, act as preprocessors and produce C code. One danger, noted by many authors (e.g., Korson and McGregor, 1990), in using such (hybrid) C-extensions is that many may claim to be doing object-oriented programming, while up to 90% of their design and implementation is in the paradigm of the base procedural language (here, C).

A pragmatist would argue that for wholesale use of an OOPL in a commercial/industrial organization, there must be a transition period, even in the most

O-O-F	O-O-O	F-O-O
1. Object-oriented systems requirements specification		Functional systems requirements specification
2.	Identify objects	Draw DFDs
3.	Establish interactions	Semantic data modeling
4.	Lower-level detailed design	Transform to lower-level detailed design
5. Use of libraries and simulation of inheritance	Bottom-up use of library classes	
6. Revision to transform into a design compatible with procedural code	Add inheritance hierarchies	
7. Code using procedural modules	Aggregation/generalization	

EXHIBIT 84   Copyright © B. Henderson-Sellers, 1991

CONVERGENT METHODOLOGIES

Integration of object-oriented and procedural techniques

Difficulty of using *two* paradigms concurrently

Use of structured techniques at lowest level

Tools with navigation paths between OOD and SD

EXHIBIT 85   Copyright © B. Henderson-Sellers, 1991

object-committed organization, when this type of hybridization is vital. Further-more, it remains unclear which model will ultimately prove the easier in which contexts (Page-Jones *et al.*, 1990), especially in the interest of extendibility (Constantine, 1990a). It is argued by some that hybrid architectures in dual-paradigm languages, such as C++, may prove to be the most robust implementations, not merely convenient compromises during a period of transition, although it should be emphasized that the difficulty of programming in *two* paradigms, both fully understood, is not to be underestimated.

As noted above, in an O-O-O approach, objects are used at all stages from requirements analysis through to implementation, thus providing a "seamless transition" or nearly one-to-one mapping at all stages (Section 2.4). Nevertheless, this O-O-O methodological framework (e.g., Henderson-Sellers and Edwards, 1990a) does not totally neglect structured tools and experience; rather it defers them to a more detailed design level. The system can be fully designed in terms of objects, yet the internal structure of the object, largely "private" to that object, consists of attributes together with methods that are themselves simply functions or procedures. Design, at this detailed level, of these functions and procedures is essentially identical to structured, functional decomposition as developed over the last twenty years or so. Generally, each method can be designed independently, but each can be considered using, for example, functional design charts (Alabiso, 1988), mini-structure charts, DFDs, ERDs, etc., since at this level, functional considerations become paramount. This does not contradict the object-oriented paradigm, since at this level the implementation of the features is hidden and changes in the implementation therefore have, at least in principle, no repercussions on the rest of the software system. Object encapsulation must be maintained, as should minimum external coupling (goals also common to structural analysis and design techniques). The necessity of a functional decomposition at this lowest design level has not been stressed in the object-oriented design literature but is evident in many published examples of code. The utilization of some structured techniques at the lowest level of detailed design is thus assured (see also Coad and Yourdon, 1990, pp19–20). Of course, within a single object method, the complexity of a fully structured *system* will never be duplicated. Thus DFDs might have only a small-scale use. Indeed, Page-Jones and Weiss (1989) have been led to comment that "the days of DFDs are limited and may only be drawn to please management or the users."

In a similar vein of developing useful convergent methodologies, Bailin (1989) chooses to adopt and adapt DFDs to become EDFDs (entity data flow diagrams) for object-oriented requirements analysis, since this provides a "representation method with which most analysts were already familiar." Similarly, Wasserman *et al.* (1990) include both object-oriented and functional tools in the OOSD (Object-Oriented Structured Design) notation which takes, essentially, an F-O-O approach (Section 4.3.3). They utilize existing structured design tools, such as structure charts, directly while adopting a graphical notation representation of objects similar to that of Booch (1987) but with methods arrayed horizontally rather than vertically (see Exhibit 91 in next section). Indeed, one of their stated aims is "to build on a familiar and proven notation and set of concepts" while providing a general-purpose architectural design methodology. This notation, which constitutes somewhat of a compromise between conventional structured design and object-oriented models, includes features that may be considered by some to be undesirable for purely object-oriented approaches. As with some other elaborate notations, the particular visual conventions of OOSD can result in diagrams that are too complex to be intelligible. Furthermore, as the notation permits separation of data from behavior, violations of encapsulation are possible.

Such software tools that have "switches" and navigation paths between object-oriented and structured design can provide the software engineer with a useful product, but they must be coupled with clear guidelines to support the different mindset required to produce a good object-oriented design. Object-oriented techniques are not simple extensions or modifications of structured techniques, but represent a new software paradigm. On the other hand, fully successful application of object-orientation builds on the underlying reusable/successful principles and past experience of the software engineering discipline. In any case, it is important at some point to take the essentially discrete step toward a full understanding of the object-oriented paradigm.

The admixture, or alternation, of object-oriented and functionally-oriented techniques within analysis or within design (sometimes called "convergent design") (Exhibit 85) is discussed in more detail by Jalote (1989), Constantine (1989a, 1990a), Ladden (1989), and Henderson-Sellers and Constantine (1991). A crucial question in a convergent methodology is whether an object class can consist of functions only with no attributes or with only a degenerate encapsulated data structure (cf. Wegner, 1990). In other words, can an abstract data type be purely functional and yet remain an abstract data type? From a pragmatic viewpoint, there appears to be a possible role for library classes of so-called "function-objects." Consider, for example, the classes *COMMAND* and *TEXT_EDITOR* from the Eiffel reusable class library which have both state and behavior. The semantics of the names themselves encompass both an abstract noun and an action. This gray area of function-objects again suggests possible limitations of an "orthodox" object-oriented modeling approach and potential advantages to dual-paradigm approaches. A similar hybrid object-type is that of the "mixin" (e.g., Bobrow, 1989; Booch and Vilot, 1990b — see also Section 5.6). Of course, such borderline cases can be accommodated within the object-oriented paradigm, but care must be taken that cases of functions masquerading as objects do not proliferate, although it is generally recognized that active objects, such as tools and parsers, provide good components of a fully object-oriented system. A surplus of function-objects may be an indicator of poor design or the use of architectures more appropriate to an object-based environment (Wegner, 1989), such as Ada. The proper use of function-objects and inheritance hierarchies of function-objects may be akin to what is now considered by most proponents of object-orientation to be the true role of multiple inheritance: a practice to be used thoughtfully and, probably, sparingly (Henderson-Sellers and Constantine, 1991). One good guideline is to ask whether the functionality that is being proposed can be equated to a cohesive role in the overall model/design. If so, consideration as an object (with the caveats given above) seems worthwhile. Functionality with no cohesion should *not* be encapsulated as an object.

4.4 Analysis and Design

The reason for separating analysis from design is related to the target of the modeling at each level. At the analysis or conceptual modeling phase (Pun and Winder, 1990), we are trying to represent a part of the real world, whereas at the design stage we are representing an information systems design. Thus "information systems *analysis* is the process of creating a *model* of (the human perceptions of) the real system to be represented in the information system," while "design is the process of creating a model of the information system (artifact) to be constructed based upon the model of the real system" (Wand and Weber, 1989, p82).

The analysis-level model is then primarily concerned with providing an accurate picture of the real-world situation, and an object-oriented analysis (OOA) model must have this as its primary objective. The object-oriented design (OOD) model's major objective is to support "good" software engineering design in terms of correctness, modularity, reusability, and abstraction (Meyer, 1988). The goal of a "seamless" transition between phases should be subsumed by the primary goals of each level of modeling identified above.

It is important to note that object-oriented technology has been driven by the availability of object-oriented languages during its relatively recent rise to prominence in software engineering, and only now are analysis and design methodologies being developed that tackle the earlier stages of the life cycle. Therefore, as the technology and model move from one domain to another, it is important to be aware of the model's limitations and applicability to environments different from those in which it was originally developed.

The current object-oriented programming model, at its most general, provides syntactic and semantic constructs to support classification, identification, generalization, and some form of message-passing or client–server mechanism (Stroustrup, 1988; Wegner, 1989). Current methodologies support these concepts at the design stages, yet overload many of the constructs with multiple names to try to help clarify different types of real-world relationships. Relationship types such as "inheritance," "contains," "uses," "instantiation," and "has-knowledge-of," "is-part-of," and "is-analogous-to" (Booch, 1991; Wirfs-Brock *et al.*, 1990; Pun and Winder, 1990) are just some of the many different named relationships that are used throughout the design literature, despite many of them not being supported at the language level. The reason for so many relationship types is that they provide useful semantic information to a designer on how the real world is to be modeled. This suggests that the object model, as currently employed in object-oriented languages, is not sufficient for the analysis phase of many applications. We therefore suggest that at the level of analysis, where it is important to capture real-world semantics, a small number of extra semantic constructs that are to be found in many data modeling techniques be added. The three relationships identifiable at the analysis stage are (Exhibit 86) (1) generalization/classification

— the **is-a** relationship will be designed and implemented using inheritance; (2) association — a named relationship typified by the phrase **uses-a**; and (3) aggregation — the **is-composed-of** relationship between a high-level object and its constituent lower-level object components.

At the design phase the object-oriented constructs can be overloaded with names to provide a methodological guide to designers in the transition from analysis to design. The extra constructs introduced are the explicit recognition of aggregation and association at the analysis level, with the client–server mechanism used to simulate both of these at the design level, and the separation of implementation and specification inheritance at the detailed design level. The transition from analysis to design (Exhibit 87) is thus marked by the transformation of the three analysis relationships into the (currently) two design relationships, concomitant with an increased level of resolution as well as the switch from the "real world" (problem space) to the "software world" (solution space) (cf. Exhibit 60).

This separation of analysis and design, and the explicit recognition of language constructs and analysis constructs, are reflected in, and supported by, currently emerging analysis and design methodologies, e.g., Coad and Yourdon (1990, 1991), Wirfs-Brock *et al.* (1990), Booch (1991), Henderson-Sellers and Edwards (1990a), and Rumbaugh *et al.* (1991). For example, Coad and Yourdon (1990, 1991) talk of aggregation structures and inheritance of specification at the analysis level, while the discussion by Booch (1991) of inheritance implicitly covers both implementation and specification, and class–class relationships in terms of the "uses" relationship at the design level. This therefore leads us to offer a notation that is slightly modified at the OOA level, compared with the OO broad design and detailed design levels. However, the graphics of the two stages should be as compatible as possible to provide as seamless a transition as possible from analysis to design, yet support powerful enough concepts to be useful modeling tools at each stage.

4.4.1 Statics and dynamics of systems

Object-oriented systems at compile time consist of classes whose structure and relationships represent the static aspects of the system. At run-time the system state consists of objects, instances of classes, and references. In order to show the dynamics of the system graphically, objects must be displayed as a network of methods and the messages passing between them. A relationship between any two objects, whether expressed by aggregation and association or represented by client–server, provides a connection channel that allows messages (or events) to be sent. These messages trigger methods (or processes) that lead to changes of state in the object to which the messages were sent (Rosenquist, 1982). By recognizing that a static relationship exists between two O/Cs, providing a link for many different events, processes, and state changes to occur in a server object, we explicitly recognize the dynamic and static aspects of the system. One static architecture, therefore, does not imply a one-to-one mapping with any single dynamic arrangement of calls to the supplier class. The static link allows the client to call any exported feature of the supplier in whatever way

Relationships at Analysis

1) Generalization/Classification
is-a

2) Association
named relationship
(e.g. **uses-a**)

3) Aggregation
is-composed-of

Transition from Analysis to Design

1) Generalization ⟶ Inheritance Hierarchies

2) Association ⟶ Client–Server

3) Aggregation ⟶ Client–Server

EXHIBIT 87   Copyright © B. Henderson-Sellers, 1991

its implementation sees fit. Thus the sequence of calls to the supplier may be changed, altering the dynamic arrangement while the static structure remains unchanged.

Object methods provide the sequencing of calls to other objects and thus the dynamics of object interaction. Methods or services are simply procedures and functions such as would be found in normal procedural design. Therefore, the use of a program design language (PDL) or structure charts would seem to be appropriate to detail individual methods. Additional notation may be added to show event-neighborhood (Page-Jones *et al.*, 1990) or run-time object-diagrams (Booch, 1991), although in general a PDL would suffice to detail object dynamics.

The diagrammatic representation for the dynamics of OO systems remains to be thoroughly investigated, but work by Page-Jones *et al.* (1990), Booch (1991), Wirfs-Brock *et al.* (1990), Rumbaugh *et al.* (1991), and Pun and Winder (1990), suggests several possibilities, including the use of state-transition diagrams (STDs) and timing diagrams. In this book, however, we concentrate upon the static graphical notation, while acknowledging that notation for object dynamics is also of importance.

4.5 Available Notation

Notation is interesting (Exhibit 88). If we are to expect software developers to provide us with CASE tools for OO, then notation is of concern. We have to consider the representation of objects (i.e., objects, classes, etc., at all life cycle stages). I will show that essentially the same notation can be applied to design and also to analysis as well as to run-time execution (with only a few modifications that reflect, essentially, differing degrees of resolution ONLY). There is NO need for the equivalent of a (poor) mapping between DFDs and hierarchy charts as in functional design, for example.

Object notation/object-oriented graphics pertains to the analysis- and design-level objects, to the classes of run-time objects prior to implementation, and to object–object/class–class relationships. A general, non-language-specific notation is ideally required (Edwards and Henderson-Sellers, 1991). Since analysis objects, design objects, and also classes can be represented similarly, but at different stages of the life cycle, we will refer to such generic applicability by "O/C" (objects *or* classes). Such a "seamless" transition presents the opportunity of standardizing upon a graphical notation applicable to O/Cs *throughout* the whole life cycle. Following the presentation of icons for an individual O/C in Section 4.5.1, and graphical representation of O/C relationships in Section 4.5.2 and 4.5.3, the larger-scale concerns of representing full systems using ideas of leveling and subsystems (Section 4.5.4) and inheritance hierarchies (Section 4.5.5) will be addressed. Finally, individual classes must be specified in detail, immediately prior to implementation (Section 4.5.6). The suite of notational tools is then summarized in Section 4.5.7.

Available Analysis and Design Notation

Concentrating on

Static Notation

4.5.1 Icons for objects

Firstly, we need a basic icon to represent an object (Exhibit 89). We need to add to the chosen shape: a class name, and a list of attributes (state) and operations (behavior/functionality offered), which together comprise the (public) interface. In addition (Section 4.5.2), we need to represent O/C–O/C relationships. A commonly used icon is a rounded-edge rectangular box (though several versions of this exist), although circles are also used (i.e., Meyer, 1988), as are rectangles (Wirfs-Brock *et al.*, 1990), rectangles with domes (Page-Jones *et al.*, 1990) and amorphous blobs (Booch, 1991) (Exhibit 90). Alternatively, the graphical notation for "packages" Booch (1987) (Exhibit 91), despite being conceived originally as Ada-specific, has been further refined for object-oriented application by, e.g., Wasserman *et al.* (1990), Page-Jones *et al.* (1990), Edwards and Henderson-Sellers (1991), as well as by Booch (1991) himself — although none of these notations are, as yet, standard. These latter typify successfully the discrimination between the private, hidden part of the object and the public portion, as represented by protrusions (the class interface, i.e., services offered). Booch points out this is the analog of a building of concrete with window boxes providing access to the interior. The bulk of the body remains hidden from view. A concern with this representation is that the icon could be disproportionately large (Constantine, 1990a). Alternatively, the size of the icon may provide an indication to the designer for the need for further decomposition of an object. The notation should also consider the space limitations of display monitor/screen/VDU and paper representation, and aim to minimize the space occupied by the symbols. There is little point in having a graphical representation for all features of the paradigm if this leads to an overly complex representation. The aim of a graphical representation should be to simplify the design at various levels of detail in order to highlight those characteristics pertinent *at the scale of resolution currently being addressed*. Consequently, we have proposed a suite of complementary diagramming notations, which is reviewed briefly in Section 4.5 and used in the case study material there.

During *analysis*, ideas of aggregation and object attributes are prominent in data modeling techniques (Peckham and Maryanski, 1988). At this stage, the issues of implementation are of no concern and the notation should therefore reflect semantically important concepts rather than be concerned with later design issues that may or may not be object-oriented (Henderson-Sellers, 1990). At the analysis stage, then, the concepts of aggregation and object attributes are important semantic constructs that must be recognized explicitly, while at the design level, when the concepts of uniform reference and information hiding are paramount, the distinction between attributes and operations becomes unnecessary (see discussion below).

Exhibit 92 depicts our recommended icon for an object at the *analysis* stage, a dotted icon indicating an "abstract object", i.e. one that will never be instantiated in the run-time system and serves as a "superobject" in a generalization hierarchy. (see further details in Section 5.3). It essentially takes the Ada-like notation of Henderson-Sellers and Edwards (1990a) but rationalizes the complexity. Instead of depicting each operation and attribute individually, following Coad and Your-

Graphical representation of object needs to show

Object Name

Attributes(State)

Operations

(Functionality offered/Behavior)

+ method of showing O/C to O/C relationships

with respect to 1) Inheritance

2) Aggregation + association or
client–server

EXHIBIT 89   Copyright © B. Henderson-Sellers, 1991

CLASS ICONS

Coad and Yourdon (1990)

Wirfs-Brock *et al.* (1990)

CLASS NAME
List of Attributes
List of Services

CLASS NAME

Coad and Yourdon (1991)

Booch (1991)

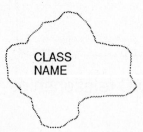

CLASS NAME

CLASS NAME
List of Attributes
List of Services

EXHIBIT 90

Notation not standard (yet!)

Booch's notation

— Developed for Ada

— May be able to be modified to be more generally applicable

Wasserman *et al.* (1990)   Page-Jones *et al.* (1990)

Formal
output control
parameter

Exception
parameter

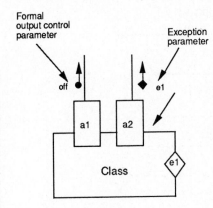

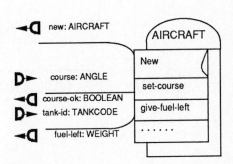

© 1990 IEEE

EXHIBIT 91

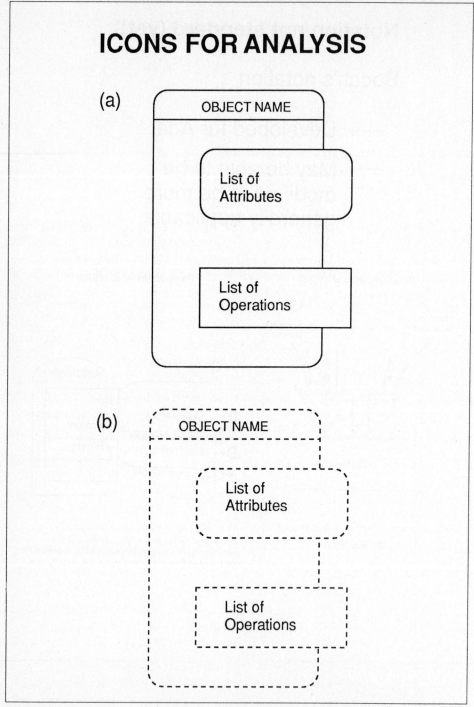

EXHIBIT 92   Copyright © J.M. Edwards and B. Henderson-Sellers, 1991

don (1990) and Wilson (1990), these are grouped into a single rounded symbol containing the attributes and a single rectangular symbol containing the operations. In order to retain a visual indication of the ideas of information hiding, the notation of Coad and Yourdon (1990) is not adopted directly. Rather there is a displacement of these attribute and operation symbols to protrude slightly outside the object border — to maintain the representation of the external interface and private sections of the object (see also Page-Jones *et al.*, 1990). However, this is minimized and offers a more "space saving" notation than that of Henderson-Sellers and Edwards (1990a), a simpler notation than that of Wasserman *et al.* (1990), a more suggestive notation than that of Coad and Yourdon (1990), and a more useful and concise notation than that of Alabiso (1988).

At the *design* stage, the recommended icon thus shows only a set of services and a class name, again displaced to represent information hiding (Exhibit 93). Again, to represent an abstract or deferred class (one that cannot be instantiated but may be inherited from) the icon is dotted. This notation represents the concepts of uniform reference and information hiding by not specifying the way results or actions are implemented, for example, by storage or by computation (the "principle of uniform reference": Meyer, 1988).

At the detailed design stage it may be necessary to show services that are secret, being available to other services of the class but not to other classes, since the programmer needs to know what services are required in order to "cut the code." In this notation the service name can be placed within the icon yet not in the interface portion, graphically implying that the service is not visible from outside the class (Exhibit 93(c)). The notation could thus be used to show the full set of a class's services, both those visible and nonvisible.

The internal structure of an O/C, largely "private" to that object, consists of code to implement the services offered. These are coded as a set of features that encompass attributes and methods, the latter being simply functions or procedures. Design, at this detailed level internal to the class, of these functions and procedures is essentially identical to structured, functional decomposition as developed over the last twenty years or so. This does not contradict the object-oriented paradigm, since at this level the implementation of the features is hidden and changes in the implementation therefore have no repercussions on the rest of the software system.

4.5.2 Class–class (object–object) relationships

Diagrammatic notation requires representation not only for individual object classes but also of object–object (class–class) aggregation, association, and generalization. At analysis it is important that these three semantically different concepts be differentiated. However, since OOPLs don't currently support aggregation and association directly, but rather simulate both by client–server mutual responsibilities (Rumbaugh, 1987; Loomis *et al.*, 1987), during the design phase a single client–server relationship can be used to subsume the aggregation and association relationships identified and depicted at the analysis stage. This means that relationships identifiable in the real world, and hence that should be represented at the analysis stage, are not necessarily discriminated between at the

ICONS FOR DESIGN

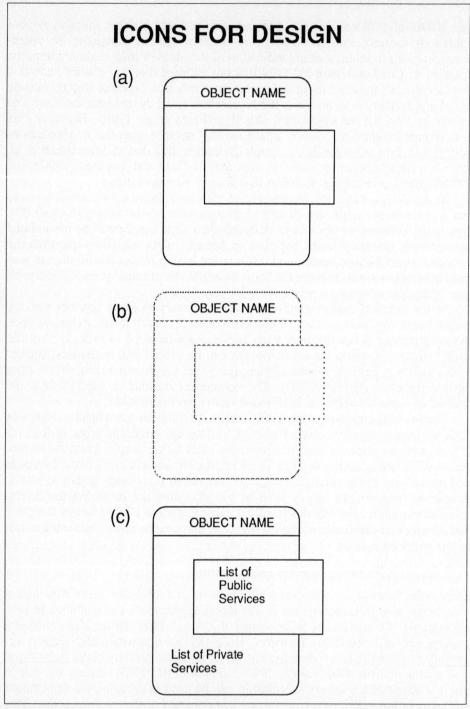

design and implementation stages.

Object–object (or class–class) relationships at the *analysis* stage therefore include generalization, aggregation, and association (Exhibit 94). Aggregation represents the **has-a**, **consists-of**, or **contains** (see also Pun and Winder, 1990) relationship (e.g., a room consists of four walls, a floor, and a ceiling); association is a named meaningful relationship between one object and another (e.g., a customer object uses the services of a bank object); and inheritance represents a taxonomic hierarchy or **is-a** relationship. As discussed earlier, it is important that these three semantically different concepts be differentiated at the analysis stage.

The Object Modeling Technique (OMT) notation of Loomis *et al.* (1987) and Rumbaugh *et al.* (1991) provides an object model for the analysis stage that supports these relationships (Exhibit 95). In this notation, which has some similarities with that of Coad and Yourdon (1990), association is shown simply by an undirected line connecting the two objects with associated cardinalities indicated; aggregation is shown by an arrow from the "component" to the "aggregate"; and generalization is shown by lines connecting objects with a triangle at the join of subclasses to superclasses. This symbol may be adapted for the use of expanded modeling constructs as supported in the EER notation (Elmasri and Navathe, 1989), such as disjoint and overlapping mappings of subclasses (see further discussion in Edwards and Henderson-Sellers, 1991).

However, the OMT model uses a thin line for both association and inheritance. One further problem occurs with respect to the direction of the arrow in an aggregation relationship, since in design, this would have to be translated into a client–server arrow from the aggregate to the component, i.e., a reversal of direction between analysis and design. (In Rumbaugh *et al.*, 1991 this has been obviated by the use of diamond symbols rather than directed line symbols.) Thus we recommend a notation that uses a thick arrow to represent inheritance that has a circle, an adaptation of the notation of Loomis *et al.* (1987), to represent disjoint and overlapping mappings (following Elmasri and Navathe, 1989). Exhibit 96 shows the relationship types and their recommended notations. The notation is basically that of Loomis *et al.* but replacing the inheritance graphic, adding a new object icon, and showing disjoint and overlapping mappings. For association (Exhibit 96(a)) and aggregation (Exhibit 96(b)), cardinalities may be shown on the lines, and a label on the association line may be used to clarify the relationship between the O/Cs. Within the circle on the inheritance arrow can be placed either an "o" or a "d." An "o" in the circle implies an overlapping mapping, so that an instance can be of subtype 1 and subtype 2 (something not currently supported by object-oriented languages), while a "**d**" implies a disjoint mapping, so that an instance can only be of type 1 or type 2 (the norm for current OO languages). For example, Elmasri and Navathe (1989, p417) give examples of engineering parts that could be manufactured or purchased, or both; while in other universes of discourse, subclasses may be totally disjoint (e.g., an employee can be categorized into one specific subclass: secretary, technical, engineer, etc.). Finally, an abstract (or deferred) class (which must always be a superclass) is shown dotted (Exhibit 96(c)) and multiple inheritance is easily

Object/class — Object/class interactions

<u>Analysis</u>   translates to   <u>Design</u>

Generalization/   ⟶   Inheritance
classification

Association
                    }   ⟶   Client –server
Aggregation

EXHIBIT 94   Copyright © B. Henderson-Sellers, 1991

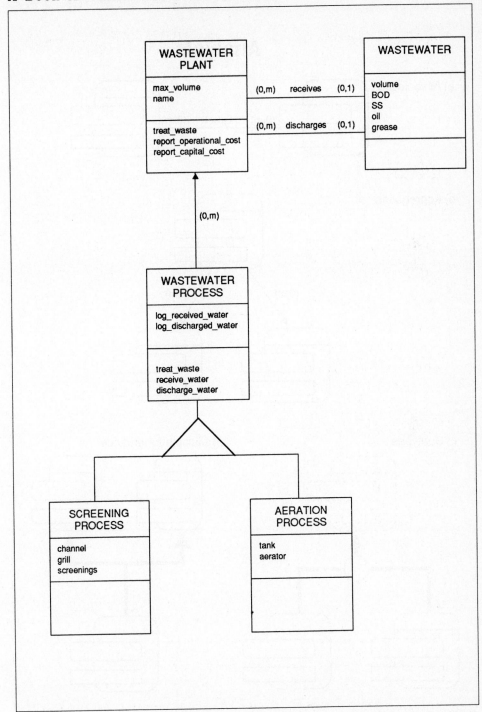

EXHIBIT 95   Copyright © J.M. Edwards and B. Henderson-Sellers, 1991

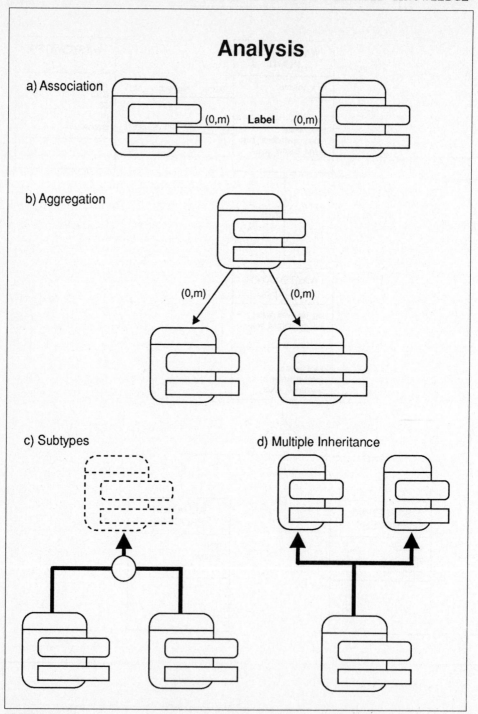

EXHIBIT 96   Copyright © J.M. Edwards and B. Henderson-Sellers, 1991

accommodated (Exhibit 96(d)).

At the program *design* level (Exhibit 97), most OOPLs only support generalization (the inheritance construct), classification (the class construct), and identification (provided by the run-time system). Association and aggregation are generally simulated similarly by reference to other objects (pointers) using client–server. When an attribute of an O/C is of an abstract data type and hence requires reference to another O/C for its realization, a thin arrow from the O/C to the server O/C is recommended (Exhibit 97), a notation useful for both aggregation and association.

Booch (1991) includes a notion for specifying use of a class in the interface and implementation. This may be important at a detailed design stage and thus, following Booch, we suggest that the connection circle may be left blank to represent the fact that the class uses the other class in its interface, or solid to represent the fact that a class uses another class in its implementation (Exhibit 97(a)) (white to represent the "clarity" of openness, black to represent "hidden"). This may be useful at the detailed design level, when the implementation of a class is being designed, but could be removed by a software tool to show the conceptual, or broad design, only. Inheritance is again shown by a thick arrow that is directed toward the superclass from the subclass (Exhibit 97(b)). To represent multiple inheritance the notation used at the analysis level is sufficient, the only difference being that the object-oriented language model does not yet allow one object to be of multiple types concurrently. Thus the disjoint mapping and overlapping mapping of the analysis level are unnecessary and must be simulated at implementation. Multiple subtypes are shown by a lattice of subclasses with an arrow pointing to the superclass (Exhibit 97(c)), while multiple inheritance is shown by a similar structure with the arrows pointing from the one subclass to the two superclasses (Exhibit 97(d)).

Other notations are used for modules and subsystems (see Booch, 1991, for full details of his notational and design approach). A collaboration diagram from the Uniform Object Notation (UON) of Page-Jones *et al.* is shown in Exhibit 98. Here, arrows indicate client–server and lines relationships as yet undecided. Also illustrated are the many connectional variants in Booch's notation. These support the use of a second class for implementing the interface of the original class or for its own internal implementation. The instantiation relationships are relevant to languages supporting genericity. Other connections shown here are more relevant to certain environments than others.

4.5.3 Contract diagrams

As well as using a graphical representation for object–object interactions, a second concept should be applied to each and every client–server relationship: the notion of a contract (Meyer, 1989b). The terms of these contractual obligations/benefits are spelled out in a 2×2 matrix (Meyer, 1989b) (Exhibit 18), which can be clarified in a contract diagram (CD) as a table of features and requirements (Exhibit 99).

The idea of contracts is related to that of "responsibilities" by, e.g., Wirfs-Brock and Wilkerson (1989b) and Wirfs-Brock and Johnson (1990), in which

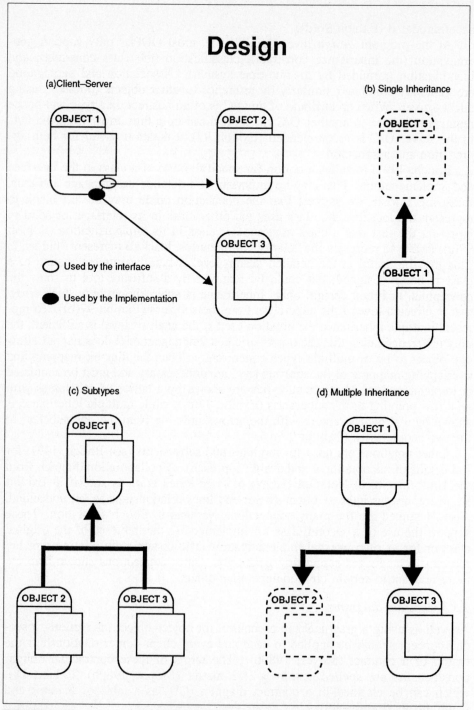

EXHIBIT 97 Copyright © J.M. Edwards and B. Henderson-Sellers, 1991

Page-Jones *et al.* (1990) Collaborations Diagram

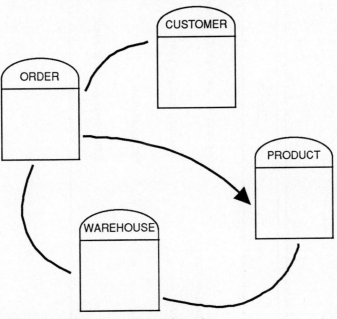

Reprinted by permission of Larry Constantine and Computer Language Magazine, Miller Freeman Inc., 600 Harrison Street, San Francisco, CA, 94107, USA

Booch (1991) Icons for Relationships and Cardinalities

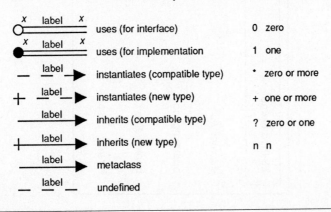

EXHIBIT 98

Method Name	Require	Result
depreciation	historic cost valid historic cost > residual value	depreciation per year on value
operating_cost	book value not void	operating cost per year
book_value	asset is tangible	net asset value
historic_cost	asset is tangible	actual original cost of asset

EXHIBIT 99   Copyright © J.M. Edwards and B. Henderson-Sellers, 1991

a contract is seen as defining a cohesive set of responsibilities that a client can depend on. Wirfs-Brock and Wilkerson (1989b) stress the need to use a responsibility-driven conceptual approach since a data-driven approach "inherently violates encapsulation." Furthermore, a CD is necessary not only for association relationships but also for aggregation responsibilities, as both are represented by client–server at the design level.

4.5.4 Systems representations

We have seen that notationally the difference between OOA and OOD relates to whether we can discriminate between aggregation and association and thus whether we have two sorts or one sort of protruding box on the O/C icon. Bearing this duality in mind, the remainder of the discussion will utilize the *design* notation, although an analogous analysis stage description is also perfectly feasible.

Small systems can be designed by simply building up a diagram showing the relationships between all the classes and indeed to the base library classes. However, it is evident that in any reasonably complex system such a full systems diagram is nevertheless likely to become rapidly highly complex (e.g., Seidewitz, 1989; Jalote, 1989). Consequently, the idea of leveling (Exhibit 100), taken from DFDs and data modeling, can be applied here for both analysis and design (e.g., Feldman and Miller, 1986; Bailin, 1989; Seidewitz, 1989; Simsion, 1989; Laranjeira, 1990; Henderson-Sellers and Edwards, 1990b). At each level of abstraction around 7 ± 2 (Miller, 1956) object icons should be shown. The levels are numbered (1, 2 ...) as internal details of the objects are subsequently expanded and viewed (see following discussion). A general level is referred to as "level-n" and the top level as "level-1."

At this topmost level (level-1) the basic interacting objects should be identified and interrelated (largely association in the first instance) (Exhibit 101). In other circumstances, it may be useful to remove the interface details ("selective visibility off"). This can be done at any level of design diagram (DD). At the top level, this removal of detail could be considered as a special case (Exhibit 101) and referred to as a level-0 diagram. These are referred to as "subjects" by Coad and Yourdon (1990). Most of these objects will however contain references to other objects as a result of aggregation, inheritance, or possibly further association relationships, but at this level such supporting features do not appear. An even more simplified graphics notation, using only icon shapes and object names but no protruding rectangles/ellipses, is more than adequate. Note that a leveled *analysis* diagram will show the association relationships, while in a *design* diagram the notation of client–server is used. For example, in Exhibit 102, the *CUSTOMER_PORTFOLIO* object contains instance variables of type *BANK_ACCOUNT, TELEPHONE_ACCOUNT, CREDITCARD_ACCOUNT, DRIVER'S_LICENSE*, etc., which are all available to clients of the *CUSTOMER_PORTFOLIO* object. Although *DRIVER'S_LICENSE* may be an attribute (e.g., with values "Current" or "not-Current"), it may equally be a reference to a *DRIVER'S_LICENSE object* that contains information on ID number, convictions, duration held etc., while

LEVELING DIAGRAM

Aggregation

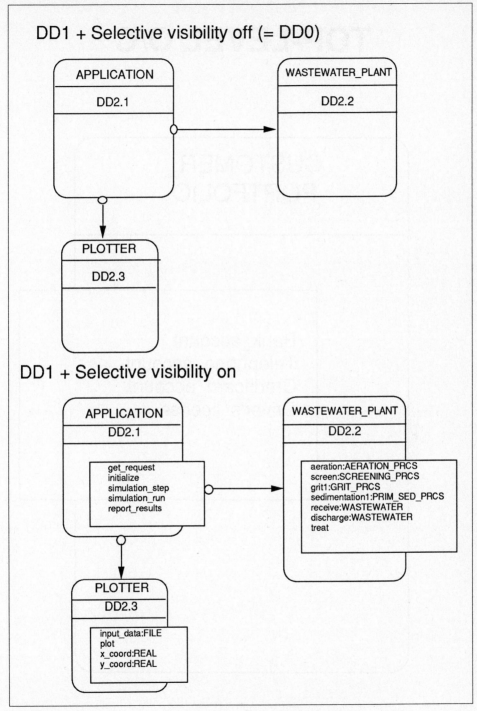

TOP-LEVEL O/C

CUSTOMER_
PORTFOLIO

Bank_account
Telephone_account
Creditcard_account
Driver's_license

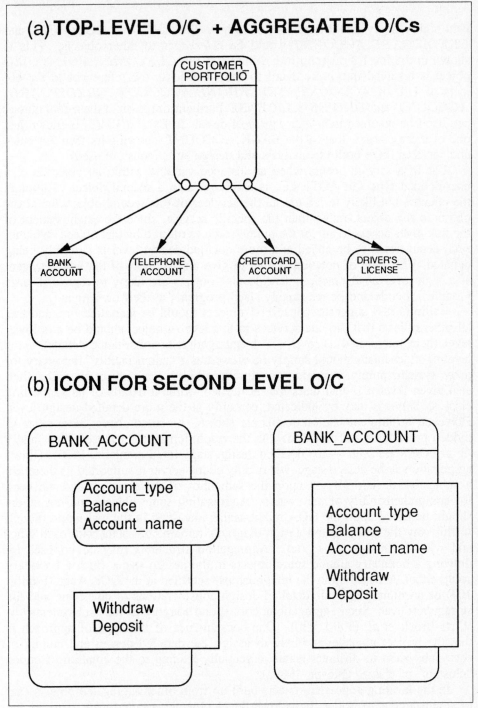

(a) TOP-LEVEL O/C + AGGREGATED O/Cs

CUSTOMER_PORTFOLIO

BANK_ACCOUNT

TELEPHONE_ACCOUNT

CREDITCARD_ACCOUNT

DRIVER'S_LICENSE

(b) ICON FOR SECOND LEVEL O/C

BANK_ACCOUNT

Account_type
Balance
Account_name

Withdraw
Deposit

BANK_ACCOUNT

Account_type
Balance
Account_name

Withdraw
Deposit

EXHIBIT 103   Copyright © J.M. Edwards and B. Henderson-Sellers, 1991

it is highly likely that *BANK_ACCOUNT, TELEPHONE_ACCOUNT,* and *CREDITCARD_ACCOUNT* would be *references* to other objects. This is shown in the level-1 diagram in Exhibit 103: the *CUSTOMER_PORTFOLIO* object is resolved into more detail to show explicitly the references to the objects of *BANK_ACCOUNT, TELEPHONE_ACCOUNT, CREDITCARD_ACCOUNT,* and *DRIVER'S_LICENSE.* Furthermore, each of these four classes can itself be resolved to a finer degree of detail. In Exhibit 103(b) is shown just one of these classes, that of the BANK_ACCOUNT, showing its own attributes and services (here both the analysis and design style icons are used).

Use of a service occurs when an instance variable within an object is of a user-defined type (an ADT), i.e., is a reference to a second object. Although the client is not likely to require all the services of this second object, the arrow points to the object, rather than the specific service, since the establishment of the link gives access to any of the public services offered by that object. Whether such detail needs to be added at a more detailed design level is currently being debated. This type of notation is able to give an overview of the whole system at a high level of abstraction. The level-1 objects are likely to represent large modules of code and be reasonably sized programs in their own right.

Bailin (1989) suggests that level-1 objects should be identified first and that all other objects that provide services to this level-n object should be at a lower level (here interpreted as level-$n + 1$ aggregation or inheritance details). This leveling mechanism should simply be viewed as a "zoom facility" necessary for *large* systems purely as an aid to comprehensibility. Each object class identified at a given level-n is that class that is needed, without details of its supporting classes. Services may be indicated, certainly at the more detailed design level. However, no implementation details are shown. As noted above, these relate to hidden procedures and functions. As the resolution level increases, then finally library O/Cs are seen — the detailed design stage (cf. Laranjeira, 1990). Object aggregation at the design stage, where only client–server is supported, is therefore a subjective decision based upon the semantics of the situation and the need for comprehensibility of the system. Aggregating some objects and not others should be based upon the OOA relationships identified in the real-world model. In this way the analysis and design diagrams remain consistent with each other and with the real-world model. Aggregation structures may be imposed by drawing a boundary around some objects in the design stage. Such a boundary could either be based upon the relationships identified at the OOA stage (Exhibit 104) or on more pragmatic detailed design considerations of clustering and file storage/retrieval. Such aggregations correspond roughly to the "subsystems" of Wirfs-Brock *et al.* (1990, p30). One consequence of this type of approach is that the project manager is likely to assign the detailed design and coding of each subsystem to different teams, essentially leading to the creation of coded "clusters" of classes (Meyer, 1989a).

In the leveling approach, objects built up from other aggregated objects can, to some degree, consider these lower-level objects as component parts of the higher-level object. They need not appear in the level-1 diagram. Indeed, at this stage their presence is essentially irrelevant, so long as the contracting protocol

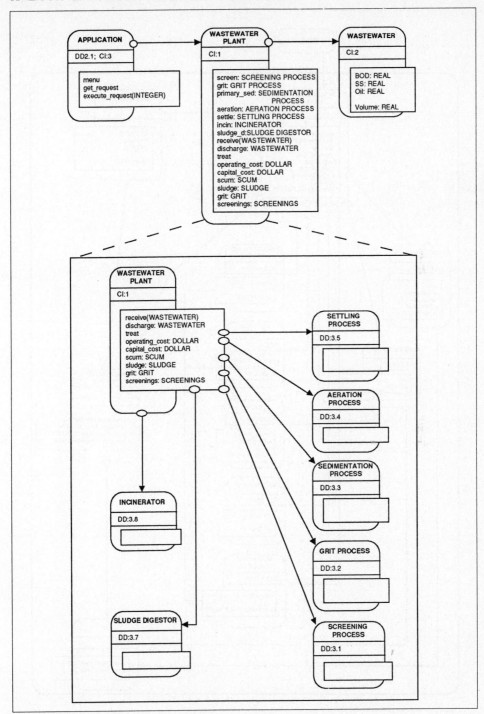

EXHIBIT 104   Copyright © J.M. Edwards and B. Henderson-Sellers, 1991

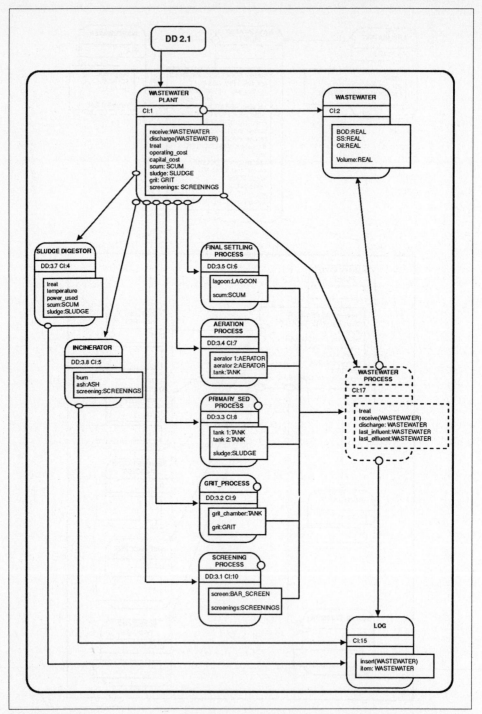

EXHIBIT 105   Copyright © J.M. Edwards and B. Henderson-Sellers, 1991

has been clearly defined in the appropriate contract diagram (see Section 4.5.3). Using the zoom facility, an expansion of the upper-level class reveals lower-level details and any further object–object association interactions. The zoom facility means that a part of the system can be examined in more and more detail. For example, the level-1 design diagram (DD) (Exhibit 101) can be expanded to a set of level-2 DDs (Exhibit 105), and so on. However, in large systems where only a part of the whole can be shown at any one time, it is important that the subsystem be placed in context. The need for specifying context and the connection to other parts of the system, as well as expanding the detail for the subsystem to be examined, can be represented by diagrams similar to Exhibit 105 (DD2.2) but showing details of objects in only a subsystem while showing relationships to other subsystems (Exhibit 104). Notation with the O/C icon shows the particular subsystem connections, using either association plus aggregation (analysis) or simply client–server (design) connections as appropriate.

4.5.5 Inheritance hierarchies

Client–server and inheritance object–object relationships have often been confused (see discussion in Thomas, 1989a). In a large system, a combination of the two types of relationships into the same diagram (such as the Structure Layer of Coad and Yourdon, 1990) could be adding unnecessary and confusing detail. Similarly, Figure 7 of Korson and McGregor (1990) uses the diamonds of the ER diagram to represent both inheritance and client–server. A clear distinction can perhaps best be drawn by visualizing client–server (when it represents association) essentially as a "horizontal" relationship and the inheritance mechanism as being orthogonal to this (Exhibit 106). (An alternative multidimensional visualization can be found in Booch, 1991, Figure 1–1.) In some cases, access may be made to a parent class, in others (especially when the upper-level classes are deferred or abstract classes) to one of the descendants. In yet other cases, different members of the inheritance hierarchy may be required at different portions of the design. Nevertheless, the actual class required should be within the plane of the full system. "Vertical" description of the hierarchy may well be described "off-line" using an inheritance diagram (ID) (Exhibit 73) rather than as a third dimension (cf. Exhibit 107); again, choice will be influenced strongly by the need for clarity. In this visualization of the mutual orthogonality, aggregation is shown on the left as an "expansion" to a lower-level design diagram; association connections are essentially horizontal. In this case, two members of the same inheritance hierarchy are accessed at the topmost level.

The level of information required in any inheritance hierarchy also requires discussion. This concept is known as "selective visibility." In Exhibit 73 again only class names are shown, although this would be just one view of a set of increasingly detailed inheritance hierarchy charts or IDs. At a more detailed level of resolution, information on attributes and services is required in parallel to the level-n diagrams discussed above. However, since, in general, objects inherit *all* features (attributes + methods) from their ancestors (although in some languages this can be overridden), any features declared in an ancestor class and not redefined in any subclass *do not* require explicit representation at all

ASSOCIATION AND INHERITANCE

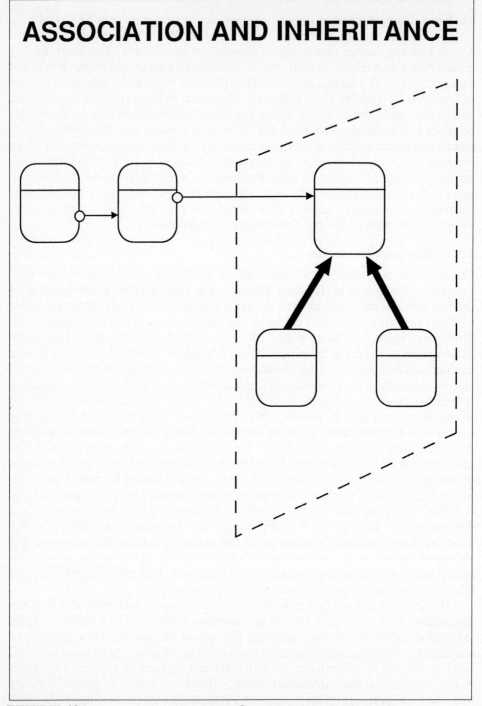

EXHIBIT 106 Copyright © B. Henderson-Sellers, 1991

THREE INTERRELATIONSHIPS

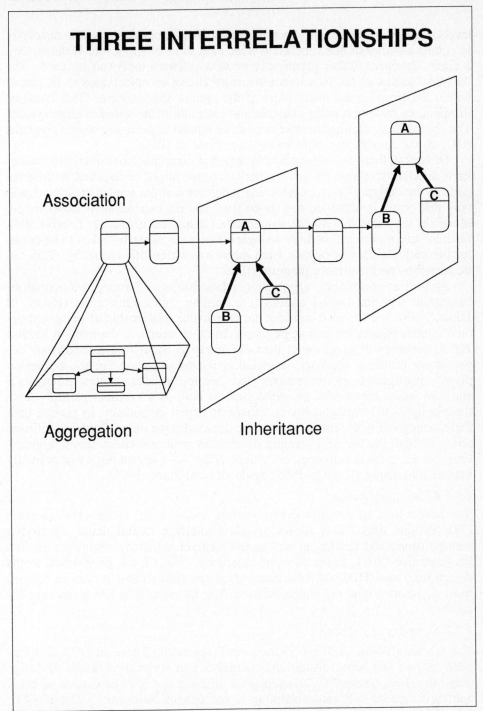

Association

Aggregation   Inheritance

EXHIBIT 107   Copyright © B. Henderson-Sellers and J.M. Edwards, 1990

levels, else the representation becomes unnecessarily complex. If it is necessary to collect together in one subclass a clear indication of applicable features, then a class "flattener" (either graphically or as a software tool) can be used. The "off-line" nature of the inheritance structure allows an object/class to be placed within the structure for many parts of the system specification. This localizes information, making it more readable and easier to locate within a large system. The objects in an inheritance structure can be related to particular design diagrams (DD) by the suitable use of indexing (e.g., Exhibit 105).

Of course, there are other possible apparent complications, since two entities from different levels of the same inheritance tree might be required at different parts of the design. Again, considering inheritance at the implementation detail, only that object is identified at a given level and the expansion (if used) simply illustrates the same inheritance structure but displaced vertically (Exhibit 106). In an off-line representation only a single inheritance hierarchy needs to be drawn for the multiple uses of objects from anywhere within this hierarchy. This can be shown by an inheritance diagram (ID).

As well as considering aggregation relationships as forming orthogonal relationships with the level-1 entities (the Problem Space Object Set (PSOS) of Jalote, 1989), one can also consider the inheritance relationship as being orthogonal to both association and aggregation. In other words, as depicted in Exhibit 106 (a summary diagram rather than one likely to occur in a real software development process), the basic association relationships are "in the horizontal plane"; aggregations are projections (and therefore in some senses orthogonal); and inheritance hierarchies are orthogonal to both as a "vertical plane." Since three-dimensional orthogonality is difficult to depict graphically, in general both these orthogonal relationships need to be depicted separately. (Further confusion arises through the use of a leveling diagram to represent client–server aggregations but using the terminology of "parent–child" — a terminology that normally implies inheritance (Rajlich, 1985; Seidewitz and Stark, 1987)).

4.5.6 Class specification

The lowest level of detail in design (before source code) is the class interface (CI) (Exhibit 108). This shows the class interface in full detail, specifying method names and results, as well as the contract, either by comments or, in a language like Eiffel, in the form of assertions. The CI can be indexed to the design diagrams (DD) and inheritance diagrams (ID) so that it may be located from anywhere within the documentation. The CI essentially forms the basis for coding.

4.5.7 Summary of notation

The schema (Exhibit 109) shows the overall approach of how an OOA is developed into an OO broad design and thereafter into succeeding levels of design detail (level-n). These OO DDs represent different levels of expansion of detail and their number will vary according to the system complexity. The ID, CD, and CI diagrams all localize important information, yet relate back to design diagrams of the system. The indexing mechanism needs further refinement, but the notation suggested should be applicable to any chosen method.

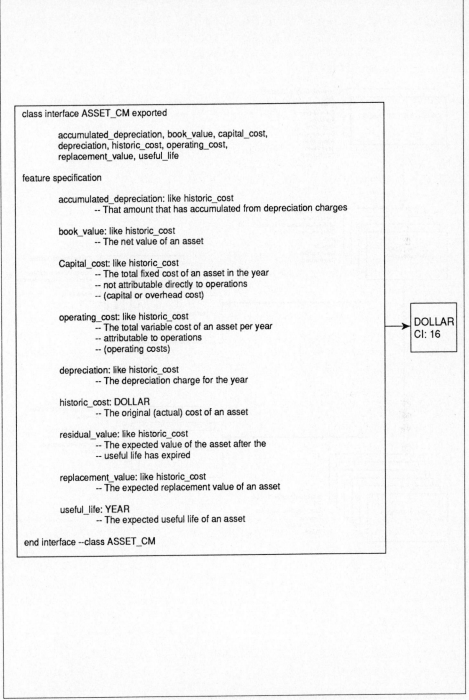

```
class interface ASSET_CM exported

        accumulated_depreciation, book_value, capital_cost,
        depreciation, historic_cost, operating_cost,
        replacement_value, useful_life

feature specification

        accumulated_depreciation: like historic_cost
                -- That amount that has accumulated from depreciation charges

        book_value: like historic_cost
                -- The net value of an asset

        Capital_cost: like historic_cost
                -- The total fixed cost of an asset in the year
                -- not attributable directly to operations
                -- (capital or overhead cost)

        operating_cost: like historic_cost
                -- The total variable cost of an asset per year
                -- attributable to operations
                -- (operating costs)

        depreciation: like historic_cost
                -- The depreciation charge for the year

        historic_cost: DOLLAR
                -- The original (actual) cost of an asset

        residual_value: like historic_cost
                -- The expected value of the asset after the
                -- useful life has expired

        replacement_value: like historic_cost
                -- The expected replacement value of an asset

        useful_life: YEAR
                -- The expected useful life of an asset

end interface --class ASSET_CM
```

DOLLAR
CI: 16

EXHIBIT 108   Copyright © J.M. Edwards and B. Henderson-Sellers, 1991

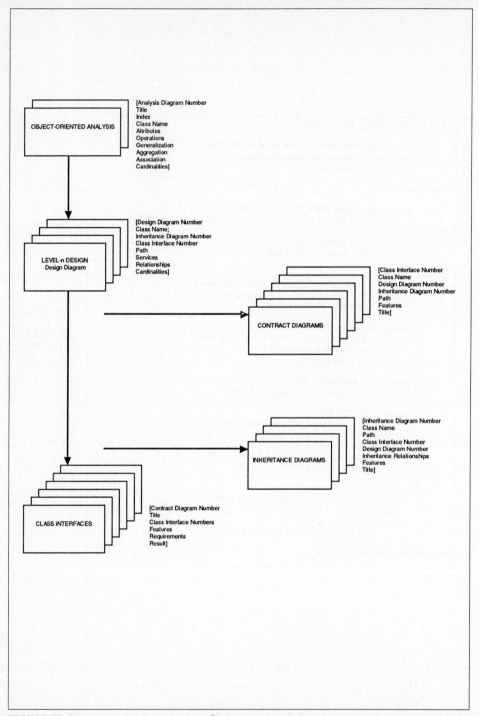

In the analysis diagrams, association, aggregation, and some generalization relationships are used between O/Cs which themselves exhibit an external interface in terms of attributes and operations. These are then easily translated into design diagrams showing services and client-server relationships. To complement these, more detailed diagrams are developed to show the class contracts (CDs) and inheritance hierarchies (IDs), together with appropriate indexing between these and the systems (leveled) design diagrams. Finally each class is fully specified in the class interface (CI) diagrams which provide the basis for coding.

Each design diagram should represent a semantically cohesive set of classes, similar to the idea of cluster (Meyer, 1989a) or information areas (Feldman and Miller, 1986). The means by which this may be achieved is the subject of continuing study.

We therefore propose that the leveling diagram with the "zoom" option be adopted for association and aggregation relationships (client–server at implementation) and that association, aggregation, and inheritance can be depicted by structures shown on orthogonally intersecting planes (cf. Exhibit 106), but that in general this will provide excessive complication and that this "view expansion" be considered off-line in associated inheritance diagrams and design diagrams. This is especially appropriate when we consider inheritance as an implementation detail rather than a design detail.

For the diagramming component of software CASE tools, it would seem that a level-1 diagram would first show the main object–object interactions (association or client–server). Any one of these nodes could be "exploded" to give a more detailed view of the supporting classes (aggregation or client–server). Other nodes might represent classes that are supported within an inheritance hierarchy that could be viewed by rotating a frame of reference into view or overlaying more detailed information. Note this orthogonal representation might also be required to be viewed at a more detailed level. In addition, there would seem to be a detail requirement. Initially, only O/C names might be visible. Then, upon option, the user/developer might wish to see details of the attributes and/or services. Such overlays could be required in combination with any of the resolution levels discussed above for object–object interactions. (Further details are to be found in Edwards and Henderson-Sellers, 1991.)

4.6 Illustrative Example

As a brief, further illustration, these notational techniques and methodologies are applied to a small teaching example of a bibliography system (Exhibit 110) and then to a bank account system that is partially completed with gaps left for the reader to complete in order to encourage you to gain first-hand experience by trying your hand. Let's consider the reference system. First we need a bibliography, which is a collection of a large number of references. Each reference relates to a given book or paper and therefore describes features such as author name, date, paper/book title, and publication details.

ANALYSIS AND DESIGN

WORKED EXAMPLE

Design of Bibliographic

Storage and Retrieval System

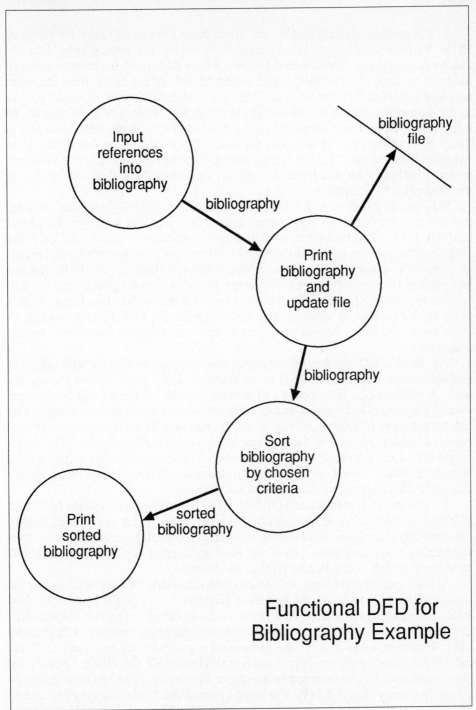

Functional DFD for
Bibliography Example

In a functional decomposition we would have the bibliography file (Exhibit 111). Bubbles would then show functions by which the bibliography data file can be manipulated. These would include a data flow from the input routine to the print routine. Data initially input would "flow," as indicated, from the input area to the print and update area, and then the updated information would be sent to the data store, shown by the straight line segment, known as a terminator. In a logical DFD, this represents the stored information; in a physical DFD this is likely to be related to, for instance, the actual file stored on the hardware. Data from the "print/update" bubble is then moved into the sort function that produces a sorted bibliography and these data would then flow from this sort routine to the final print functionality.

How would you do that in OO? At the topmost level (level-1) we can consider two interrelated O/Cs: an Application object that uses the Bibliography object (Exhibit 112). Note that since, in this diagram, selective visibility is "off," the diagram relates to the concept of subjects and can thus equally usefully be labeled as a "level-1" diagram. Of course, at this top level, there is grossly inadequate information for implementation. Reference to the design diagrams from the full set that give more specific information is indexed below the class name. In this case, DD2.1 is able to serve as a level-2 diagram for both level-1 objects; in other cases, the index names are likely to refer to different lower-level design diagrams.

The level-2 DD for this bibliography example can be shown with selective visibility either off (Exhibit 113) or on (Exhibit 114). Now further classes are seen. A bibliography is composed of several journal references and book references. The aggregation arrow points from composite to component object. The component parts of journal_ref (for example) can also be seen in their interfaces. Again, indexing below the name gives reference to further details. The application object uses a set of five "commands." These are included as part of the bottom-up design detail, since in the implementation we foresee using library classes in the language environment of our choice.

An alternative representation (Exhibit 115) in terms of subsystems (still here at level-2 resolution) is of more utility in larger systems, but is included here to illustrate this technique. When using subsystems, boundary connections to other subsystems *must* be shown. Here we need to interact with the "Application" subsystem, which is detailed in DD2.2, as shown.

At even greater resolution, individual class icons may be magnified and/or the further detail of library classes portrayed (Exhibit 116). At the individual class level, contract diagrams (Exhibit 117) are vital to detail the agreed responsibilities. Implementation details are then outlined in the class interface (CI) (Exhibit 118). However, even in a CI the procedural algorithms are not shown. These can be described using structured methodologies *inside* the object. Finally, all the classes may be documented in an object dictionary as an obvious analog to a data dictionary (Exhibit 119). For large systems the dictionary may become so massive as to be known as an object encyclopedia. The entries in this dictionary are the object/class name, its ancestors, the services it offers, and the services it requires.

LEVEL-1 DESIGN DIAGRAM WITH NO INTERFACE DETAILS (LEVEL-0 DD, "SUBJECT")

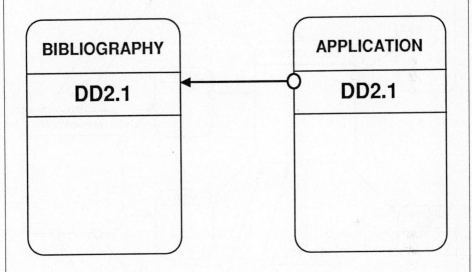

For further information
consult the design diagram number
indicated beneath the class name

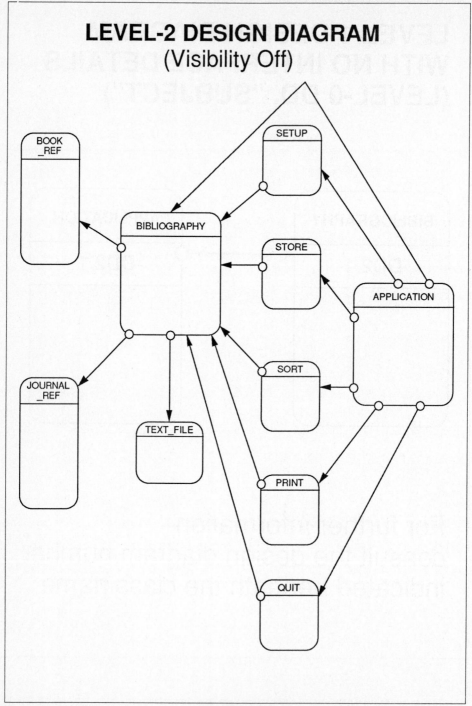

LEVEL-2 DESIGN DIAGRAM
(Visibility Off)

EXHIBIT 113   Copyright © B. Henderson-Sellers, 1991

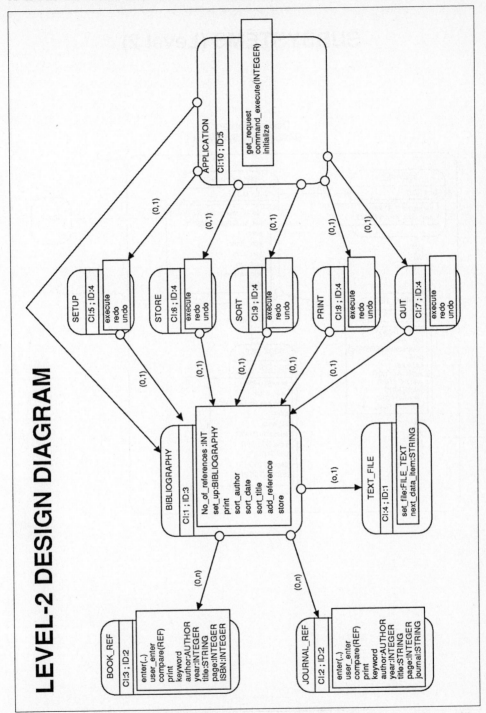

LEVEL-2 DESIGN DIAGRAM

EXHIBIT 114 Copyright © J.M. Edwards and B. Henderson-Sellers, 1991

SUBSYSTEMS (Level 2)

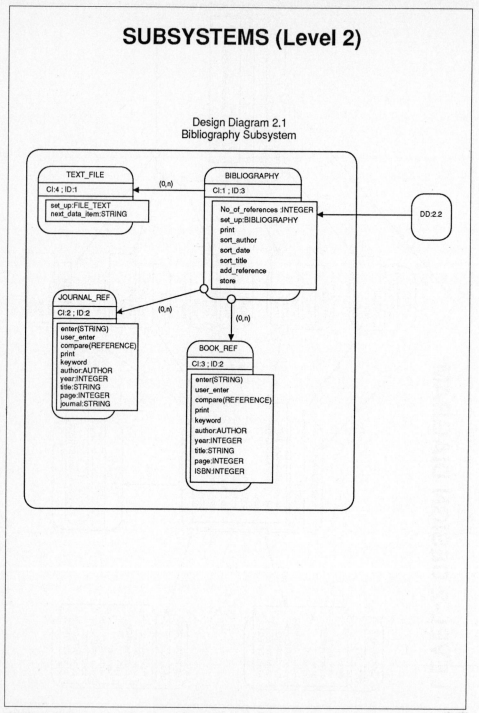

Design Diagram 2.1
Bibliography Subsystem

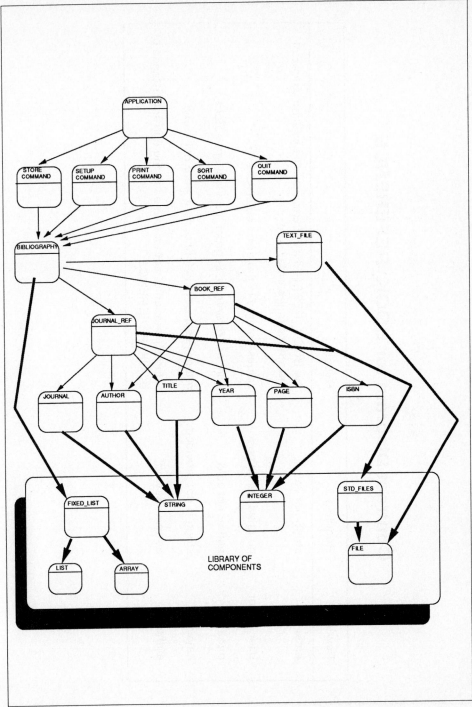

EXHIBIT 116   Copyright © B. Henderson-Sellers, 1991

Contract Diagram for BOOK_REFERENCE

Feature	Requires	Result
enter	string not void	the BOOK_REFERENCE instance will have the values of the strings in the order sent
user_enter	no previous values	values entered in the order entered
printout	author not void	print out reference, in order, on standard output
keyword	string is not provided	return yes if word is found, no if word not found
author	author not void	returns instance of author related to the current instance of BOOK_REFERENCE

EXHIBIT 117   Copyright © B. Henderson-Sellers and J.M. Edwards, 1990

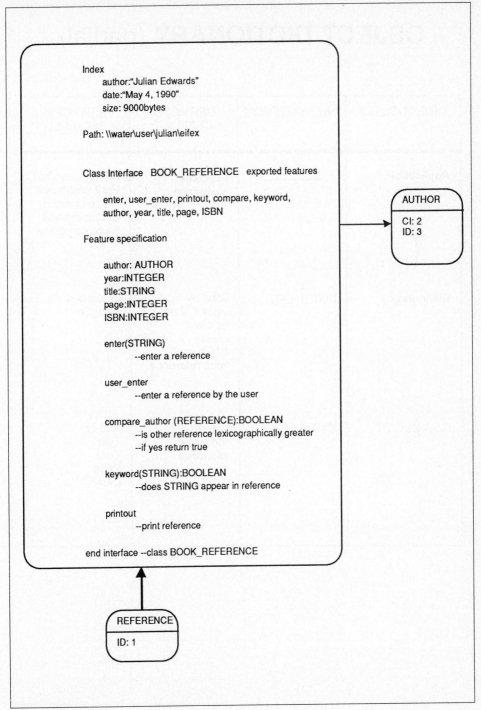

Index
    author:"Julian Edwards"
    date:"May 4, 1990"
    size: 9000bytes

Path: \\water\user\julian\eifex

Class Interface BOOK_REFERENCE exported features

    enter, user_enter, printout, compare, keyword,
    author, year, title, page, ISBN

Feature specification

    author: AUTHOR
    year:INTEGER
    title:STRING
    page:INTEGER
    ISBN:INTEGER

    enter(STRING)
        --enter a reference

    user_enter
        --enter a reference by the user

    compare_author (REFERENCE):BOOLEAN
        --is other reference lexicographically greater
        --if yes return true

    keyword(STRING):BOOLEAN
        --does STRING appear in reference

    printout
        --print reference

end interface --class BOOK_REFERENCE

AUTHOR

CI: 2
ID: 3

REFERENCE

ID: 1

EXHIBIT 118   Copyright © B. Henderson-Sellers and J.M. Edwards, 1990

OBJECT DICTIONARY (partial)

OBJECT/CLASS	INHERITS FROM	SERVICES OFFERED	SERVICES REQUIRED
Application	————	Executes command	Setup command Print command Quit command Sort command Store command
Bibliography	FIXED_LIST	Sorts by author, date, or title Prints bibliography Adds reference	Reference Text_file
Book_ref	STD_FILES	Enters individual reference	Author Title Year Page ISBN

EXHIBIT 119   Copyright © B. Henderson-Sellers and J.M. Edwards, 1990

Second Systems Development Example

Banking System (Part Only)

+ Exercise for Student

EXHIBIT 120

The second example we will consider is that of a banking system (Exhibit 120). On the next few pages we have some information that will permit you to attempt to develop your own inheritance hierarchy as part of this example OO software development project. Let's follow through those 7 steps of Henderson-Sellers and Edwards (1990a) (Exhibit 69). Step 1 was a requirements specification in terms of objects (underscored) rather than functionality (Exhibit 121). The real world is about CUSTOMERS depositing CHECKS or CASH into one or more ACCOUNTS, perhaps involving the services of an ATM or a TELLER. We might identify objects in the problem space (Exhibit 122), such as passbook account, savings account, savings investment account, etc., as well as customers, tellers, and so on, although we should note that this example is meant to be illustrative and by no means complete.

In Step 2, we identify those objects/classes. This gives us, in our limited example, entities of customer and several account types (labeled A through F in Exhibit 122). Now how do you find the objects? What about cash and checks? These might be objects. In other cases they might be simply attributes. Generally, if the candidate object is only needed to provide a single data value, then it should be stored as an attribute. If, on the other hand, it is likely to play a more important role in the specific domain in terms of a number of services offered, then it should be an object class in its own right. However, these considerations are largely a concern of the detailed design level, not of the current analysis stage.

Step 3 was establishing interactions. Exhibit 123 shows a customer (ignoring cash and checks for the moment) who interacts with tellers in respect of several bank account types (but usually not ALL the accounts). Identify those interactions, differentiating (in analysis) between attributes (such as *name* and *address* for *CUSTOMER*, *owner* and *balance* for *PASSBOOKACCOUNT* (Exhibit 124). The operations available in *PASSBOOKACCOUNT*, shown here, are *open*, *withdraw*, and *deposit*. All these are available for clients to use, although as yet there is no indication as to what constraints there may be between the *CUSTOMER* and *PASSBOOKACCOUNT* objects.

Move a step forward toward detailed design (Step 4). Identify interactions between customer and checking account: we could deposit a check or cash (Exhibit 125). We might request a balance; or we might actually withdraw cash or get a bank draft. Although we might identify these interactions at this stage, questions remain regarding their implementation details — resolving these details is not necessary until *much* later in an object-oriented systems development.

Now Step 5 would be to try to find library classes (Exhibit 126). Now that's a bit hard in this small example because we don't have the full problem and we don't know what is in the library. Neither have we built up our own library classes, because this is day one of the project. It's a bit hard to identify these steps in this small example; but we might have a library class of type *REAL* and a subtype of this with two fixed decimal places, called, say, *FIXEDPOINT2*, and we may identify cash as being of this type. We may identify account-name as a library class or a customer class with several fields.

There are often several ways of doing the same thing. You may have attributes

Methodology

Step 1. Requirements Specification

e.g., <u>customers</u> deposit or withdraw <u>cash</u> or <u>checks</u> into one or more <u>accounts</u>. Available <u>accounts</u> are:

a) <u>Checking Account</u>

b) <u>Passbook Account</u>

c) <u>Savings Investment Account</u>

d) <u>Security Plus Investment Account</u>

e) <u>Term Deposit Account</u>

f) <u>Short-Term Call Account</u>

EXHIBIT 121   Copyright © B. Henderson-Sellers, 1991

Step 2.   Identify Entities

Fairly easy:

1) Customer

2) Checking Account (A)

3) Passbook Account (B)

4) Savings Investment Account (C)

5) Security Plus Investment Account (D)

6) Term Deposit (E)

7) Short-Term Call Account (F)

But what about:

8) Cash

9) Check

These could be attributes or objects
in their own right

EXHIBIT 122   Copyright © B. Henderson-Sellers, 1991

Step 3. Establish Interactions

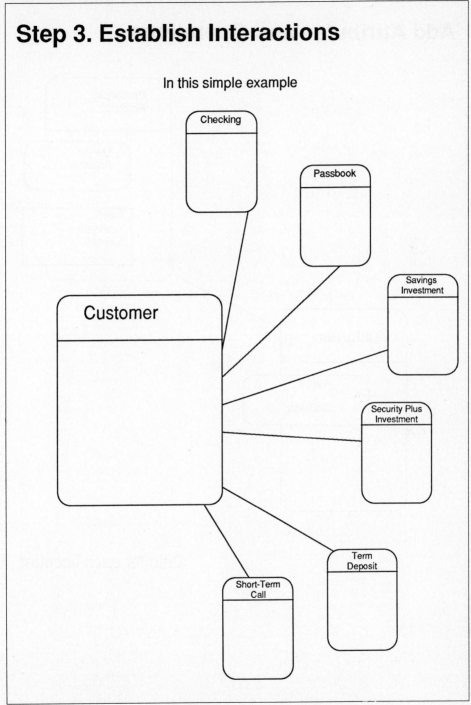

In this simple example

Checking

Passbook

Savings Investment

Customer

Security Plus Investment

Short-Term Call

Term Deposit

EXHIBIT 123   Copyright © B. Henderson-Sellers, 1991

Add Attributes and Operations

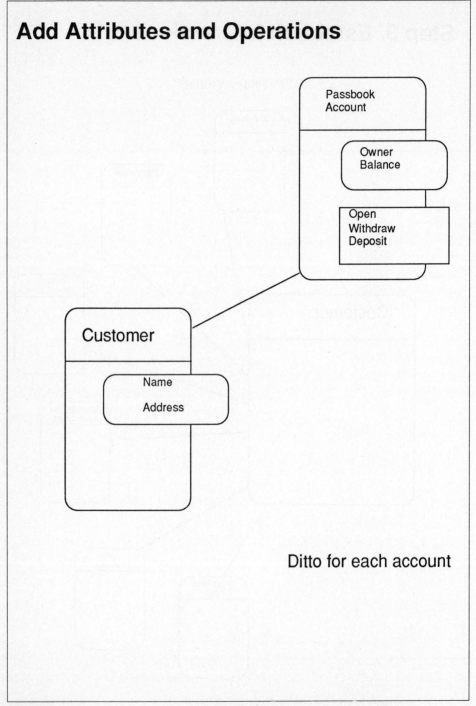

Ditto for each account

EXHIBIT 124   Copyright © B. Henderson-Sellers, 1991

Step 4. More Detailed Design

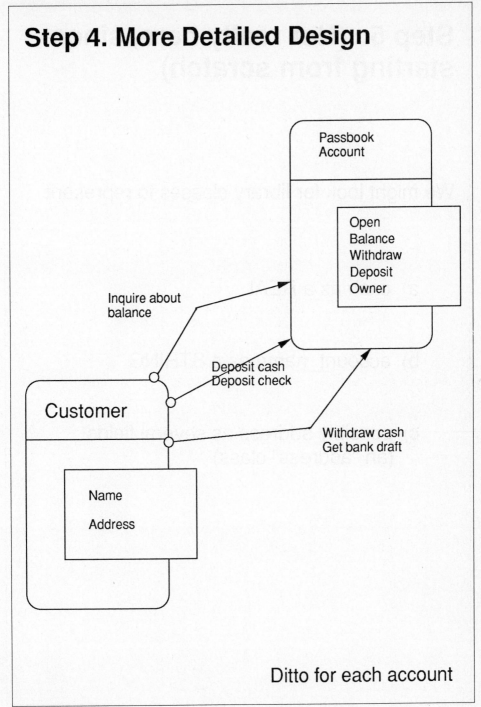

EXHIBIT 125   Copyright © B. Henderson-Sellers, 1991

Step 5. (Not really here, since starting from scratch)

We might look for library classes to represent

    a) cash as a REAL

    b) account_name as a STRING

    c) possibly address as several fields
       (an "address" class)

EXHIBIT 126   Copyright © B. Henderson-Sellers, 1991

Step 6.   Look For Inheritance Hierarchies

Required knowledge

a)   No interest on Checking Accounts. Must maintain minimum $250 balance.

b)   Passbook. No minimum balance. Interest rate dependent on balance.

c)   Savings Investment. Minimum balance $500. Withdrawals must be $100 or more. Interest rate dependent on balance.

d)   Security Plus Investment. Minimum balance $5, 000. Minimum transaction $500. Interest rate dependent on balance.

e)   Term Deposits. Fixed term. Minimum deposit $500. Interest rate depends on both term and deposit.

f)   Short-Term Call Account. Minimum deposit $10,000. Minimum period of deposit 7 days. All transactions minimum $1, 000. Interest calculated daily (single rate).

EXHIBIT 127   Copyright © B. Henderson-Sellers, 1991

Table of Interest Rates

Passbook

$1 – $1,999	10%
$2,000 – $9,999	12%
$10,000 – $19,999	13%
≥ $20,000	15%

Savings Investment

$500 – $1,999	9.5%
$2,000 – $9,999	12%
$10,000 – $19,999	13%
≥ $20,000	14%

Security Plus Investment

$5,000 – $9,999	13%
$10,000 – $19,999	14%
≥ $20,000	15%

Term Deposits

Term	$500 – $49,999	≥$50,000
1 mth to < 3 mths	15%	15.5%
3 mths to < 6 mths	16%	16%
6 mths to < 12 mths	16.5%	16.5%
12 mths to <13 mths	17%	17%
13 mths to < 33 mths	18%	18%
34 mths to ≤ 60 mths	18%	18%

Short-Term Call Account

11%

EXHIBIT 128   Copyright © B. Henderson-Sellers, 1991

Exercise for Student
Work Page

EXHIBIT 129 Copyright © B. Henderson-Sellers, 1991

of a base class or of a complex type. The question I wish to put to you, the reader, is that of the inheritance hierarchy, where again there is no *one* correct description. In Exhibits 127 and 128 you have information relating to the six accounts and Exhibit 129 is intentionally blank for you to have a go at deriving the inheritance structure for this problem. These figures give a plethora of information regarding the rules for each of these accounts. You can see that they each have names. Some have to have different minimum balances, some of them have rules about withdrawals. They have different rules about interest, minimum transaction, minimum period of deposit, and so on. You have that information and also information on interest rates (Exhibit 128). Some accounts have restrictions on interest calculations regarding the period of deposit of the money. My own interpretation follows in Exhibits 130–132. Try not to read on until you have attempted this small challenge yourself.

Here is one possible route. First, a basic Bank Account object/class is sketched out (Exhibit 130). Here we have an analysis icon and a design icon. Since we have seen that inheritance hierarchies are usually sought during design, it is this design diagram that we will use in the following exhibits. There are several ways of approaching this particular example — you might construct an object class to represent *each* of the bank accounts. However, it is soon recognized that all of the accounts have a balance, and a method for deposit and withdrawal. Hidden inside the object is further information on how deposits and withdrawals are made and how the balance is calculated. These different accounts can then be interrelated by identifying commonality. Some accounts have common rules regarding minimum transfers and minimum deposits, whether or not they have interest rates and whether these are in tables or a flat rate and so on.

A useful tool to help to recognize commonalities is a check list (Exhibit 131). For example, is there an interest rate? All accounts, as specified here, except checking accounts, have this feature. Is it a flat rate interest? The only one to qualify is the STCA (F), whereas account types B through E had tables. We can identify other characteristics, such as whether there is a minimum balance required. That seems to be be applicable to everything except passbook accounts. Is there a minimum transaction? This occurs in three of the account subtypes. Is there is a minimum deposit and a minimum period? You can see some commonality there. For instance, Savings Investment and Security Plus Investment have the same entries in those tables, except that the actual numerical values are different. So there might be a commonality that you might home in on. There is a distinct difference, however. For instance, you could argue between A and B–F that while A (checking) has no interest, B–F (all examples of "savings accounts") do have interest payable. Hence a "top" (abstract or deferred) account superclass could be identified (Exhibit 132) with two immediate subclasses differentiating on this characteristic: a checking account (with no interest) and a general savings account (for all those account types that pay interest). Note that although we have observed differences in interest structure, this is not a public feature, only being used internally to calculate or adjust the "balance." Similarly, Exhibit 131 suggests that two subclasses of savings account can be identified. In this case their parent class, Passbook account, is not abstract and can be instantiated (as account type B). This split between Minimum Term Deposit (E) and Investment (C, D) accounts is accomplished by discriminating on minimum transaction, minimum deposit, and minimum period of deposit (Exhibit 132). Again these features are hidden so that we can see that this diagram is essentially that of a late design when implementation details are beginning to be considered.

One interesting question that arises is "At what level in this inheritance hierarchy are these features defined?" You could argue that there's a minimum balance on all accounts — except for the passbook account (B). However, you could consider having a common attribute of minimum-balance, defined in class *ACCOUNT*, which has a value of zero for this passbook account type. Hence you would argue that minimum balance is an attribute that can be located at the topmost (parent/common ancestor) class and then assigned different values in

One Suggested Route

Construct an object class for each type of account

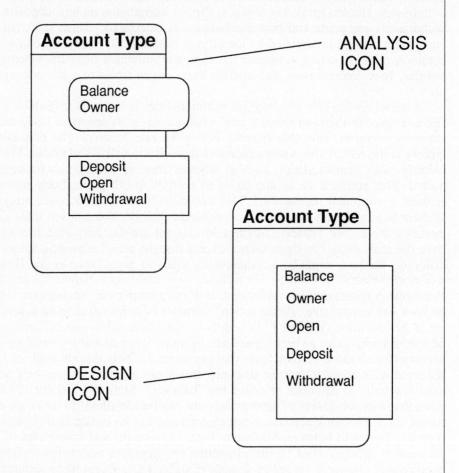

ANALYSIS ICON

DESIGN ICON

"Hidden" is how deposits are made, how withdrawals
are made, how balance is calculated, current
interest rate structure, etc.

EXHIBIT 130   Copyright © B. Henderson-Sellers, 1991

Recognize commonality

		Interest	Flat Rate Interest	Interest Table	Value of Min. Balance	Value of Min. Transaction	Min. Deposit	Min. Period of Deposit
A	Checking				250			
B	Passbook	✔		✔				
C	Savings Investment	✔		✔	500	100		
D	Security Plus Investment	✔		✔	5,000	500		
E	Term Deposits	✔		✔	(500)		500	✔
F	Short-Term Call Account	✔	✔		(10,000)	1,000	10,000	✔

EXHIBIT 131   Copyright © B. Henderson-Sellers, 1991

Generalization

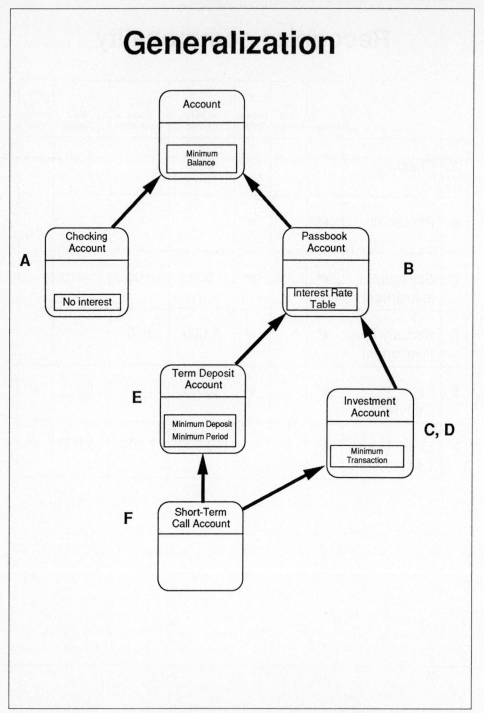

EXHIBIT 132   Copyright © B. Henderson-Sellers, 1991

each subtype. Similarly, interest could be deferred until the class *PASSBOOK ACCOUNT* (B) and implemented as a lookup table. Since *SHORTTERM-CALLACCOUNT* (F) has a fixed interest rate, this class would redefine the feature as a constant or consider it as a one-line table. (Information hiding suggests any chosen implementation would be suitable independently of the design specification — so long as that specification is met.) In other circumstances, it might be more useful to declare the interest feature in the top class (*ACCOUNT*) and overwrite it as zero in *CHECKINGACCOUNT*. Indeed, there is likely to be no unique solution, which is obviously "best"; although as the design develops, some of these initial uncertainties and ambiguities tend to dissolve away. One further guideline is to remember to mirror the real world as far as possible.

The inheritance structure seen here thus gives a framework for the final coded classes. The upper-level classes ("upper" meaning here at a higher level of abstraction; but note also the use of the name "base class" for the uppermost class — the ultimate ancestor!) will contain most of the code and the derived classes simply new features or redefined features. Here classes C and D add the feature of *minimum_transaction*, while class E adds both *minimum_deposit* and *minimum_period* for that deposit. Since the class F (STCA account) inherits from both classes E (Minimum Term Deposit) and C/D (Investment accounts), it will have features of *minimum_deposit*, *minimum_period*, *and minimum_transaction*.

In some senses, what we were doing here is generalization (Exhibit 133) (going up) and specialization (which is going down). In some projects, you do it one way; and in some cases you use the alternative. That can arise from the fact that, for example, you identify classes in a transport system, such as a car class and truck class. That was fine, because you then added a bicycle class and a bus class and a plane class. These, however, are all subclasses of a more general transport vehicle class and factor out the commonality and create the superclass. Or you might add more and more attributes to a class until you realize that a division into two or more subclasses might be more appropriate. It partly depends upon your initial information; it partly depends upon the initial specification and your domain of interest.

At this stage (Step 7) we are looking for commonality and groupings to allow us to build useful classes and clusters of classes. We may look for aggregations, e.g., ceiling, wall, floor, to be aggregated as a cluster of classes constituting a room cluster. We can therefore construct client–server at a relatively detailed design stage (corresponding to either association or aggregation at analysis). Generalization is constructing inheritance hierarchies by factoring our commonalities; and specialization is creating subclasses that are just like the parent classes but just a little bit more specialized. Both of those are extendibility concepts.

One further step leads to code (implementation details). Exhibit 134 shows what an account class might look like in a pseudo-object-oriented language, a little like Eiffel. Exhibit 134 shows a class *ACCOUNT* with an interface given in the **export** clause that is the statement of the visibility, i.e., the explicitly stated public interface. This lists the features that can be accessed from *outside*

Step 7
Further Possible
Clustering/Generalization

Aggregation and Clustering

    —— **has-a** relationship

    —— constructing network of
    clients and servers that
    are closely related (clusters)

Generalization

    —— constructing inheritance
    hierarchy by factoring
    out commonality to
    superclass

Specialization

    —— constructing subclasses
    i.e., more restricted
    but also exhibiting
    extendibility

EXHIBIT 133   Copyright © B. Henderson-Sellers, 1991

Brief Code for Class Account

```
class ACCOUNT export
        open, deposit, withdraw, balance, owner
feature
        balance: INTEGER;
        owner: STRING;
        min_balance: INTEGER is 1000;
        open (who:STRING) is

            do
                  owner:=who
            end;

        deposit (amount:INTEGER) is

            do
                  balance:=balance+amount
            end;

        withdraw (amount:INTEGER) is

            do
                  balance:=balance - amount
            end;
    end -- class ACCOUNT
```

EXHIBIT 134   Copyright © B. Henderson-Sellers, 1991

the specific class (i.e., services offered to other client objects). In this class, the only things that any other object can ask of this class account are the routines *open, deposit, withdraw* and the attributes *balance* and *owner.* Following this public interface is the implementation that has code for publicly available features and also private routines and attributes needed by these public features in order to do their job. Here *balance* is simply an integer, so it is an attribute; *minimum_balance* is a private feature (here an attribute) of the class because it's not declared in the export clause. It is hidden. Here it has an integer value of 1000. (For simplicity of presentation we have ignored the existence of cents and permit only integer numbers of dollars to be transacted.) Then we have code for the procedures *open, deposit,* and *withdraw.* Here the open procedure needs a single argument with type *STRING.* So if we use the feature *open,* we need to pass a single argument. To deposit we presumably increment the balance by the amount deposited. So the feature *deposit* has to have a single argument that is an amount of type *INTEGER.* (In the real world, all the features of type *INTEGER* would, as noted above, require instead a two decimal place fixed point representation.)

In refining the design, there may be discussion as to *where* you locate particular lines of code, for instance, whether you have it all as high as possible (in a parent) and redefine any characteristics lower down, or whether you defer all feature that look even slightly different in lower object classes to be defined at that lower level (see example above). You might also need to use the concept of an abstract class (see Section 5.6 for further details). In the former case you would have a largish piece of code in *ACCOUNT* describing the rules for withdrawals and then in, say, the specialized passbook account you might redefine that particular functionality by adding the restriction that withdrawals must occur in chunks of $250. In the latter case, the top class, *ACCOUNT,* would defer the description of withdrawal and this particular function would have to be derived in *all* the children (here *CHECKING, PASSBOOK*). Of course, this argument could then be applied iteratively, with *PASSBOOK* now being considered as the parent and *TERM DEPOSIT, SAVINGS INVESTMENT,* and *SECURITY PLUS INVESTMENT* being the children. Indeed, during a dynamically iterative design, shifting implementation details up (and possibly down) the inheritance hierarchy is commonplace (e.g., Goldstein, 1989; Booch and Vilot, 1990a), as is the need to revise the evolving inheritance hierarchy to ensure semantic validity (Kerr, 1991).

How do we use this class *ACCOUNT* and its subclasses as well as their available features? Consider the *PASSBOOKACCOUNT* class as a server. This is then used by a client, which might be a customer object or a teller object. Exhibit 135 shows how a client object would use the server object (i.e., class *PASSBOOKACCOUNT*). In the customer class is a variable *myaccount,* which is of type *PASSBOOKACCOUNT.* Type *PASSBOOKACCOUNT* is simply a reference to the class *PASSBOOKACCOUNT* shown in Exhibit 134: a user-defined type. Note this code is essentially in Eiffel syntax — other languages are slightly different. To create *myaccount,* in Eiffel I use the word Create. In C++ I use a constructor, which is a user-supplied member function (the equivalent of

Examples of Using Code

(e.g., part of customer or teller) to
use class ACCOUNT

myaccount: ACCOUNT
         - - type declaration
myaccount.Create
         - - create an object
myaccount.open("Brian")
myaccount.deposit(5000)
myaccount.balance.print

BUT

myaccount.min_balance

         is illegal since the feature
         "min_balance" is secret

EXHIBIT 135   Copyright © B. Henderson-Sellers, 1991

Eiffel routines) named with the tag name of the class. It is invoked whenever an object is defined or allocated through the operator **new** (e.g., Lippman, 1989, p232). The notation here of client–server in both Eiffel and C++ is that of variable dot method (i.e., variable.method) (see further discussion in Section 5.5). This is interpreted as: go to the run-time object of a given type (the object name before the dot) and in that class definition pick out the feature that is specified following the dot. The next line (ignoring lines starting with hyphens that are comments) says go to newly created account and open the account in my name. Then deposit an amount, i.e., go to the object *myaccount*, which is an instantiation of the class *PASSBOOKACCOUNT*, utilize the feature *deposit* that you will find there and that I am allowed to use because it is declared in the public interface.

I can therefore legally make the request (pass the message) of *myaccount. deposit(5000)*. I can also say *myaccount.balance* and *myaccount.print*. However, in this case, *print* is not defined in this class and must be inherited from one of the basic library classes. But I can't do *myaccount.minimum_balance* because this is a private feature NOT declared in the public interface. That is how information hiding is implemented and that is how classes are used. This use is generally referred to as message passing, a terminology originally from Smalltalk but now widely used, although Meyer prefers "invoke a procedure."

The principle of uniform reference says that "clients of a module should be able to use any service provided by the module in a uniform way regardless of whether the service is implemented through storage or through computation" (Meyer, 1988, p95). In other words, the syntax of the language is identical in both cases, so that the programmer and program user do not have to *know* anything but the module's internal representation, either by storage or calculation. This also means that a feature originally coded as a routine/method can, at a later date, be recoded as an attribute without being visible to the user of the service. For example, conceptually a bank balance is an attribute, a number. However, in implementation we may code this as a call to a cumulative sum object rather than having stored the balance as a single number in a field within the object itself. However, this is an implementation detail, i.e., hidden information, and thus irrelevant at the broad/logical design stage.

Exhibit 136 illustrates the ease of adding an account subtype in an object-oriented language/design. *CHECKING* and *PASSBOOK* are the main children of class *ACCOUNT*. Remember a checking account was just like an account except it had no interest paid. Class *CHECKING* inherits from *ACCOUNT*. In Eiffel this is specified with an **inherit** clause; in C++ it is written as class *CheckingAccount : public Account{. . . }* (the keyword "public" could be replaced by the keyword "private", depending upon the required visibility of inherited members within the derived class — for more details see, e.g., Lippman, 1989, p257 et seq.). You inherit a *minimum_balance*, set as 1000, from the parent. But a checking account has a minimum balance of only 250. So in this case we inherit not only only public features but also private features that can, if necessary, be redefined in the subclass. Inheritance is the only way in a pure object-oriented language to gain access to hidden features. However, in a hybrid language, there may be other constructs, such as friend functions in C++.

Adding Inheritance

```
class CHECKINGACCOUNT
inherit
      ACCOUNT
redefine min_balance
feature
      min_balance:INTEGER is 250;
end - - class CHECKINGACCOUNT


class SAVINGSACCOUNT
inherit
      ACCOUNT
redefine withdraw
feature
      interest: TABLE [INTEGER, INTEGER]
      withdraw (amount:INTEGER) is
            do
- - calculate interest whenever a withdrawal is made
                  balance:= balance – amount +
                  interest. value (savings, balance)
            end;
end - - class SAVINGSACCOUNT


etc.
```

EXHIBIT 136   Copyright © B. Henderson-Sellers, 1991

Here the minimum balance was stated in the parent class and inherited. But we could just as validly have deferred the implementation of minimum balance to the class level of checking and savings account. In savings account we inherit a procedure for *withdrawal* that needs to be redefined. *Withdraw* passes an argument, this is subtracted from the *balance* and the interest to date is added to the *balance*. That makes a call to another object, which we haven't yet defined. It requires the services of another object called *interest*, with a feature called *value*, and that feature will require two arguments, one on the current savings and one on balance. We have chosen not to go further into this here; but that interest object will relate to the table of interest values we had in our original documentation in this problem (Exhibit 128).

4.7 Summary

To summarize Chapter 4 (Exhibit 137), we have taken an extensive look at systems development methodologies, including consideration of the development of individual clusters of classes within that overall systems life cycle. Object-oriented analysis and design techniques are still being developed, so that the methodologies examined can be regarded more as prototypes or methodological frameworks. As part of a necessary suite of tools for object-oriented project management, graphical notation is required. Again, although notations are not yet agreed upon, some common threads can be seen and several options, as well as personal recommendations, have been presented.

It is important to try to use these methodologies and notations. In many cases, the choice will depend upon your particular situation, especially if you have special demands for concurrency, real-time, large volume of transactions, etc. Within the confines of a relatively small text, a small, illustrative study was presented with some "exercises for the student." For a more detailed working out of specific and more extensive examples (but using very specific methodologies), the reader could gain great insight and experience by consulting the examples in Wirfs-Brock *et al.* (1990), Booch (1991), and Rumbaugh *et al.* (1991).

Chapter 4

Summary

Systems
Development
Methodology

Notation

Case Study of
Bibliography and
Bank Accounts

Chapter 5

SOME IMPLEMENTATION CONCEPTS

In this last chapter we concentrate on implementation details across languages. This includes language-specific examples and also tightens up the terminology. We have in fact discussed many of these ideas already since describing object-orientation is essentially circular, or rather spiral. Now we can "spiral round" once more and consolidate those ideas while adding more detail.

In this chapter, I have divided the material into 10 areas for consideration (Exhibit 138). Firstly, what is an object-oriented *programming language* (OOPL)? We have discussed in considerable detail so far the object-oriented paradigm/philosophy. Now it is appropriate to consider in a little more detail current implementations of that paradigm in available OOPLs. Hence in Section 5.1 definitions of OOPLs are considered. In Section 5.2 we consider a tight definition of objects and classes from the language viewpoint and then relate these to ADTs in Section 5.3. Class features and associated terminology are discussed in detail in Section 5.4. With tighter definitions comes a more rigorous basis that is extended, in Sections 5.5 and 5.6, to encompass messages, subclasses, superclasses, and inheritance. Polymorphism is introduced in Section 5.7 — an important and slightly more difficult concept. Polymorphism is generally implemented by the use of dynamic binding, a discussion of which leads us to operator overloading and genericity (Section 5.8). We conclude by a further look at exception handling and automatic garbage collection (Section 5.9), plus a coda on specific languages (Section 5.10).

5.1 Definitions of OOPLs

You should now have a broad idea of what an OOPL is and be able to identify the characteristics you would wish to have in an OOPL that don't exist in other languages. Although there is no totally agreed definition, there are some strong

Chapter 5 Overview

* 1. Definitions of an OOPL

*2. Objects and Classes

*3. Abstract Data Types

*4. Class Features

*5. Messages

*6. Subclasses, Superclasses, and Inheritance

*7. Polymorphism, Operator Overloading, Dynamic Binding

*8. Genericity

*9. Exception Handling and Autogarbage Collection

*10. Language Examples

guidelines on what characteristics permit the appellation "object-oriented." We will look first at Peter Wegner's (1989) classification scheme for OOPLs and then at Bertrand Meyer's (1988) definition.

Wegner's classification is shown in Exhibit 139. A language, such as Ada, is said to be *object-based* when it supports objects but not classes or inheritance. In other words, encapsulations are possible representing individual objects (akin to multiple-entry subroutines). *Class-based* languages, such as CLU, support not only objects but also classes, thus giving a degree of object management. An *object-oriented* language then adds inheritance. This, then, gives us a basic working definition of an OOPL (see also discussion in Blair *et al.*, 1989). Wegner then goes further and adds other refinements. Object-oriented languages that support data abstraction and strong typing are a narrower set of OOPLs, which incidentally exclude two of the most well regarded (Smalltalk and Simula67). A further subset of those strongly typed languages are those with types determinable at compile time. An example here would be Eiffel. Then we could also consider concurrency and persistency — not characteristics generally found in OOPLs, but nevertheless topics of much current research and development. Persistency, especially for the database community (discussed only briefly in this book — see Section 1.1), is very important.

As a contrast to Wegner's language classification, consider Meyer's (1988) "seven steps to OO happiness" (Exhibit 140). These steps describe seven levels attained along the way to becoming fully object-oriented, although, unlike Wegner, Meyer does not give names to these phases. At level 1 there is an object-based modular structure with a high degree of modularization. At this stage, many 3GLs, like FORTRAN using tightly encapsulated subroutines, pass this test. As we encounter successive levels in Exhibit 140, more of these languages fall by the wayside. At level 2, we introduce data abstraction. Again many 3GLs are still in this category. At level 3, automatic memory management is introduced. This entails automatic allocation and deallocation of memory space when objects are no longer referenced, which eliminates the dangling pointer syndrome "beloved" of C programmers. Although there is some overhead (1–3%) with automatic garbage collection, it is easier to use than malloc in C and can prevent you running out of memory at a crucial time. In some language environments (such as Eiffel) there is an On/Off switch in the configuration file; in others, such as Smalltalk, the garbage collector is always available. When operational, it runs in the background, reclaiming memory incrementally when the cpu has less work. It doesn't just wait until the memory is full and then halt the system for garbage collection. This would be unacceptable, especially in a real-time control system in which accurate knowledge of the scheduling of memory reclamation is vital.

Moving on to the idea of ADTs (which you can see in procedural languages like C and FORTRAN), and hence to classes, leads us to Meyer's level 4. Classes are sets of objects from which you can generate lots of instantiations by using the class as a "template." Few procedural languages meet this level. Meyer also states that every nonsimple type is a module and every module is a type. This means not only that we have classes but also that the idea of classes, i.e., the col-

Wegner (1989) classifies languages as:

1) Object-based: objects are supported, e.g., Ada

2) Class-based: objects belong to classes, e.g., CLU

3) Object-oriented: classes support inheritance, e.g., C++, Eiffel, Smalltalk

Further Refinements

4a) OO data-abstraction: classes support information hiding, e.g., Smalltalk

4b) Strongly typed OO: types determinable at compilation, e.g., Simula 67

4c) OO + data-abstraction + strong typing, e.g., Eiffel

5a) + Concurrency

5b) + Persistence

EXHIBIT 139

1. Definition of an OOPL

Level 1 *(Object-based modular structure)*: Systems are modularized on the basis of their data structures.

Level 2 *(Data abstraction)*: Objects should be described as implementations of abstract data types.

Level 3 *(Automatic memory management)*: Unused objects should be deallocated by the underlying language system, without a programmer intervention.

Level 4 *(Classes)*: Every non simple type is a module and every high-level module is a type.

Level 5 *(Inheritance)*: A class may be defined as an extension or restriction of another.

Level 6 *(Polymorphism and dynamic binding)*: Program entities should be permitted to refer to objects or more than one class, and operations should be permitted to have different realizations in different classes.

Level 7 *(Multiple and repeated inheritance)*: It should be possible to declare a class as heir to more than one class and more than once to the same class.

B. Meyer, 1988. *Object-oriented Software Construction*

EXHIBIT 140

lection idea and the abstract data type concept, are fused together. Hence every nonsimple type (i.e., excluding simple types such as *CHARACTER, REAL, INTEGER*, etc.) is a module. An example might be *ACCOUNT* or *CUSTOMER*. Each of those nonsimple types is a module. Level 4 says that you can't have modules that are not types. You can, in contrast, in procedural languages like FORTRAN and COBOL. Although these languages have modules with (potentially) high information hiding, these modules may be conceptually and semantically unrelated and therefore have no relevance whatever to the concept of type. They are just collections of bits of code that were hung together for some arcane reason. Once we have reached level 4, we have a class-centered language that is the very basis of object-oriented programming. Whether levels 5–7 simply enhance a level-4 OOPL, or whether only languages at level 7 can justly be called OOPLs, is a matter of debate. For our purposes, a combination of Meyer (1988) and Wegner (1989) does, I feel, give the proper perspective of increasingly sophisticated OOPLs.

Inheritance (level 5) is a key new idea that most consider must be present in an OOPL. Inheritance can be considered both as an extension and as a specialization — or sometimes as a restriction. It depends upon how you wish to view it — either from a module or a type perspective. You can consider Savings Account as an extension of a bank account in that it augments the services of the parent class, but at the same time it's more restrictive, in the sense that the collection of objects (subset) to which you can apply it is smaller than the collection of the more general set of bank accounts.

Polymorphism and dynamic binding belong to level 6. Polymorphism is essentially the ability to refer to an object at run-time that may be from more than one class, and for operations to have realizations from different classes. We could, for instance, have a routine called print, and if I send the message to an object that happens to be a circle, or print to an object that happens to be a square, then those objects will respond correctly (but differently) to the same message, *print*. In other words, I can overload the operation *print*, giving it different realizations in different classes.

Multiple and repeated inheritance is level 7. One of the current arguments is how much of this is necessary. The extent to which these ideas should be utilized in practice is arguable, but it is undeniable that the trend in languages *is* toward inclusion of multiple inheritance (for example, Version 2.0 of C++ included this in 1990) — few languages fail to include this in either present versions or soon-to-be-available versions. It is probably good to have as a feature of your language, but a feature that shouldn't be overused. Meyer's typical example is that of a windowing environment where a window has "graphical" features and thus inherits from some graphical or geometric type of hierarchy (for instance, including class *RECTANGLE*), yet also has the capability of nesting windows on the screen and therefore must also belong to a tree/node-type hierarchy (for example, inheriting from a *TREE* superclass).

Although it is considered by Meyer that these features are in increasing order of sophistication, there are obvious incompatibilities with Wegner's classification, which would give a different classification under the two schemes. Perhaps the most notable of these is the position of automatic memory management available in Smalltalk and Eiffel but not in C++ — three languages commonly regarded as OOPLs.

5.2 Objects and Classes

In this section, we will tighten up the definition of objects and classes (Exhibit 141), first introduced in Chapter 2. At the design stage, "object" refers to a collection of things, in other words there is some loose connection with concepts identified by nouns. At implementation, the code is a class. When you run the system, you have a specific example(s) (an instantiation) of that class and that also is known as an object(s).

The *definition* of a run-time object is therefore an instantiation of a class, created as and when required. So you could have three bank accounts, myaccount, heraccount, hisaccount, which are all individual instantiations (objects) created from the single class template *ACCOUNT*. More graphically depicted (Exhibit 142), a bank account object at analysis and design refers to a *set* of things. The code is the class of ALL accounts, with features such as account number, account name, balance, and so on. At run-time we have run-time objects. Now we have very specific values for each of these attributes (fields). Account number now has a very specific *INTEGER* value and the account name a specific character string representation.

We now need to relate classes to ADTs in the next section.

5.3 Classes and ADTs

A class is an implementation of an abstract data type (Exhibit 143). Therefore, it is a generic template with which to describe shared characteristics. Object-oriented systems comprise coded classes. Classes therefore exist at *compile time*. A class could represent all animals, all bank accounts, etc., whereas what exist at *run-time* are individuals. The class is the implementation of the ADT. The ADT describes the external view. Conversely, the ADT is the class without the implementation. For instance, the external view of a vector doesn't tell me whether the implementation of a vector requires cartesian, polar, or complex representation. Indeed, since the ADT is the *specification* and the class the *implementation* of the ADT, it is in fact possible to construct more than one version of a class that implements an ADT (in the same way that at a lower level one of several algorithms would be used to implement a sort functionality.)

An ADT is exactly comparable with the data types with which you are familiar, data types such as *INTEGER, CHARACTER*. User-defined types (ADTs) are extensions or developments of concepts like structures in C, like COBOL records (the nearest two analogies in procedural languages). The definition of an ADT is a type name plus a valid range plus appropriate functions, preconditions, including associated axioms, but with no detail on implementation (how we do things). Exhibit 144 exemplifies the difference between an ADT and a class for

2. Objects and Classes

Design-level object
— identifiable set of things (nouns)

At implementation, a set of objects is coded as a class

At run-time, a specific example of a class is an object

Definition: "An object is an instantiation of a class"
— created at run-time as and when required

e.g., 3 bank accounts

      myaccount

      heraccount

      hisaccount

all examples created from class *BANKACCOUNT*

EXHIBIT 141 Copyright © B. Henderson-Sellers, 1991

Example

Design
Set of bank accounts

Implementation

Code representing:

Class of all accounts with features such as "account number," "title," "date commenced," "balance," "can have deposit," "can have withdrawal"

Run-time

Object

Example of account class with "account number" = "1111/123-456" "title" = Mr O. Oriented "date commenced" = 1990 etc.

EXHIBIT 142   Copyright © B. Henderson-Sellers, 1991

3. Classes and abstract data types

a) Class is an implementation of an ADT

Generic description template of shared characteristics

Classes exist at compile time
e.g., bank accounts
animals
furniture

b) Abstract Data Type (ADT) ("User-Defined Type")

describes external view
(no implementation details)

cf. INTEGER, REAL, CHARACTER
C-structure
COBOL group or record

DEFINITION: ADT is type name + valid range
+ appropriate functions
(not the implementation)
+ preconditions

Counter Example

1. Abstract Data Type

```
TYPE COUNTER
CONDITIONS
        integer range 0 . . . 59;
        Counting is by steps of one,
        modulus 60
ROUTINES
        up;
        down;
        zero;
END(COUNTER);
```

2. cf. the implementation (class)

```
Class COUNTER
ATTRIBUTE
        a: INTEGER
ROUTINE
        up;
        begin
            if a=59 then a:=0 else a:=a+1;
        end; - - up
ROUTINE
        down;
        begin
            if a=0 then a:=59 else a:=a-1;
        end; - - down
ROUTINE
        zero;
        begin
            a:=0;
        end; - - zero
END - - counter
```

EXHIBIT 144

a counter. The ADT has a type name, a range of integers and routines (such as count up, count down, and zero). My ADT tells me WHAT I can do, but not HOW I can do it. The implementation of that (which is deferred as long as possible) is of a CLASS for the *COUNTER*. In pseudocode, as shown here, these are routines that are essentially procedural.

The set of messages to which the class responds is called the protocol. It essentially represents those methods defined in the class interface, together with some notion of contract or class responsibility (see also earlier discussion in Section 2.6).

5.4 Inside an Object/Class

Looking inside an object more closely, we typically talk about features, which are the characteristics of the interior. Some typical terminology is shown in Exhibit 145, although this terminology is language-dependent to a degree. Features may be attributes or methods (also known as routines or member functions). (Method is essentially the Smalltalk word, routine Eiffel, and member function C++.) Methods include both procedures and functions. Adopting the word "method" generically, we can divide methods into functions, which return an object, and procedures, which don't return a value, but just do something. In other words, functions provide a query facility on the state of the object, whereas procedures implement commands, thus changing the state of the object. In Smalltalk, a method is always a function; you just may choose to ignore its returned object. At this stage we are now at the level of procedural code and can use all the expertise we've developed over the years in functional decomposition and procedural coding. However, the style of programming, even within a class, should be in sympathy with the overall aim of object-orientation. This does lead to the development of a new programming style, even in designing and coding internal procedural elements. The use of inheritance, at the code level, requires acquisition of new skills, as does the use of complex types and of instance variables, and of message sending. Unfortunately, such stylistic guidelines are not possible to demonstrate within the small examples that must be used here. Once the introductory learning phase is successfully completed, however, you should consult more advanced texts on object-oriented programming style and aim to learn these new skills, so useful for programming-in-the-large.

Exhibit 146 shows Eiffel code for a class *ZOO_ANIMAL*. It has an export clause delimiting the interface, exporting the methods *draw, locate, inform*. Each of these is then defined in the body of the code, although since this is in fact an abstract class, some definitions will be deferred to subclasses. Following the export clause is the inherit clause (seen in the subclass *BEAR*). Class *BEAR* inherits from one other class: *ZOO_ANIMAL*. Features are listed next and basically occupy the remainder of the class code. The first four features are attributes in this particular class: variables that have a value stored here (i.e., not a reference/pointer to another class/object). The remaining features are all routines. The Eiffel syntax for routines is **is do end**. Routines defined in subclasses are indicated by the OO keyword **deferred**. There are a few other

4. Inside an Object/Class

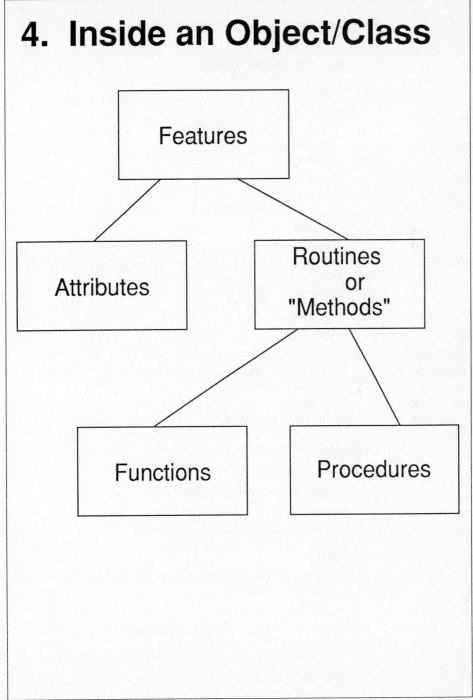

EXHIBIT 145   Copyright © B. Henderson-Sellers, 1991

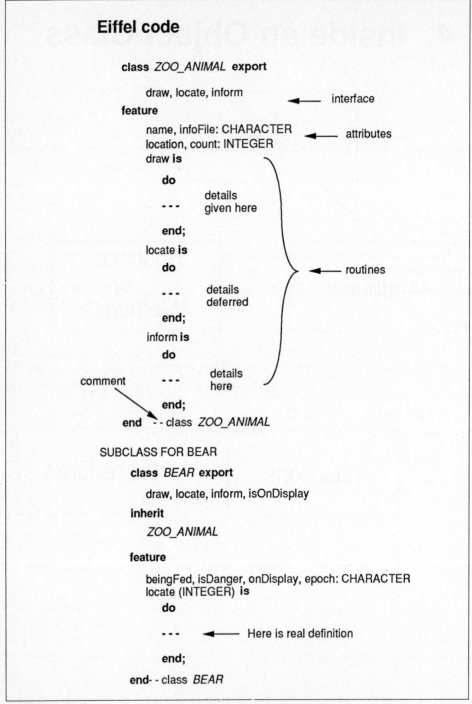

keywords in the language beyond the scope of our present discussion (for further details see, e.g., Meyer, 1988, 1991).

Exhibit 147 shows a brief example of the code for the same class written in C++ (after Lippman, 1989, pp308–309). This is an early prototype for the class *ZooAnimal* and its derived class *Bear*. The C++ class is split into public, protected, and (here not shown explicitly) private — the default. Member functions are contained in the class body and may be defined in-line, after the main class definition in a separate section or even in a separate file. In this example, the member function *locate*, if defined external to the class body, has to indicate to which class it pertains. So for the subclass *Bear* it would appear as

```
Bear::locate() {
        // Definition of function goes here
}
```

If a member function is void, then it is a procedure rather than a function in the nomenclature used previously; if a member function is declared virtual, then it will be bound dynamically and can thus be used for inheritance. Conversely, if you wish to utilize an inheritance hierarchy, then it is necessary to add a virtual definition to the member function. Inheritance in C++ is illustrated in the code for the class *Bear*, which inherits from class *ZooAnimal*. A colon is used in the class name to indicate the superclass(es) and a #include statement is needed.

Attributes are essentially the variable values of the class that represent the characteristics of the class (i.e., its state) rather than its behavior. These may be simple data assignments or may be implemented by computation and/or reference to other objects. Often the data values are of a basic type such as *INTEGER*, *CHARACTER*, *STRING*, etc., which in most OOPLs are themselves regarded as object types. This conforms with the underlying notion of a "pure" OOPL such as Smalltalk in which *everything* is an object. Attributes are also referred to as slots (e.g., Bobrow, 1989; Harmon, 1990), especially in languages, such as CLOS, with an artificial intelligence (AI) basis, and the idea of an instance variable is sometimes referred to as an entity (Meyer, 1988). This use of the word "entity" is, however, in direct conflict with the use in the analysis/design phases, described in Chapter 4.

5.5 Message Passing

We've already talked a little about message passing (Exhibit 148). We can send a message to an account object from a customer object requesting withdrawal of an amount. In many languages it would look like this: *myaccount.withdraw(5000)*, etc. Arguments are in brackets when required. In C++ it is possible to have default arguments, especially useful for constructors. This format is common to Eiffel and C++, for example, which use the same sort of dot notation. In Eiffel the principle of uniform reference holds for both types of features — attributes and routines — and allows us to change from an implementation as a routine to an implementation as an attribute. The message invokes the features, but only those features declared in the server class's interface. Invocation may of course

Example C++ code

```
Class ZooAnimal  {
public:
        ZooAnimal ( char*, char*,short);
        virtual ~ZooAnimal();
        void draw();
        virtual void locate();
        void inform();
protected:
        char *name;
        char *infoFile;
        short location;
        short count;
};
```

Derived Class for BEAR

```
#include "ZooAnimal.h"
class Bear : public ZooAnimal {
public:
        Bear( char*,char*,short,char,char);
        ~Bear();
        void locate( int );
        int isOnDisplay();
protected:
        char beingFed;
        char isDanger;
        char onDisplay;
        char epoch;
};
```

EXHIBIT 147

5. Invoking a routine or "passing a message"

e.g., message sent to object for my bank account, myaccount

> to "deposit"
> to "withdraw"

e.g., myaccount.deposit(5000);
> myaccount.withdraw(300);

Message invokes features (routines + attributes)
that are internal to object and often
hidden from user.

EXHIBIT 148   Copyright © B. Henderson-Sellers, 1991

result in the use of other features, hidden within the class (such as *minimum-balance*). The messaging notation in Smalltalk and Objective-C is *myaccount withdraw(5000)*, whereas in CLOS the object to which the message is directed becomes the argument to the method: *withdraw (myaccount,5000)*.

Sending a message to an object performs an operation (Exhibit 149). The object responds by choosing the appropriate method, performs this operation and then passes control back to the "caller." This is a bit like a subroutine call in a procedural language, but much more because you locate the message NOT by searching sequentially through the object (and undertake the procedural commands as we do so). The nearest analog in a procedural language is a multiple entry subroutine in FORTRAN, which acts a little like an object in the sense that its procedures do not have to be accessed sequentially.

Page-Jones (1991b) identifies three types of messages: (i) informative ("what has happened"); (ii) interrogative ("what is now true?"); and (iii) imperative ("make it so"). An example of each of these might be, in a banking context: (i) "deposit made successfully, balance is $x"; (ii) "what is current balance?" and (iii) "make deposit of $x." Inside the object, Meyer (1988) identifies three types of functional behavior: (a) a constructor function, (b) an accessor function, and (c) a transformer function that are available to fulfill the message requests identified above for the client class.

If you send the message of "tell me the value of *x*" to an object with a string attribute named *x* that currently has a value "A", then the answer you get is "A" (Exhibit 150). If you send the message of "reverse" to a string object of value "anystring," its value becomes "gnirtsyna." If you send a message "at: 1 put: H" to a string object "hello" then its value becomes "Hello." The fourth line in Exhibit 150 is a second example of "at: 2 put" type of message, but sent to a very different object. And we get the appropriate, but different, response, although the message notation is essentially the same. Here the new value is (1 2 3 4 5) — a string one longer than the original (Howard, 1988). Lastly, two similar messages are sent to 2 different graphics objects — one a circle, one a square — and we get a different response to the same message because the objects are different. The graphic object selects the implementation appropriate to the particular form of run-time object. This is polymorphism (see Section 5.7). Rotating a circle presumably has a null implementation; for a square there would be extensive calculation to get new coordinates, etc. (assuming the particular method implementation to be correct!).

5.6 Classes and Subclasses

Classes, subclasses, and inheritance were considered briefly in Chapter 2. In Exhibit 151 is shown another way of looking at the same thing, here using a Venn diagram to represent sets. Within the collection of all programming languages (outer box), we see a set of OOPLS, a set of logic PLs, a set of procedural PLs, and a set of functional PLs. Assuming single inheritance and completeness of our decomposition, these subsets would be space-filling such that all PLs fell into only one of the subsets of PLs, as indicated. Within the

Object = private data + set of operations

Message sent to object requesting
performance of one of its operations

Object responds by choosing method
appropriate to message, executing this,
and then returning control to caller

(after Cox, 1986, p50)

EXHIBIT 149   Copyright © B. Henderson-Sellers, 1991

Messages and Responses

e.g.

Object	Message	Response
x	Value	A
"anystring"	reverse	"gnirtsyna"
"hello"	at: 1 put: H	"Hello"

Same message could provoke different response

(1 0 4 5)	at: 2 put: (2,3)	(1 2 3 4 5)
circle on screen ◯	rotate thru 45 degrees	◯
square on screen ▢	rotate thru 45 degrees	◇

(adapted from Howard, 1988)

EXHIBIT 150   Copyright © B. Henderson-Sellers, 1991

6 Classes and Subclasses

Inheritance

(a) Single

Programming Languages (PLs)

PROCEDURAL PLs	OOPLs	
	C-extensions	non-C extensions
FUNCTIONAL PLs	LOGIC PLs	

(b) Multiple

Programming Languages (PLs)

PROCEDURAL PLs	C-extensions	OOPLs non-C extensions
FUNCTIONAL PLs	LOGIC PLs	

OOPLs we then have a subset of C-extensions and one of non-C-extensions. If we then recognize that the subset of C-extensions describes languages that can be better regarded as hybrid languages, with the full capabilities of not only providing language support for the OO programming paradigm but also retaining the procedural paradigm, then the Venn diagram must be modified (lower part of Exhibit 151).

An alternative representation for inheritance is the inheritance hierarchy which is a tree for single inheritance (Exhibit 152) and a network for multiple inheritance (Exhibit 153). Here we have the same example using classes, subclasses, and superclasses. The base class here is *PROGRAMMING LANGUAGES*, with four derived classes. In this example, we have included only subclasses from the one class, OOPLs. The whole nomenclature of subclass, class, and superclass is, of course, relative and in any inheritance structure it is likely that there will be many more "levels" than these three. To accommodate this, Meyer introduces names that permit differentiation between one "generation" removed (up as parent and down as heir) and more than one generation removed (up as ancestor and down as descendant). He also notes that this avoids the apparent contradiction in the use of the word "subclass" since this implies a subset. Although this is true in an inheritance sense, from a module perspective derived classes are seen to *extend* the base class, since the services available to the subclass can be greater in number than those available in the class itself (Meyer, 1988, p233). Also shown in Exhibit 152, at the bottom of the diagram, are examples of each of the lowest-level classes. These are instances and would be the run-time objects in this system. Any class that can be instantiated is sometimes known as a "concrete" class — in contrast to the abstract class (here Programming Language and OOPL) that cannot be instantiated. Note that if hybrid OOPLs are included explicitly, then the inheritance hierarchy shows a subset (here hybrid OOPLs) inheriting from more than one "parent" (Exhibit 153).

One potential problem with such multiple inheritance (MI) is the potential for a clash of names of inherited features. In principle, the subclass inherits every feature, although in the hybrid language C++, for example, there are other choices. Resolution of name clashes of a pair of features (one from each parent class) is language-dependent. In OO LISP clashes are resolved by depending on the order of declaration, an ordering that can be made more explicit in CLOS. In C++ extra function qualifiers are added. Eiffel uses renaming in which the subclass inherits both and then renames one of the "twins." Multiple inheritance also gives rise to the possibility of repeated inheritance where a class inherits from one superclass by two or more routes. For example, in Exhibit 153, the hybrid PL class inherits from the programming language class via procedural PLs as well as via OOPLs.

Within an inheritance hierarchy, it is likely that some (or all) of the topmost classes may contain features whose definitions are deferred to the subclasses. In other words, there are no *implementation details* for these features within the base (parent) class. This means that this uppermost class cannot be instantiated and this type of class is subsequently known either as a deferred class (e.g., Meyer, 1988, p234) or as an abstract class (e.g., Goldberg and Robson, 1983;

Inheritance

Avoids code duplication

a) Single inheritance (supported by many languages)

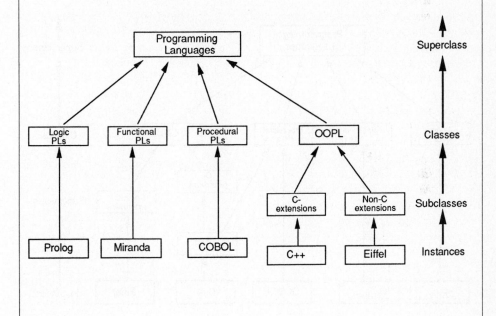

EXHIBIT 152   Copyright © B. Henderson-Sellers, 1991

Inheritance

b) Multiple inheritance
   (supported by some languages)

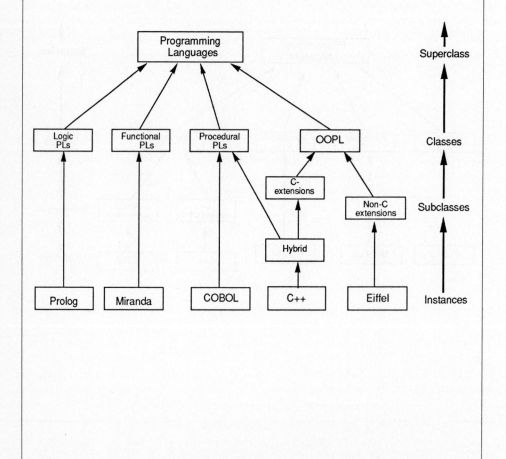

EXHIBIT 153   Copyright © B. Henderson-Sellers, 1991

Lippman, 1989; Booch and Vilot, 1990b, p304; Wirfs-Brock *et al.*, 1990). The design and use of abstract classes is discussed by, e.g., Johnson and Foote (1988); Wirfs-Brock and Johnson (1990).

One particular type of abstract class (i.e., one that will never by instantiated *per se*) is the "mixin" (e.g., Bobrow, 1989; Booch and Vilot, 1990b). This is a class that is probably not a full ADT, but rather an encapsulation of several closely associated features bundled together as a class available to be "mixed in," via multiple inheritance, to add capabilities to a wide variety of classes, possibly not related. The behavior of the mixin is seen as orthogonal to the behavior of the classes with which it is to be combined (Booch and Vilot, 1990b), insofar as they add in "sideways" extra characteristics, thus not requiring *all* classes in the inheritance hierarchy to support the mixin behavior. Bracha and Cook (1990) compare the use of mixins in the languages CLOS, Smalltalk, and Beta — in the latter two languages, which have only single inheritance, they discuss how this can be simulated instead. They view a mixin as an "abstract subclass" — for example, a subclass that might add a border to a wide variety of window classes.

Wegner (1990) discusses single versus multiple inheritance. He notes that in many senses the language PL/I can be said to have three "parents" in FORTRAN, ALGOL 60, and COBOL. The problem is that of resolving clashes (as noted above) in feature inheritance (mostly in method inheritance). He gives seven possible resolution rules:

- *call the first method in a specified linear ordering*

- *call all methods in order (of the linear ordering)*

- *execute first method that returns a non nil value*

- *collect values of all methods into a list*

- *compute the arithmetic sum of values*

- *call all before demons, then the first method, then all after demons*

- *use an argument to select one or a subset of methods*

However, his example, using a "pie hierarchy," which purports to show multiple inheritance, is depicted as a network in Exhibit 154. Here we appear to have examples of both multiple and repeated inheritance (the latter not discussed in the cited paper). Further inspection reveals that only the upper part of the chart is really an inheritance hierarchy, since (1) an apple **is-a** fruit, which **is-a** food, and (2) cinnamon **is-a** spice, which **is-a** food. The relationships between pie, apple, and cinnamon are NOT those of inheritance; rather a pie **is-composed-of** apple and cinnamon (plus a few other things like pastry and sugar) — i.e., it is an aggregation relationship (Exhibit 155). It is NOT TRUE to say that pie *inherits* from apple and cinnamon, since this would imply that a pie is a type of apple (not true) *and* a pie is a type of cinnamon (again not true). This illustrates

Multiple Inheritance?

Food

Fruit   Spice

Apple   Cinnamon

Pie

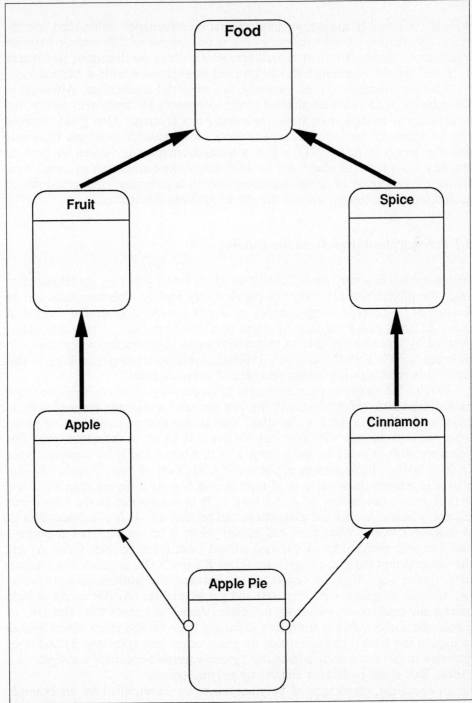

EXHIBIT 155 Copyright © B. Henderson-Sellers, 1991

the use (or possibly misuse) of implementation inheritance rather than specification inheritance. It is therefore, to my mind, crucial to differentiate between inheritance, aggregation, and association relationships, as discussed in Chapter 4. Stated simply, inheritance should be used to implement an **is-a** relationship.

Multiple inheritance, used correctly, is a powerful mechanism. Although in the majority of cases a well-planned single inheritance hierarchy will suffice, the availability of multiple inheritance provides extra leverage. One good example can be found in the technical environment of wastewater treatment (Edwards and Henderson-Sellers, 1991), where a wastewater plant is viewed by both an engineer (as a piece of plant) and by an economist/accountant as an asset, illustrating the simplicity of design based on this "dual parentage" that could not be accomplished succinctly without the use of multiple inheritance.

5.7 Polymorphism and Dynamic Binding

Polymorphism is a very powerful tool to which I will give only an introduction since the subject becomes very complicated very rapidly. Polymorphism can be defined as "a concept in type theory in which a name may denote objects of many different classes related by some common base class. Thus, any object denoted by this name is able to respond to some common set of operations in different ways" (Booch and Vilot, 1990b). Dynamic binding (see later in this section) is needed to implement this idea of polymorphism.

Exhibit 156 shows an example that is often quoted to illustrate what we mean by polymorphism (after Meyer, 1988). We can send a message that will refer to objects of a different form *at run-time*. That means that we don't have to know, when we start the run, what type our objects have to be. A definition states that when we wish to make an assignment a := b, when a and b are complex types (ADTs) and are instantiations of the same ADT, then of course that's OK. But also it is reasonable when a is of type A and b is of different type B, if and only if B is a descendant of A. So long as B is somewhere in the inheritance hierarchy below A, then the assignment can be realized. If A is a descendant of B it doesn't work. What does that mean? Here is an analogy that is perhaps easier to understand. I go to a restaurant and I ask for vegetables (class A) and the waiter brings me green vegetables (class B); that's OK because B is a subset of A (green vegetables are vegetables). However, the converse doesn't work, i.e., if I ask for green vegetables (B) and get vegetables (A) that might include carrots and cauliflower, which are not green, then I will reject this. Not OK. In a software context, this is necessary since my code (in the client class) wishes to exploit the known characteristics of green vegetables (subclass B) and does not want to run the risk of addressing "green-vegetable-specific" messages to a carrot. This is the basic idea underlying polymorphism.

In code, the advantages of polymorphism are exemplified by an example given by Winblad *et al.* (1990) for showing an object that can be of either type *POINT* or *CIRCLE*. In C, with no polymorphism possible, a `Switch` statement is needed. When *POINT* and *CIRCLE* inherit from *OBJECT*, a polymorphic

7. Polymorphism

The ability to refer to objects of different form at run-time

Assignment a:=b OK
      not only if a, b of same type
      but also if a is of type A
               b is of type B
where B is a descendant of A

Analogy

Ask for	Get	OK/Not OK?
Vegetables (A)	Green Vegetables (B)	✔ OK
Green Vegetables(B)	Vegetables (A) (say including carrots)	✗ Not OK

EXHIBIT 156

response to the message requesting the current object to show itself is possible in a language like C++, and the corresponding code is significantly smaller:

Solution with no polymorphism

```
void show(obj)
     struct object *obj;
{
     switch (obj→objectType)
     {
     case POINT:
          showPoint(obj);
          break;
     case CIRCLE:
          showCircle(obj);
          break;
     default:
          printerror("incorrect object type");
     }
};
```

Solution with polymorphism

```
void show(obj)
     struct object *obj;
{
          obj.show
};
```

Furthermore, if more object types, such as *LINE, SQUARE, POLYGON*, etc., are required, in a language with no polymorphism, each new type requires an extra `Case` — here an additional three lines of code per new type. No additional lines of code are required in a language with polymorphism. (In both cases the implementation of the method show, showCircle, etc., is not shown, so the comparison of code length is perfectly valid.)

In most object-oriented languages, polymorphism is strongly linked with dynamic or late binding (Exhibit 157) (see also Winblad *et al.*, 1990, p37). The use of dynamic binding allows us to defer binding until run-time. Remember binding is the specification of the exact nature of the attribute: its name, type, and storage location. Binding can be at various stages: it can be at language definition time, so *INTEGER* in FORTRAN is part of the language. It can be at compile time, which is early or static binding — and consequently doesn't permit the use of polymorphic calls. Sometimes the use of dynamic binding is mandatory; in other languages it is optional (e.g., in C++).

Operator overloading is an associated concept. Operator overloading you are aware of already: it is using the same operator symbol to mean two different things. So a simple example is if you say A := B + C, the + means something different when B and C are integers or whether they are reals (because the bit patterns used for reals and integers are very different). We are used to that since, for instance, addition in a procedural language of two variables of type integer is accomplished differently from adding two reals or concatenating (adding) two characters. We use the same symbol "+" but with a different implementation.

Associated Concepts

Dynamic Binding

Where type is not known at compile time

Binding = specifying exact nature of an attribute,
e.g., variable name, type, and storage location

Binding can be

1) Language definition time, e.g. ,type "integer" in
   FORTRAN or Ada

2) Compile time. Static (or early) binding cannot
   be changed at run-time

3) Run-time. Dynamic (or late) binding can be
   changed.

Operator Overloading

e.g., + means different implementation for reals and complex

So now you can do anything you like. You could overload the operator plus and now make it an operator that is valid for the addition of matrices because now *MATRIX* becomes an abstract data type. If you define plus for tables, where "table plus table" could mean anything you wished, then this also would make adding tables allowable. For example, plus for tables might mean gluing them together. However, it should be noted that overloading can be dangerous (cf. Ferguson, 1991). It can confuse types and generally make for poorly understood code, etc.

5.8 Genericity

A special type of class is one which has one or more arguments of unspecified type. This is known as either a parameterized type (e.g., Stroustrup, 1988) or a generic class (e.g., Meyer, 1988) (Exhibit 158). Using this feature of an OOPL allows, for instance, a generic array to store sometimes integers, sometimes reals, and sometimes cabbages. Genericity is available in CLU, Eiffel, and Ada but not currently in C++ (but cf. Booch, 1991, p118). In C++ it can be simulated using type conversions, or casts, a technique viewed by Meyer (1990b) as defeating any attempt at maintaining a secure static typing system.

I may wish to write classes that have a generic type associated with them. For example, I could write a class *ARRAY* (although I would actually just use the class from my class library and never have to write an array description again!). In procedural languages, if I had an array in which I wished to store integers, I would have to state *ARRAY* to be of type *INTEGER*. If I wanted to use an array later in the program to store reals or, in object-oriented languages, cabbages, I would have to declare a second array of this different type. In object-orientation I can have generic type of *ARRAY* in which I can store elements of any type. This is a single class to be coded that will have certain instantiations in integers. At other times, the same class may be instantiated to hold characters, or cabbages, etc. I can even have a mixed set of types, so long as they are all part of the same inheritance hierarchy. Those types of the element that are stored in the array here, say of type *ACCOUNT*, are defined at run-time. Running the program, you sometimes instantiate an array as containing integers, another time accounts, etc. At compile time, you don't know what type of elements are going to be stored in this class array. For further discussions on genericity, see Meyer (1988).

5.9 Other Characteristics

We mentioned previously (p53) the idea of asserting correctness. With Eiffel this is done using invariants (Exhibit 159). This is not available in C++, Objective-C, or Smalltalk yet. Our class description is similar to that shown in Exhibit 134, but now we have an additional constraint: when we deposit, it would seem reasonable that the contract for depositing should be valid only if I try to deposit a positive number. Up to now (as in Exhibit 134) if I said in my

8. Genericity

e.g., generic type of stack, array, or list contains elements of type NOT predetermined

e.g., ARRAY[T] could be
      ARRAY[INTEGER]
      ARRAY[ACCOUNT] etc ...

Defined at run-time

LEADS TO reusable classes

9. Other Characteristics

a) Adding Safety (Assertions)

Use of **Assertions:**

      Preconditions
      Postconditions
      Invariants

within object (class definition)

```
class  ACCOUNT  export
          as before

BUT
deposit (amount:INTEGER) is

        require
            amount > 0
        do
            balance := balance + amount
        ensure
            balance = old balance + amount
        end;
etc.

Plus "class invariant"

invariant
balance >= min_balance
end - - class ACCOUNT
```

EXHIBIT 159

calling (client) class, *myaccount.deposit*(-30) the code would have to accept that (illogical though depositing a negative amount might be). Therefore, we also need some correctness checks within the class (actually within the feature for preconditions and postconditions and within the class for class invariants). Before a client can use the deposit routine, these checks now ensure that the argument is positive. This precondition (here expressed by **require**) puts the responsibility of correctness *within* the object. In procedural code, you'd call this *outside* the call, e.g.,

    IF amount > 0 THEN
        CALL subroutine CALCULATE
    ELSE
        Flag error

In object-oriented code, the responsibility lies inside the object, so that *every* time a call to that object is made, the check will be made. The programmer no longer has to remember to place every call to the subroutine within a IF THEN ELSE structure like the one above. In addition to a precondition tested upon routine entry, there may also be a postcondition at the end of the routine (in Eiffel, this uses the keyword **ensure**). Although trivial in this example, in a lengthy procedure it is useful to ensure at the end of the routine that (here) balance equals old balance + amount. Again, postconditions are aimed at correctness. The set of assertions can be related to the software contract in the design, the contract specifying the class obligations in terms of each of its features (collectively known as the responsibilities — as discussed earlier). Violation of the contract, in terms of its pre- and postconditions is discussed elsewhere in this section. Postconditions and preconditions could be violated in the middle of a class, but the class invariant must be satisfied at all times.

Exception handling (Exhibit 160) is important to provide a good traceback whenever anything goes wrong. Exception handling is done in Ada, CLU, Eiffel, Smalltalk, and CLOS, but not in Objective-C and not really in C++ (but see Koenig and Stroustrup, 1990, and the ANSI C library header file **assert.h**, e.g., Eckel, 1989, p128). The use of assertions, preconditions, postconditions, and class invariants, as already mentioned, is vital to ensure safety. Assertions are Violation of one of these assertions will result in a run-time error and the program will terminate with a clear message using the exception handling capabilities of a language (when available). Violation of the precondition implies a bug in the client object; violation of the postcondition implies a bug in the object's own method (Meyer, 1989b). In addition, in Eiffel, the exception handling mechanism includes both an optional retry and/or rescue clause. If an exception/error occurs you may wish to try again before terminating the program, for example. If you were ringing a number via a modem and the number was busy, you might well wish to try again after a short interval rather than abort your attempt to connect to your favorite remote computer. The rule might be "if busy, wait 10 seconds and try again." Only after several attempts might you decide that today was a bad day (perhaps there is systems time scheduled on the mainframe) and try again much later.

b) Exception Handling

— done in Ada, CLU, Eiffel

— not done in C++

Violation of contract
(e.g. as specified by use of
Assertions)

Rescue clause in Eiffel

plus

Retry option

c) Autogarbage Collection

Release for reuse of no longer required memory locations

Costly in time ("therefore" not for time-critical programs)

But useful

— Avoids dangling pointers problem (very nasty bug)

— avoids clogging up of memory by unwanted values

(considered very important by Meyer)

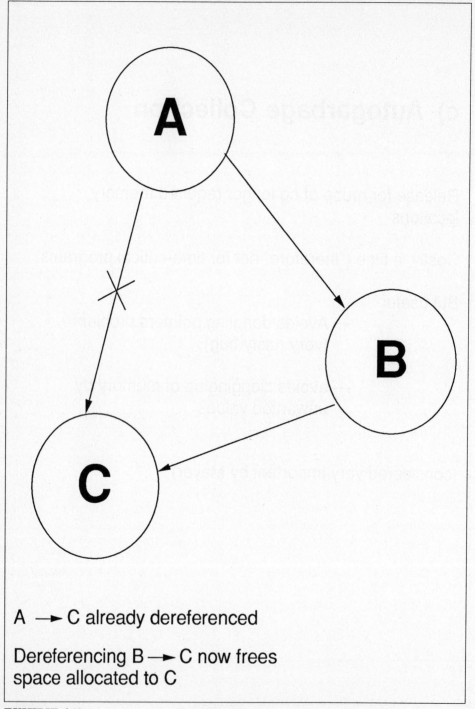

A → C already dereferenced

Dereferencing B → C now frees
space allocated to C

Meyer placed garbage collection (Exhibit 161) high on his list of important characteristics of an OOPL. This really means autogarbage collection (or "automatic memory management") in which the release and reuse of memory locations that are no longer required is undertaken automatically, rather than a manual system such as free in C. Unused objects have space reallocated at run-time, as soon as there are no references (not just deletion of the present reference) to that object (Exhibit 162). This also prevents stuffing up of memory with unused (and no longer usable) objects. So if all the references to an object are cut, then the object is no longer needed as a run-time object. Garbage collection does have a run-time penalty, so again you may wish not to utilize this option all the time. It avoids nasty dangling pointer bugs that frequently occur in C, for instance, the significant fraction of programming time spent writing memory alloc/deallocate code (Wirfs-Brock et al., 1990, p183). Automatic memory management exists in Smalltalk and CLOS (Thomas, 1989b) and Eiffel (Meyer, 1988), but not in C++ (Stroustrup, 1988) or Objective-C.

5.10 Language Examples

In the last section, a few final comments on OOPLs are appropriate (Exhibit 163). Mostly OOPLs run on PC and Unix workstation platforms. Little support for OOPLs is found in the mainframe environment. In contrast C++, Smalltalk, and Actor run on a DOS platform, and DOS and Macintosh versions of Eiffel have been announced as imminent (at the time of writing).

Smalltalk is the archetypal OO language (Goldberg and Robson, 1983; Goldberg, 1985) (Exhibit 163), although the first OOPL really was Simula (e.g., Birtwistle et al., 1973; Papazoglou et al., 1984). However, this was made available, in the late sixties, as a simulation language and so was used extensively for simulation but not really for anything else — it had no life as a real general-purpose programming language despite having these capabilities and being a superset of ALGOL–60. More recently, it has found a new lease of life and is currently being heavily advertised.

In Smalltalk, everything is an object. Even classes are objects, being members of a metaclass. Smalltalk is more than a language, it is a complete environment. It is well supported by the availability of extensive class libraries, debuggers, inspectors, and interactive browsers. Smalltalk is type checked at run-time (dynamic typing) which means it is possible to be running the system and get a type violation while running. If type checking is done at compilation, as in Eiffel, these errors will be trapped then.[11] Smalltalk is certainly regarded as useful for an introduction to OO ideas (e.g., LaLonde and Pugh, 1990), for a prototyping environment, but not currently for very large applications, although current work in this area may invalidate such concerns regarding commercial applicability.

---

[11]Meyer (1989d) notes that "wherever $x.f$ appears in a class text and the compiler accepts it, it is guaranteed that any object associated with x at run-time will have at least one feature corresponding to f."

10. Language Examples

Simula 67, one of the first, most used for simulation,
　　　but intended as a general-purpose language

Smalltalk most well known

C++ only recently multiple inheritance ⌐　　Extension of
Objective-C no operator overloading ⌐　　non-OO
　　　　　　　　　　　　　　　　　　　　　　　designs

Eiffel new, but produces C code, uses some
　　　characteristics of Ada (for syntax) + Simula 67

Loops, Flavors, Ceyx, extensions to Lisp

Icon/Mac interface is OO derived from Smalltalk

Ada, sometimes mentioned but not really because
of early binding, no garbage collection,
no inheritance

Extensions of non-object-oriented designs, typically C++ and Objective-C, are well accepted in which OO ideas are grafted on to existing procedural languages. In addition to C, base languages used in this way include Pascal (OO version in Turbo Pascal), BASIC (Visual BASIC and Extended Visual BASIC), and, probably in the near future, COBOL (see Adams and Lenkov, 1990). This means that it's easier to learn because you know the rootstock, but also more difficult because it is easy to drop back to the base language.

The C++ language (Stroustrup, 1986) is perhaps the most popular of these so-called "hybrid languages" at present, with a very wide user-base worldwide. It's a language that has been largely adopted especially in areas where organizations are already using C, where it is seen as a natural successor. Indeed, many programmers have adopted C++ simply as a newer, better version of C — with no intention of adopting the OO paradigm (e.g., Shaw, 1991). C++ adds the **class** construction as an extension to **struct**. The features of the class are known as data members (instance variables) and member functions (methods) (e.g., Dewhurst and Stark, 1987). (Exhibit 164 compares the terminology for a range of OOPLs.) Member functions are private by default, when they are available only to the class itself and to friends; and may be declared as public (total visibility) or as protected (available only to the class and to derived classes) (see also Booch and Vilot, 1990b.) Although there is no strict compiler-enforced ordering of these various elements, Kirslis (undated) recommends an ordering (Exhibit 165) whereby interface information is declared first and protected and private parts (hidden information) last, followed by implementation details of data members.

Furthermore, member functions are statically bound by default, but may be declared as *virtual*, which indicates that they will be bound dynamically to permit polymorphic usage. Meyer (1990b) notes that this need for the programmer to choose to define member functions as virtual in order to be useful in an inheritance context is likely to lead to violations of the "Open–Closed Principle of OOP" (Meyer, 1988, p23) — see also Section 3.5. In C++, deciding to extend a previously isolated class is likely to require opening and modifying the base class. In addition, Antebi (1990) suggests that the use of "friends" in C++ "is a violation of the discipline of information hiding, but it is a disciplined violation."

Being a language nearer to the machine, explicitly using pointer arithmetic (as does C), C++ has been criticized by Meyer (1990b) as potentially unsafe, and compared by Potter (1990) to a dragster alongside Eiffel's Porsche (the dragster may be faster, but when it comes to cornering … !).

Eiffel is a new, pure object-oriented language (Meyer, 1988, 1991) with syntax derived (ancestrally) from Simula and Ada, using, at present (Version 2.3), C code as an intermediate stage for enhanced portability. The syntax contrasts markedly with that of C++. Version 2.2 was reviewed by Potter (1990) and is also summarized by Hopkins (1990a), their texts supplementing the vendor's printed material. Version 2.3 began shipping in late October 1990 and Version 3.0 is imminent. Unlike C++, which uses **make** and **include** files, Eiffel's four-pass compiler is "intelligent" enough to recognize the need to compile only those classes changed since the last compilation and to undertake the necessary class linking without programmer prescription or intervention. Its syntax and structure

Language Comparison of OO Terminology

Smalltalk	C++	Objective-C	Object-Pascal	Eiffel	CLOS
Object	Object	Object	Object	Object	Instance
Class	Class	Factory	Object type	Class	Class
Method	Member function	Method	Method	Routine	Method Generic function
Instance variable	Member	Instance variable	Object variable	Attribute	Slots
Message	Function call	Message expression	Message	Applying a routine	Generic function
Subclass	Derived class	Subclass	Descendant type	Descendant	Subclass
Inheritance	Derivation	Inheritance	Inheritance	Inheritance	Inheritance

© Winblad et al. (1990)

EXHIBIT 164

A Style for C++ Classes

```
File: C.h
        //   Specification (External)
    class C {
            friends
    public:
            constructor(s)
            destructor
            member-function-decls
        //   Specification (Internal)
    protected:
            constructor(s)
            member-function-decls
    private:
            constructor(s)
            member-function-decls
        //   Implementation
    protected:
            data-members
    private:
            data-members
    }
    inline      member-function-definitions

File: C.c
    #include "C.h"
    member-function-definitions
            (except inlines)
```

EXHIBIT 165   Copyright © P. Kirslis, undated are seen by many as being "clearer" and easier to learn than, say, C++. However, that same characteristic (of a readily learnable yet brand new syntax) makes many managers cautious of endorsing what they see more as an abrupt change in programming environment than a perceived smooth evolutionary transition to a hybrid language such as C++ or Objective-C. In the long run, however, it is likely that many programmers, encouraged by their managers to follow this evolutionary course, will never come to appreciate and utilize the full power of the OO paradigm, compared with their compatriots/competition that adopt one of the "pure" OOPLs such as Eiffel, Smalltalk, or Actor.

Within the OOPL arena, concerns such as persistency and concurrency are not yet established in commercial releases. While Eiffel has some ability to store objects *as* objects, true persistence is yet to be incorporated. Dynamic versus static binding was discussed in Section 5.7. These and other features are summarized in Exhibit 166 for some of these languages.

There are many other languages, which I have not described, and many have not even been mentioned in passing. In early 1989, a survey by Saunders (1989) revealed the existence of 69 general-purpose OO languages. These include languages associated with database management systems still under development, AI-based languages, and LISP-based languages. In this last category are LOOPS and CLOS. Several hypermedia and the Apple Mac interface have object-oriented roots. Finally, Ada is often put forward as an object-oriented language. On the basis of the arguments in Section 5.1, it could certainly be classified as object-based, but its use of early binding eliminates the possibility of polymorphism. Neither is inheritance currently supported, although it can be simulated (Donaldson, 1990). One version of Ada, Classic Ada, has been released with OO features and the possible consolidation of object-orientation into mainline Ada has been under discussion since 1990.

Taking a more pragmatic viewpoint, if I insist on programming in COBOL, C, or FORTRAN, then of course I can, if I am determined enough, enforce an OO style, since in any Turing-complete language I can do anything if I put my mind to it (Exhibit 167). The difference is between those languages that support (and thereby help) the paradigm and those that simply permit the programmer to implement an OO concept within the standard procedural language framework, grudgingly. Meyer (1988) discusses how far you can go toward OO implementation in a range of specific procedural languages. For example, in FORTRAN there is encapsulation in terms of subroutines. These are *not* ADTs, but you can make a subroutine into a type by programmer-control. However, it is specifically not a class and cannot therefore be instantiated multiple times. In C, you can do everything you can in Eiffel or C++ by definition, since both these languages compile into C code. However, it is significantly easier in C++ than in C to produce truly object-oriented code (but cf. Linowes, 1988).

I have not mentioned languages for the artificial intelligence (AI), knowledge-based information systems (KBIS), or object-oriented database (OODB) environments (other than a brief review on pages 3 and 4), since these extend beyond what most students wish to cover in acquiring basic object-oriented knowledge and technical skills.

Comparison of OO Language Features

Feature	Smalltalk	C++	Eiffel	Turbo Pascal
Persistence	Some (whole system)	No	Yes	No
Multiple inheritance	No	Ver 2.0	Yes	No
Typing	Dynamic	Static	Static	Static
Binding	Dynamic	Default static Optional dynamic	Dynamic	Default static Optional dynamic
Autogarbage collection	Yes	No	Yes	No
Exception handling	No	No	Yes	No
Assertions	No	No	Yes	No
Libraries	Yes	From some vendors but mainly third party	Yes	Yes

EXHIBIT 166   Copyright © B. Henderson-Sellers, 1991

Note:

Can apply OO paradigm to other languages
contrast languages that **support** OO
cf. those that **permit** it

e.g., FORTRAN — encapsulation of subroutines
                 — abstract data types
                    via multiple "entry" points

C — can be done without extensions
    — typedef struct {
                                }

Applications — already
        1) Smalltalk/Apple Mac
        2) DBMS esp. spatial DB + GIS
        3) KBIS/ES

?? OO COBOL??

    — currently under discussion/development

EXHIBIT 167

5.11 Summary

In this last chapter, I have delved a little deeper into the language constructs (Exhibit 168), many of which have already appeared in the discussion of analysis and design. Nomenclature of classes, objects, ADTs, messages, polymorphism, inheritance, exception handling, etc. has all been tightened up, although a detailed understanding of many of the implementation details of, for example, polymorphism and genericity goes beyond this text. Inheritance has been considered in the context of coded examples from a small number of languages and in the last section some brief comparisons have been made between current, commercially available object-oriented programming languages.

In the **final summary**, shown in Exhibit 169, I have stressed the software engineering aspects of this book in which the advantages of the object-oriented approach have been clarified and details of recommended development methodologies and notation have been presented. The emphasis on the book has been on analysis and design as a better vehicle for understanding the object-approach to software engineering, rather than on teaching object-orientation[12] through the syntax of one specific language. This is especially important since no currently available language supports all the aspects of OO that are discussed in Chapters 3 and 4. Learning OO independently of language syntax thus also prepares the reader for future OOPL implementations as well as providing a firm foundation for current object-oriented software development.

As we saw in Chapter 1, object technology is still immature although developing rapidly. In the near future I would anticipate consolidation of methodologies into CASE tool support, the maturation of object database management systems, and the wider adoption within commerce, industry, and technical and scientific establishments of an object-oriented philosophy — first in a prototyping environment and then throughout the organization.

Opportunities for better, safer, more reliable software development engendered in a more productive (and hence satisfying) environment are now being presented to us. It is now up to us, the users of technology and developers of applications software, to adopt the mindset and mature along with this exciting leading edge software development technology.

---

[12]I still don't like this term even after using it for a whole book!

Chapter 5
Summary

Definitions in OOPLs of

Objects, Classes, ADTs

Features

Messages

Polymorphism

Inheritance

Exception Handling

Final Summary

Aspects of Object-Oriented Software Engineering (Analysis, Design, Implementation)

Advantages of an Object-Oriented Approach

Terminology of Object-Oriented Systems Development and Object-Oriented Programming

EXHIBIT 169

References

Abbott, R.J., 1983, Program design by informal English descriptions, *Comms. ACM*, **26(11)**, 882–894

Adams, M., and Lenkov, D., 1990, Object-oriented COBOL: the next generation, *Hotline on Obj.-Oriented Technology*, **2(2)**, 12–15

Alabiso, B., 1988, Transformation of data flow analysis models to object oriented design, *OOPSLA '88 Proceedings*, ACM, 335–353

Allaby, A. and Allaby, M. (eds.), 1990, *The Concise Oxford Dictionary of Earth Sciences*, Oxford Univ. Press, Oxford, 410pp

Antebi, M., 1990, Issues in teaching C++, *J. Obj.-Oriented Programming*, **3(4)**, 11–21

Auer, K., 1989, Which object-oriented language should we choose?, *Hotline on Obj.-Oriented Technology*, **1(1)**, 1, 3–6

Bailin, S.C., 1989, An object-oriented requirements specification method, *Comms. ACM*, **32(5)**, 608–623

Balda, D.M., and Gustafson, D.A., 1990, Cost estimation models for the reuse and prototype software development life-cycles, *ACM SIGSOFT Software Engineering Notes*, **15(3)**, 42–50

Bancilhon, F., and Delobel, C., 1991, Recent advances in O-O DBMS, TOOLS '91 Tutorial Notes, 4th International Conference and Exhibition, March 4–8, Paris

Barber, G.R., 1991, The Object Management Group, *Hotline on Obj.-Oriented Technology*, **2(5)**, 17–19

Beck, K., and Cunningham, W., 1989, A laboratory for teaching object-oriented thinking, *SIGPLAN Notices*, **24(10)**

Berard, E.V., 1990a, Life-cycle approaches, *Hotline on Obj.-Oriented Technology*, **1(6)**, 1, 3–4

Berard, E.V., 1990b, Understanding the recursive/parallel life-cycle, *Hotline on Obj.-Oriented Technology*, **1(7)**, 10–13

Berard, E.V., 1990c, Object-oriented requirements analysis, *Hotline on Obj.-Oriented Technology*, **1(8)**, 9–11

Berman, C., and Gur, R., 1988, NAPS — a C++ project case study, *Procs. USENIX C++ Conference*, 137–149

Bielak, R., 1991, The guessing game. A first Eiffel program, *Eiffel Outlook*, **1(1)**, 16–18

Bird, R., and Wadler, P., 1988, *Introduction to Functional Programming*, Prentice Hall, New York, 293pp

Birtwistle, G., Dahl, O.-J., Myrhaug, B., and Nygaard, K., 1973, *Simula Begin*, Studentliteratur (Lund) and Auerbach Pub. (New York)

Blair, G.S., Gallagher, J.J., and Malik, J., 1989, Genericity vs inheritance vs delegation vs conformance vs ..., *J. Obj.-Oriented Programming*, **2(3)**, 11–17

Blair, G.S., Malik, J., Nicol, J.R., and Walpole, J., 1990, A synthesis of object-oriented and functional ideas in the design of a distributed software engineering environment, *Software Engineering Journal,* **5(3)**, 194–204

Bobrow, D.G., 1989, The object of desire, *Datamation*, May 1, 1989, 37–41

Bollinger, T.B., and Pfleeger, S.L., 1990, Economics of reuse: issues and alternatives, *Inf. Software Technol.,* **32**, 643–652

Booch. G., 1983, *Software Engineering with Ada*, Benjamin/Cummings, Menlo Park, CA

Booch, G., 1987, *Software Engineering with Ada*, 2d ed., Benjamin/Cummings, Menlo Park, CA, 580pp

Booch, G., 1991, *Object Oriented Design with Applications*, Benjamin/Cummings, Menlo Park, CA, 580pp

Booch, G., and Vilot, M., 1990a, Object-oriented design. Evolving an object-oriented design, *The C++ Report,* **2(8)**, 11–13

Booch, G., and Vilot, M., 1990b, Object-oriented design. Inheritance relationships, *The C++ Report,* **2(9)**, 8–11

Bracha, G., and Cook, W., 1990, Mixin-based inheritance, *ECOOP/OOPSLA '91 Procs.,* ACM, 303–311

Burnham, W.D., and Hall, A.R., 1985, *Prolog Programming and Applications*, Macmillan, Basingstoke, UK, 114pp

Caldiera, G., and Basili, V., 1991, Identifying and qualifying reusable software components, *IEEE Computing,* **24(2)**, 61–70

Card, D.N., Cotnoir, D.V., and Goorevich, C.E., 1987, Managing software maintenance cost and quality, *IEEE*, 145–152

Coad, P., and Yourdon, E., 1990, *Object-Oriented Analysis*, Yourdon Press/Prentice Hall, New York, 232pp

Coad, P., and Yourdon, E., 1991, *Object-Oriented Analysis*, 2d ed., Yourdon Press/Prentice Hall, New York, 233pp

Coleman, D., and Hayes, F., 1991, Lessons from Hewlett-Packard's experiences of using object-oriented technology, in *TOOLS4* (Procs. 4th Int. Conf. TOOLS Paris, 1991) (eds. J. Bézivin and B. Meyer), Prentice Hall, New York, 327–333

Collins, R., 1990, Object orientation changes the face of computing, *Professional Computing*, March 1990, 10–11

Constantine, L.L., 1989a, Object-oriented and structured methods. Toward integration, *American Programmer*, 2(7–8), 34–40

Constantine, L.L., 1989b, Object Oriented and Structured Design Seminar, Digital Consulting Pacific, Sydney, 1989

Constantine, L.L., 1990a, Objects, functions, and extensibility, *Computer Language*, 7, 34–56

Constantine, L.L.., 1990b, 'The Object-Oriented Systems Symposium', Digital Consulting Pacific, Sydney, June 1990

Constantine, L.L., 1990c, Objects by teamwork, *Hotline on Obj.-Oriented Technology*, 2(1), 1, 3–6

Cox, B.J., 1986, *Object Oriented Programming: An Evolutionary Approach*, Addison-Wesley, Reading, MA, 274pp

Cox, B.J., 1990a, There *is* a silver bullet, *Byte*, October 1990, 209–218

Cox, B.J., 1990b, Planning the software industrial revolution, *IEEE Software*, Nov. 1990, 25–33

Davis, A.M., 1988, A taxonomy for the early stages of the software development life cycle, *J. Systems and Software*, 8, 297–311

DeMarco, T., 1978, *Structured Analysis and System Specification*, Yourdon Press, New York

Deutsch, L.P., 1989, Comment made during a panel session at OOPSLA '89, October, New Orleans

Dewhurst, S.C., and Stark, K.T., 1987, Out of the C world comes C++, *Computer Language*, February 1987, 29–36

Dittrich, K.R. (ed.), 1988, *Advances in Object-Oriented Database Systems, Lecture Notes in Computer Science, 334*, Springer-Verlag, Berlin, 373pp

Dobbie, G., 1991, Object oriented database systems: a survey, Procs. 14th Aust. Comp. Sci. Conf., UNSW, Feb. 6–8, 1991, *Australian Computer Science Communications*, 13(1), 10-1 – 10-11

Donaldson, C.M., 1990, Dynamic binding and inheritance in an object-oriented Ada design, *J. Pascal, Ada and Modula-2*, 9(4), 13–18

Eckel, B., 1989, *Using C++*, McGraw-Hill, Berkeley, CA, 617pp

Eckel, B., 1990, C++ notes, *The C Gazette*, Spring 1990, 70–72

Edwards, J.M., and Henderson-Sellers, B., 1991, A coherent notation for object-oriented software engineering, *Technology of Object-Oriented Languages and Systems: TOOLS5* (ed. T. Korson, V. Vaishnavi and B. Meyer), Prentice-Hall, New York, 405–426

Elmasri, R., and Navathe, S.B., 1989, *Fundamentals of Database Systems*, Benjamin/Cummings, 802pp

Feldman, P., and Miller, D., 1986, Entity model clustering: structuring a data model by abstraction, *The Computer Journal,* **29,** 348–360

Ferguson, T., 1991, Operator overloading in C++, *J. Obj.-Oriented Programming,* **4(1),** 42–48

Ghezzi, C., and Jazayeri, M., 1987, *Programming Language Concepts* 2d ed., J. Wiley and Sons, New York, 428pp

Gibbs, S., Tsichritzis, D., Casais, E., Nierstrasz, O., and Pintado, X., 1990, Class management for software communities, *Comms. ACM,* **33(9),** 90–103

Gibson, E., 1991, Flattening the learning curve: educating object-oriented developers, *J. Obj.-Oriented Programming,* **3(6),** 24–29

Goldberg, A., 1985, *Smalltalk-80: The Interactive Programming Environment,* Addison-Wesley, Reading, MA

Goldberg, A., 1991, Object-oriented project management, TOOLS '91 Tutorial Notes, Paris, March 1991

Goldberg, A., and Robson, D., 1983, *Smalltalk–80: The Language and Its Implementation,* Addison-Wesley, Reading, MA

Goldberg, A., and Rubin, K., 1990, Talking to project managers: organizing for reuse, *Hotline on Obj.-Oriented Technology,* **1(10),** 7–11

Goldstein, S.C., 1990, Introducing OOPS through design — it's all in the words, *Hotline on Obj.-Oriented Technology,* **1(11),** 1, 4–7

Goldstein, T., 1989, The object-oriented programmer, *The C++ Report,* **1(5),** May 1989

Harmon, P., 1990, Object-oriented systems, *Intelligent Software Strategies,* **6(9),** 1–16

Hecht, A., 1990, Cute object-oriented acronyms considered fOOlish, *ACM SIG-SOFT, Software Engineering Notes,* **15(1),** 48

Heintz, T.J., 1991, Object-oriented databases and their impact on future business database applications, *Inf. Management,* **20,** 95–103

Henderson-Sellers, B., 1990, Three methodological frameworks for object-oriented systems development, *Procs. 3rd Intl. Conf., TOOLS3,* Sydney 1990 (eds. J. Bézivin, B. Meyer, J. Potter and M. Tokoro), 118–131

Henderson-Sellers, B., 1991a, Metrics necessary for object-oriented development, submitted to *ACM SIGMETRICS*

Henderson-Sellers, B., 1991b, Hybrid object-oriented/functional decomposition methodologies, *Hotline on Obj.-Oriented Technology*

Henderson-Sellers, B., 1991c, Parallels between object-oriented software development and total quality management, *Journal of Information Technology,* **6(3),** 15–19

Henderson-Sellers, B., and Constantine, L.L., 1991, Object-oriented development and functional decomposition, *Journal of Obj.-Oriented Programming,* **3(5),** 11–17

Henderson-Sellers, B., and Edwards, J.M., 1990a, The object-oriented systems life cycle, *Comms. ACM*, **33(9)**, 142–159

Henderson-Sellers, B., and Edwards, J.M., 1990b, Object-oriented graphics: old wine in new bottles?, *Procs. Graphics in Object-Oriented Software Engineering (GOOSE) Workshop*, OOPSLA '90, Ottawa, Canada, October 1990

Henderson-Sellers, B., and Freeman, C., 1991, Cataloguing object libraries, *ACM SIGSOFT, Software Engineering Notes*

Hopkins, D., 1990a, An Eiffel experience, *ACS Bulletin (Victoria Branch)*, June 1990, 5–8

Hopkins, J.W., 1990b, Object-oriented programming: the next step up, *J. Obj.-Oriented Programming*, **3(1)**, 66–68

Hopkins, J.W., 1991, What management needs to know, TOOLS '91 Tutorial Notes, Paris, March 1991

Hopkins, T., and Warboys, B., 1990, Asset management and object-oriented technology, *Hotline on Obj.-Oriented Technology*, **1(11)**, 12–13

Howard, G.S., 1988, Object oriented programming explained, *J. Systems Management*, **39(7)**, 13–19

Jackson, I.F., 1986, *Corporate Information Management*, Prentice Hall, London, 338pp

Jackson, M.A., 1983, *System Development*, Prentice Hall, London, 418pp

Jalote, P., 1989, Functional refinement and nested objects for object-oriented design, *IEEE Trans. Software Eng.*, **15**, 264–270

Johnson, R.E., and Foote, B., 1988, Designing reusable classes, *J. Obj.-Oriented Programming*, **1(2)**, 22–35

Kerr, R., 1991, Object disorientation, *Hotline on Obj.-Oriented Technology*, **2(5)**, 12–13

Khoshafian, S., 1990, Insight into object-oriented databases, *Inf. Software Technol.*, **32(4)**, 274–289

Kim, W., and Lochovsky, F.H. (eds.), 1989, *Object-Oriented Concepts, Databases, and Applications*, ACM Press New York/Addison-Wesley, Reading, MA, 602pp

Kirslis, P., undated, A style for writing C++ classes

Koenig, A., and Stroustrup, B., 1990, Exception handling for C++, *J. Obj.-Oriented Programming*, **3(2)**, 16–33

Korson, T., and McGregor, J.D., 1990, Object-oriented software design: a tutorial, *Comms. ACM*, **33(9)**, 40–60

Korson, T., and McGregor, J.D., 1991, Technical criteria for the specification and evaluation of object-oriented libraries, Clemson University Technical Report # 91–112

Kuhn, T., 1962, *The Structure of Scientific Revolutions*, Univ. Chicago Press

Ladden, R.M., 1989, A survey of issues to be considered in the development of an object-oriented development methodology for Ada, *Ada Letters*, **9** (2), 78–88

Lahire, P., and Brissi, P., 1991, An integrated query language for handling persistent objects in Eiffel, in *Technology of Object-Oriented Languages and Systems: TOOLS 4* (eds. J. Bézivin and B. Meyer), Prentice Hall, New York, 101–114

LaLonde, W., and Pugh, J., 1990, Smalltalk as the first programming language: the Carleton experience, *J. Obj.-Oriented Programming*, **3**(4), 60–65

LaLonde, W., and Pugh, J., 1991, Subclassing ≠ subtyping ≠ **is-a**, *J. Obj.-Oriented Programming*, **3**(5), 57–62

Laranjeira, L.A., 1990, Software size estimation of object-oriented systems, *IEEE Trans. Software Eng.*, **16**(5), 510–522

Leathers, B., 1990a, Cognos and Eiffel: a cautionary tale, *Hotline on Obj.-Oriented Technology*, **1**(9), 1, 3, 6–8

Leathers, B., 1990b, OOPSLA panel: OOP in the real world, *ECOOP/OOPSLA '90 Proceedings*, ACM Press, New York, 299–302

Linowes, J.S., 1988, It's an attitude, *Byte*, August 1988, 219–224

Lippman, S.B., 1989, *C++ Primer*, Addison-Wesley, Reading, MA, 464pp

Loomis, M.E.S., 1990a, OODBMS. The basics, *J. Obj.-Oriented Programming*, **3**(1), 77, 79–81

Loomis, M.E.S., 1990b, OODBMS vs. relational, *J. Obj.-Oriented Programming*, **3**(2), 79–82

Loomis, M.E.S., Shah, A.V., and Rumbaugh, J.E., 1987, An object modeling technique for conceptual design, *Procs. ECOOP '87*, Springer, New York, 192–202

Loy, P.H., 1990, A comparison of object-oriented and structured development methods, *ACM SIGSOFT, Software Engineering Notes*, **15**(1), 44–48

McCullough, P., and Deshler, N., 1990, WyCASH+: an application built within an OOP environment, *Hotline on Obj.-Oriented Technology*, **1**(10), 1, 3–4

Malhotra, A., Thomas, J.C., Carroll, J.M., and Miller, L., 1980, Cognitive processes in design, *J. Man-Machine Studies*, **12**, 119–140

Meyer, B., 1988, *Object-Oriented Software Construction*, Prentice Hall, Hemel Hempstead, UK, 534pp

Meyer, B., 1989a, From structured programming to object-oriented design: the road to Eiffel, *Structured Programming*, **1**, 19–39

Meyer, B., 1989b, Writing correct software, *Dr Dobb's Journal*, Dec. 1989, 48–63

Meyer, B., 1989c, The new culture of software development: reflections on the practice of object-oriented design, *Procs. TOOLS '89* (Paris, November 13–15, 13–23)

Meyer, B., 1989d, Course notes for two day seminar, Object-oriented design and programming: a software engineering perspective, Sydney, November 1989, Interactive Software Engineering, Inc., 235pp

Meyer, B., 1990a, Lessons from the design of the Eiffel libraries, *Comms. ACM,* **33(9),** 68–88

Meyer, B., 1990b, Eiffel and C++: a comparison, unpublished technical note, Interactive Software Engineering, March 1990, 12pp

Meyer, B., 1991, *Eiffel: The Language,* Prentice Hall, New York

Miller, G., 1956, The magical number seven, plus or minus two: some limits on our capacity for processing information, *The Psychological Review,* **63(2),** 81–97

Millikin, M., 1989, Object-orientation: what it can do for you, *Computerworld,* March 13, 1989

Moreau, D.R., and Dominick, W.D., 1989, Object-oriented graphical information systems: research plan and evaluation metrics, *J. Systems and Software,* **10,** 23–28

Mullin, M., 1989, *Object Oriented Program Design With Examples in C++,* Addison-Wesley, Reading, MA, 303pp

Norden, P.V., 1958, Curve fitting for a model of applied research and development scheduling, *IBM Journal,* **July 1958,** 232–248

Nurick, A., 1990, An OOP developer's success story, *Programmer's Update,* June 1990, 41–51

Page-Jones, M., 1980, *The Practical Guide to Structured System Design,* Yourdon Press, New York

Page-Jones, M., 1991a, Object-orientation: stop, look, and listen! *Hotline on Obj.-Oriented Technology,* **2(3),** 1, 3–7

Page-Jones, M., 1991b, TOOLS '91 Tutorial Notes, 4th International Conference and Exhibition, March 4–8, Paris

Page-Jones, M., and Weiss, S., 1989, Synthesis: an object-oriented analysis and design method, *American Programmer,* **2(7–8),** 64–67, Summer 1989

Page-Jones, M., Constantine, L.L., and Weiss, S., 1990, Modeling object-oriented systems: the Uniform Object Notation, *Computer Language,* **7 (10),** October 1990.

Papazoglou, M.P., Georgiadis, P.I., and Maritsas, D.G., 1984, An outline of the programming language Simula, *Comput. Lang.,* **9,** 107–131

Parnas, D., 1972, On the criteria to be used in decomposing systems into modules, *Comms. ACM,* **15(2),** 1053–1058

Peckham, J., and Maryanski, F., 1988, Semantic data models, *ACM Computing Surveys,* **20,** 153–189

Pfleeger, S.L., 1991, Model of software effort and productivity, *Inf. Software Technol.,* **33(3),** 224–231

Pokkunuri, B.P., 1989, Object oriented programming, *SIGPLAN Notices*, **24(11)**, 96–101

Potter, J., 1990, Eiffel 2.2, *J. Obj.-Oriented Programming*, **3(3)**, 84–88

Price, R.T., and Girardi, R., 1990, A class retrieval tool for an object oriented environment, in *Procs. 3rd Intl. Conf., TOOLS3*, Sydney 1990 (eds. J. Bézivin, B. Meyer, J. Potter and M. Tokoro), 26–36

Prieto-Diaz, R., and Freeman, P., 1987, Classifying software for reusability, *IEEE Software,* **4(1)**, 6–16

Pun, W., and Winder, R., 1990, A design method for object-oriented programming, Department of Computer Science, University College London, Research Note RN/90/51, 17pp

Purchase, J.A. and Winder, R.L., 1991, Debugging tools for object-oriented programming, *J. Obj.-Oriented Programming*, **4(3)**, 10–27

Rajlich, V., 1985, Paradigms for design and implementation in Ada, *Comms. ACM,* **28**, 718–727

Rhoades, C.E. Jr., 1990, Scientific programming, concurrency and object-oriented languages: a view from the battlements, *Procs. 3rd Intl. Conf., TOOLS3*, Sydney 1990 (eds. J. Bézivin, B. Meyer, J. Potter and M. Tokoro), 109–116

Rosenquist, C.J., 1982, Entity life cycle models and the applicability to information systems development lifecycles, *The Computer Journal*, **25(3)**, 307–315

Rumbaugh, J., 1987, Relations as semantic constructs in an object-oriented language, *OOPSLA '87 Proceedings*, ACM, 466–481

Rumbaugh, J., Blaha, M., Premerlani, W., Eddy, F., and Lorensen, W., 1991, *Object-Oriented Modeling and Design*, Prentice Hall, New York, 528pp.

Saunders, J.H., 1989, A survey of object-oriented programming languages, *J. Obj.-Oriented Programming*, **1(6)**, 5–11

Schmucker, K.J., 1986a, MacApp: an application framework, *Byte*, August 1986, 189–193

Schmucker, K.J,, 1986b, *Object-Oriented Programming for the Macintosh*, Hayden Book Company

Seidewitz, E., 1989, General object-oriented software development: background and experience, *J. Systems and Software,* **9**, 95–108

Seidewitz, E., and Stark, M., 1987, Towards a general object-oriented software development methodology, *Ada Letters,* **7**, July/Aug. 1987, 54–67

Shaw, R.H., 1991, C++ without objects, *Borland Language Express,* **1(1)**, 10–13

Shlaer, S., and Mellor, S.J., 1988, *Object-Oriented Systems Analysis: Modeling the World in Data*, Yourdon Press/Prentice Hall, 144pp

Simsion, G.C., 1989, A structured approach to data modelling, *Aust. Comp. J.*, **21**, 108–117

Snyder, A., 1986, Encapsulation and inheritance in object-oriented programming languages, *OOPSLA '86 Proceedings*, ACM Press, 38–45

Sommerville, I., 1989, *Software Engineering* 3d ed., Addison-Wesley, Wokingham, UK, 653pp

Stein, J., 1988, Object-oriented programming and databases, *Dr Dobb's Journal*, March 1988, 18–34

Stewart, M.K., 1991, Object projects: what can go wrong, *Hotline on Obj.-Oriented Technology*, **2(6)**, 15–17

Stroustrup, B., 1986, *The C++ Programming Language*, Addison-Wesley, Reading, MA, 328pp

Stroustrup, B., 1988, What is object-oriented programming?, *IEEE Software*, May, 1–19

Thomas, D., 1989a, In search of an object-oriented development process, *J. Obj.-Oriented Programming*, **2(1)**, 60–63

Thomas, D., 1989b, What's in an object?, *Byte*, March 1989, 231–240

Thomsett, R., 1990, Management implications of object-oriented development, *ACS Newsletter*, October 1990, 5–7, 10–12

Trowbridge, D., 1990, OOP needs changed programmer thinking, *Computer Technol. Rev.*, August 1990

Turner, J.A., 1987, Understanding the elements of system design, Chapter 4 in *Critical Issues in Information Systems Research* (eds. R.J. Boland, Jr. and R.A. Hirschheim), John Wiley and Sons, Chichester, UK, 97–111

Urlocker, Z., 1989, Teaching object-oriented programming, *J. Obj.-Oriented Programming*, **2(2)**, 45–47

Waldo, J., 1990, O-O benefits of Pascal to C++ conversion, *The C++ Report*, **2(8)**, 1, 5–7

Wampler, K.D., 1990, The object-oriented programming paradigm (OOP) and FORTRAN programs, *Computers in Physics*, **4(4)**, 385–394

Wand, Y., and Weber, R., 1989, An ontological evaluation of systems analysis and design methods, in *Information Systems Concepts: An In-depth Analysis* (eds. E.D. Falkenberg and P. Lindgren), Elsevier Science Publishers (North Holland), Amsterdam, 79–107

Ward, P., 1989, How to integrate object orientation with structured analysis and design, *IEEE Software*, March, 74–82

Ward, P.T., and Mellor, S.J., 1985, *Structured Development for Real-Time Systems*, Yourdon Press, Englewood Cliff, NJ, 156pp

Wasserman, A.I., Pircher, P.A., and Muller, R.J., 1989, An object-oriented structured design method for code generation, *ACM SIGSOFT, Software Engineering Notes*, **14(1)**, 32–55

Wasserman, A.I., Pircher, P.A., and Muller, R.J., 1990, The object-oriented structured design notation for software design representation, *Computer*, March 1990, 50–63

Wegner, P., 1989, Learning the language, *Byte*, March 1989, 245–253

Wegner, P., 1990, Concepts and paradigms of object-oriented programming, *OOPS Messenger*, **1(1)**, 7–87

Wilson, D.A., 1990, Class diagrams: a tool for design, documentation, and teaching, *J. Obj.-Oriented Programming*, **2(5)**, 38–44

Winblad, A.L., Edwards, S.D., and King, D.R., 1990, *Object-Oriented Software*, Addison-Wesley, Reading, MA, 291pp

Winston, A., 1990, Objective reality, *Unixworld*, April 1990, 72–75

Wirfs-Brock, A., and Wilkerson, B., 1989a, Variables limit reusability, *J. Obj.-Oriented Programming*, **2(1)**, 34–40

Wirfs-Brock, R.J., and Johnson, R.E., 1990, A survey of current research in object-oriented design, *Comms. ACM*, **33(9)**, 104–124

Wirfs-Brock, R.J., and Wilkerson, B., 1989b, Object-oriented design: a responsibility-driven approach, *OOPSLA '89 Proceedings*, 71–75

Wirfs-Brock, R.J., Wilkerson, B., and Wiener, L., 1990, *Designing Object-Oriented Software*, Prentice Hall, New York, 341pp

Woodfield, S.N., 1990, Object-oriented software development, pp715–725 **in** *Procs. Int. Symp. on Water Quality Modeling of Agricultural Non-Point Sources, Utah, 1988*, U.S. Department of Agriculture, ARS–81, 881pp

Wybolt, N., 1990, Experiences with C++ and object-oriented software development, *Procs. USENIX C++ Conference*, 1–9

Wybolt, N., 1991, Bootstrapping object-oriented CASE, *Hotline on Obj.-Oriented Technology*, **2(3)**, 13–15

Yamazaki, S., Kajihara, K., Hori, M., and Yasuhara, R., 1990, Real time OOD — object-oriented design techniques for communication control systems, *Procs. 3rd Intl. Conf., TOOLS3*, Sydney 1990 (eds. J. Bézivin, B. Meyer, J. Potter, and M. Tokoro), 199–206

Yourdon, E., and Constantine, L.L., 1979, *Structured Design: Fundamentals of a Discipline of Computer Program and Systems Design*, Yourdon Press/ Prentice Hall, New York, 473pp

Annotated Bibliography

In this annotated bibliography I have collected together some more detailed reading to help you to follow up in more detail some of the ideas presented in this book. The list is largely devoted to more specialized books, rather than journal articles. Many of these books, especially those pre-1990, have an inevitable language bias, often as a result of the author having a vested interest in one particular language. As well as listing these in alphabetical order, I have added some brief comments on their usefulness. The list is not meant to be complete but certainly includes most of the more well known books in the area of object-oriented analysis, design, and programming as well as specific language references.

Booch, G., 1987, *Software Engineering with Ada*, Benjamin/Cummings. Grady Booch has done a lot of good work in object-oriented design, although his earlier work, like this, is geared toward an implementation in Ada. Despite this, some basic OO ideas have emerged from his ideas and have been consolidated in his more recent book (see below).

Booch, G., 1991, *Object-Oriented Design with Applications*, Benjamin/Cummings. A very welcome book that takes you slowly through the concepts and jargon (152 pages) and then Booch's individual notation and design methodology (69 pages). The third section covers application case studies in a number of major languages: Smalltalk, Object Pascal, C++, CLOS, and Ada (270 pages). There is an extensive reference list, arranged by subject area. As noted in the text earlier in my book, this work is slanted more toward detailed design, but is very useful nevertheless. It has had rave reviews on the net.

Budd, T., 1991, *An Introduction to Object-Oriented Programming*, Addison-Wesley, 399pp. Stresses the need to understand the philosophy of the object-oriented approach *before* considering language syntax. CRC cards are used as a vehicle for class identification and several case studies are presented as "prototypes" for the novice programmer to emulate. (The code is also contained in the last 70 pages of the book.) While concentrating on the implementation phase, the text aims to be relatively language-independent, instead stressing concepts. However, several languages are used throughout to illustrate specific points.

Coad, P., and Yourdon, E., 1990, *Object-Oriented Analysis*, Yourdon Press/ Prentice Hall, 232pp. The first, but not likely to be the best, book on OOA. Its roots are firmly in data modeling and structured techniques (Harmon, 1990), and you are unlikely to gain much insight into OO from reading this first. However, once you are familiar with OO ideas, there are some good ideas here, although many find the notation overly messy.

Winblad *et al.* (1990) note that the data-modeling-based tools of Coad and Yourdon in this book, while containing many valuable ideas, essentially miss out on the basic OO philosophy of data-plus-functionality.

The second edition of this book was published in 1991. A five-layer method is still used, but the notation has been improved especially with respect to cardinalities. Terminology for O/Cs and their relationships has been changed. There are more guidelines on identification of objects, attributes, etc., and a new chapter has been included on introducing OOA into the business environment, although the book's overall length remains the same (233pp).

Cox, B.J., 1986, *Object Oriented Programming. An Evolutionary Approach*, Addison-Wesley, 274pp. One of the early books on OO. Proposes the idea of not just an OOPL (here that is Objective-C) but a whole software engineering factory-style environment. The author's emphasis is firmly on reusable software parts, which he likens to hardware integrated circuits and boards.

Gorlen, K.E., Orlow, S.M., and Plexico, P.S., 1990, *Data Abstraction and Object-Oriented Programming in C++*, John Wiley and Sons, Chichester, UK, 403pp. Focuses on the NIH (National Institutes of Health) Class Library to illustrate programming in C++. Probably not a first book in C++ nor in OOP in general.

Hu, D., 1990, *Object-Oriented Environment in C++. A User Friendly Interface*, MIS Presss, Portland, OR, 557pp. Arguably one of the poorer books containing a preponderance of code rather than discussion. However, if all you ever wanted was example code, then this is a book for you. But then, why not just distribute the code for those people on a diskette?

Lippman, S.B., 1989, *C++ Primer*, Addison-Wesley, 464pp. Recommended first choice for learning C++ (especially if you are already conversant with C) by many (e.g., Eckel, 1990).

Meyer, B., 1988, *Object-Oriented Software Construction*, Prentice Hall, 534pp. One of the first descriptions and arguably still the best overall description of object-oriented ideas. The slant is toward implementation; design is expressed using Eiffel as a program design language (PDL); and analysis is essentially non existent. The latter part of the book not only deals with the OOPL Eiffel (of which Meyer is the chief architect) but also contains detailed discussions of other languages.

Meyer, B., 1991, *Eiffel: The Language*, Prentice Hall. The definitive description of the language Eiffel, Version 3.0. In the style of OOSC, it contains not only an excellent description of language details, but also the rationale behind the design of the language. While not being an introductory tutorial, it is peppered with sufficient examples for the programmer to understand and learn the language well. It also highlights the features of Eiffel that have changed or been added since OOSC was published in 1988.

Mullin, M., 1989, *Object Oriented Program Design With Examples in C++*, Addison-Wesley, 303pp. Some useful insights. Again not for the C++ beginner. Also some Smalltalk influences.

Parsaye, K., Chignell, M., Khoshafian, S., and Wong, H., 1989, *Intelligent Databases*, John Wiley and Sons, Chichester, UK. The subtitle is Object-Oriented, Deductive Technologies. An introduction to OODB and hypermedia. This book covers much more than OO ideas, but in doing so helps to provide a wider perspective for OO ideas. (OO is only the subject of one of the eight chapters.) The authors propose that the areas of OO, ES, hypermedia, traditional database technology and text manipulation all merge into "intelligent databases". This provides the book's theme.

Rumbaugh, J., Blaha, M., Premerlani, W., Eddy, F., and Lorensen, W., 1991, *Object-Oriented Modeling and Design*, Prentice Hall, 528pp. Emphasis on design and bringing in substantial information from data modeling. A practical 'how-to' book and one of the better OO books with an OOA/OOD slant. The underlying rationale for the book is that of object-oriented *modeling* and a three-part OO systems development methodology is presented. The third part of the book considers language-specific implementation concerns including the contrast with relational databases. The final part describes three application case studies. Strongly recommended.

Shlaer, S., and Mellor, S.J., 1988, *Object-Oriented Systems Analysis: Modeling the World in Data*, Yourdon Press/Prentice Hall, 144pp. Largely information modeling using entity life cycles. Winblad *et al.* (1990) note that the data-modeling-based tools of Shlaer and Mellor in this book, while containing many valuable ideas, essentially miss out on the basic OO philosophy of data-plus-functionality.

Stroustrup, B., 1986, *The C++ Programming Language*, Addison-Wesley, 328pp. An authoritative view of the C++ language from its designer and developer. Better for more advanced students. Doesn't yet incorporate Version 2.0. Superceded by the second edition (1991) as this book went to press.

Winblad, A.L., Edwards, S.D., and King, D.R., 1990, *Object-Oriented Software*, Addison-Wesley, 291pp. This book has much the same market in mind as I had in writing my book. However, as with so many books, the bias is toward language details rather than analysis and design. Nevertheless, the fundamentals are well covered and there is some useful information on object-oriented databases seldom seen in books of this level. Highly recommended (see also review by R. Wiener in *Journal of Obj.-Oriented Programming*, Sept./Oct. 1990, p80).

Winder, R., 1991, *Developing C++ Software*, John Wiley and Sons, Chichester, UK, 400pp. Aims at introducing C++ as a programming language *per se*, rather than as an extension of C. It is thus a rare C++ programming text which does not have knowledge of C as a prerequisite. Certainly worth considering as a first text in C++.

Wirfs-Brock, R.J., Wilkerson, B., and Wiener, L., 1990, *Designing Object-Oriented Software*, Prentice Hall, 368pp. Well-recommended book on design. A practical "how-to" book in which several extensive examples are followed through. Thorough discussion of responsibilities, collaborations, and the use of CRC cards. Highly focused on design and therefore not an introductory book. One of the first substantial books in the design area.

Journals

Journal of Object-Oriented Programming, originally six, now nine, issues per year. Both technical papers and regular columns are featured, together with other industry news. Regular columns on C++, OODBMS, Eiffel, etc. Occasional topic-focused special issues.

Hotline on Object-Oriented Technology. A monthly newsy publication aimed at management discussing managerial and technical issues within the framework of asking "how do we do it?" Includes lots of useful firsthand experiences with OO in commercial environments. Columns and occasional articles by many well-known names in OO.

Object Magazine. Publication commenced May 1991. Published every two months. Directed at software developers and end-users using, or intending to use, object technology on a daily basis. Technical and non-technical issues are covered at a very readable level.

OOPS Messenger. Publication commenced October 1990. An ACM publication under the SIGPLAN committee. Aimed at rapid dissemination of OO ideas to the community.

The C++ Report, subtitled *The International Newsletter for C++ Programmers*. Feature articles, industry and product news, tutorials, etc.

Eiffel Outlook. Publication commenced April 1991. An independent magazine of interest to Eiffel users.

In addition, there have been special issues on OO of regular journals: for example, *Communications of the ACM*, September 1990, on OO design; *IEEE Software*, May 1988; *Byte*, August 1981, on Smalltalk, also August 1986, March 1989, and October 1990, plus occasional papers in other issues such as April 1990.

Appendix

ADDITIONAL EXHIBITS

Chapter 2

An Introduction to Object-Oriented Philosophy and Terminology

Chapter 3

Object-Oriented Software Engineering

EXHIBIT TITLE(3)   Copyright © B. Henderson-Sellers, 1991

Chapter 4

Object-Oriented Systems Development

EXHIBIT TITLE(4) Copyright © B. Henderson-Sellers, 1991

Chapter 5

Some Implementation Concepts

Index

Abstract class — see Class (abstract)

Abstract data type (ADT), xiii, 22–24, 28, 34, 43–45, 53, 61, 132, 225–228, 229–234, 247, 266

Abstraction, 16–19, 23–24, 30, 34

Acceptance testing, 63, 93, 109

Actor, 4, 261, 266

Ada, 24, 51, 63, 71, 125, 156, 254, 257, 263

ADT — see Abstract data type

Aggregation, 35–39, 63, 128, 151, 156, 163, 167, 176, 250

ALGOL 60, 247, 261

Alphard, 53

Analysis, 30, 35, 69, 108–109, 125, 142, 144, 148, 150–154, 156, 163

Areas of debate, 76–79

Assertions, 72, 182, 254–257

Association, 35–39, 63, 163, 167, 250

Attributes, 144, 156, 216, 218, 234, 238

  access to, 60

Auditability, 31

Autogarbage collection, 225, 259–261

Base class, 244

Behavior, 156

C, 3, 24, 43, 51, 53, 56, 60, 71, 75, 78, 116, 145, 225, 229, 257, 261, 263, 266

C++, 1–3, 19, 51, 56, 60, 61, 71, 78, 218, 228, 229, 234, 237, 244, 254, 257, 261, 263, 264, 266, 267

Cardinality, 163

CASE technology, 3, 71, 93, 133, 154, 185

Class, 34, 56, 79, 225–228, 229–234

  abstract, 125, 156, 161, 244

  aggregate, 175, 213

  and object, 34

  and subclass or superclass — see Inheritance

  definition of, xiii

  embedded, 125

  hierarchy — see Inheritance

  icon for, 156–161

  inside view, 41, 148, 161, 234–237

  instantiation from — see Instantiation

  interface, 56, 60, 234

  private part, 20, 237–238, 263

  public part, 20, 237–238, 263

  specification, 60, 182–183

Class-based languages, 225

Classification, xiii, 16–19, 23, 150–151, 167

Class invariant, 37, 53, 254–257

Client-server, 35–39, 72, 76, 153,

293